D0422073

ZondervanPublishingHouse
5300 Patterson Avenue SE • Grand Rapids, MI 49530
http://www.zondervan.com

May 18, 2000

Dear Pastor,

We hope you can join the wide cross-section of evangelical leaders who already have endorsed *The Gospel of Jesus Christ: an Evangelical Celebration*. This statement originally published in June 1999 aims to affirm a common understanding of the Gospel message shared by evangelical Christians. If you are not familiar with the statement, you may read it on pp. 235-48 of *This We Believe* or on the website below. If you agree with it, you may go to www.ThisWeBelieve.com and add your name to the list of endorsers.

Key evangelical leaders share their insights on specific points of The Gospel of Jesus Christ in the book, *This We Believe*. This special pastor's edition is designed to help you present the statement to your congregation. It contains sermon and worship resources, including outlines, responsive readings, suggested hymns and praise choruses, and discussion questions for your small groups, adult Sunday school, and new believers classes. Use the enclosed coupon to give your board members and congregation to purchase their own copy of *This We Believe*.

We invite you and your congregation to join other believers around the nation and around the world in this historic celebration of the one true Gospel. We pray that it will mark the beginning of a renewed understanding of the Gospel and a new commitment among Evangelicals everywhere to bring the Good News of Jesus Christ to the world.

In Christ,

Scott W. Bolinder
Executive Vice President
and Publisher

Stanley N. Gundry
Vice President and
Editor-in-Chief

Book Group
Zondervan Publishing House
www.zondervan.com

THIS WE BELIEVE

PASTOR'S EDITION

THE GOOD NEWS OF JESUS CHRIST FOR THE WORLD

John N. Akers, John H. Armstrong, and
John D. Woodbridge, General Editors

PREACHING AND WORSHIP RESOURCES
WRITTEN BY KEVIN G. HARNEY

ZondervanPublishingHouse
Grand Rapids, Michigan

A Division of HarperCollins*Publishers*

This We Believe Pastor's Edition

Requests for information should be addressed to:

ZondervanPublishingHouse
Grand Rapids, Michigan 49530

Library of Congress Cataloging-in-Publication Data

This we believe: the good news of Jesus Christ for the world / John N. Akers, John H. Armstrong, and John D. Woodbridge, general editors.
p. cm.
Includes bibliographical references.
ISBN: 0-310-23663-0
1. Evangelicalism. 2. Gospel of Jesus Christ. I. Akers, John N. II. Armstrong, John H (John Harper), 1949– III. Woodbridge, John D., 1941–
BR1640 .T48 2000
230'.04624—dc21

00-033382

This edition is printed on acid-free paper.

The editors express their gratitude to the respective publishers for permission to use stories presented on pages 30–31, 82–83, 106, 126, 146–47, 164–65, 180, 200–201, 210–11, and 228–29.

Interior design by Melissa Elenbaas

Printed in the United States of America

00 01 02 03 04 05 /❖ DC/ 10 9 8 7 6 5 4 3 2 1

CONTENTS

ACKNOWLEDGMENTS

THE EDITORS

John N. Akers is special assistant to Billy Graham.

John H. Armstrong is president of Reformation and Revival Ministries in Carol Stream, Illinois.

John D. Woodbridge is research professor of church history and Christian thought at Trinity Evangelical Divinity School in Deerfield, Illinois.

THE CONTRIBUTORS

Ravi Zacharias is president of Ravi Zacharias International Ministries in Atlanta, Georgia.

J. I. Packer is professor emeritus at Regent College in Vancouver, British Columbia, Canada, and visiting scholar for *Christianity Today*.

Kevin Vanhoozer is research professor of systematic theology at Trinity Evangelical Divinity School in Deerfield, Illinois.

Scott Hafemann is Gerald F. Hawthorne Professor of New Testament Greek and Exegesis at Wheaton College in Wheaton, Illinois.

Thomas C. Oden is Henry Anson Buttz Professor of Theology and Ethics at the Theological School of Drew University in Madison, New Jersey.

Ajith Fernando is national director of Youth for Christ in Sri Lanka and chairman of the academic affairs committee at Colombo Theological Seminary in Colombo, Sri Lanka.

Maxie Dunnam is president of Asbury Theological Seminary in Wilmore, Kentucky.

Joni Eareckson Tada is founder and president of JAF Ministries (Joni and Friends) in Agoura Hills, California.

Tite Tiénou is professor of theology of mission at Trinity Evangelical Divinity School in Deerfield, Illinois.

Lee Strobel is a teaching pastor at Saddleback Community Church in Orange County, California.

Joseph M. Stowell is president of Moody Bible Institute in Chicago, Illinois.

Timothy George is dean of Beeson Divinity School of Samford University in Birmingham, Alabama, and senior advisor for *Christianity Today*.

THIS WE BELIEVE

The Gospel of Jesus Christ is news, good news: the best and most important news any human being ever hears.

The Gospel declares the only way to know God in peace, love, and joy is through the reconciling death of Jesus Christ the risen Lord.

—*The Gospel of Jesus Christ: An Evangelical Celebration*

INTRODUCTION

Is the Gospel of Jesus Christ poised to make a major advance throughout the world? At the dawn of the new millennium, at least one encouraging sign does suggest that such an advance could take place. In recent years millions of people around the world have discovered that the Gospel is indeed "Good News"—the best and most important news any human being ever hears. They have come to understand that the only way to know God, our Creator, in peace, love, and joy is through the reconciling death of Jesus Christ the Risen Lord.

In 1800, ninety-nine out of one hundred evangelical Christians lived in Europe and North America. Now, two hundred years later, the situation is strikingly otherwise. The evangelical church has become truly global, and its center of gravity no longer remains in the West. Patrick Johnstone helps us to grasp these changes by charting the astonishing numerical growth of evangelical Christians in the last four decades:

> The growth in Eurasia, Asia, and Africa has been such that the center of gravity of Christianity moved away from the West in the early '70s. . . . Evangelicals in the West grew from 57.7 million in 1960 to 95.9 million in 1990 with an average growth 1.7%. In the rest of the world, the 1960 total of Evangelicals of 29 million grew to 208 million in 1990—an average annual growth of 6.8%.[1]

Some scholars suggest quite reasonably that the number of evangelicals in the world surpassed the 500 million mark by the year 2000.

Could this recent advance of the Gospel represent a prelude to a mighty outpouring of the Spirit of God upon the world? Such a thing is difficult to predict. The advance may only constitute a welcomed but relatively brief episode in the overall scheme of human history. Christian churches in certain parts of the world may be beaten down, overwhelmed by waves of persecution. Some churches have already suffered greatly. Sadly, the number of Christian martyrs has mounted precipitously. David Neff, senior editor of *Christianity Today*, reiterates the point that the average evangelical Christian does not live in North America but elsewhere in the world and more often than not lives in poverty and faces persecution.

The future may be uncertain concerning any further near-term advance of the Gospel, but Christ's command to work toward that goal is not. After the resurrection, Christ declared to his disciples, "All authority in heaven and on earth has been given to me. Therefore go and make disciples of all nations, baptizing them in the name of the Father and of the Son and of the Holy Spirit, and teaching them to obey everything I have commanded you. And surely I am with you always, to the very end of the age" (Matt. 28:18–20).

If we are Christian believers, this "Great Commission" from Christ applies to us. Each one of us has the joyful responsibility and privilege of compassionately sharing his Gospel with our friends and others we meet along life's way. We are "Christ's ambassadors" (2 Cor. 5:20). We are on a mission assignment. We represent the King of kings by taking his Good News to the world.

Moreover, Jesus gives us specific directives regarding our conduct as his representatives on assignment. He tells us that the world will be able to recognize us as his disciples. The identification marker is one we should always remember. It is not the cleverness of our speech or the depth of our knowledge or the brilliance of our theological arguments. Rather, it is the love we demonstrate for one another as believers. Jesus said, "A new command I give you: Love one another. As I have loved you, so you must love one another. By this all men will know that you are my disciples, if you love one another" (John 13:34–35). What we may find even more amazing is that Jesus cites the unity evidenced by his disciples as in some way helping people in the world to understand the Gospel. Jesus prayed to the Father, "I have given them the glory that you gave me, that they may be one as we are one... May they be brought to complete unity to let the world know that you sent me and have loved them even as you have loved me" (John 17:22–23). This unity is to be based on the truth of his Gospel.

Until Christ's return, then, we are commissioned to present the Gospel to our friends and neighbors and to others we meet. We are to establish new churches where the Gospel will be faithfully preached and believers will be genuinely nourished in the faith. If we call Christ Lord, we do not have the liberty to neglect our mission assignment.

REAL CHALLENGES TO THE GOSPEL'S PROCLAMATION

Yet, most of us know intuitively, either through reading or from firsthand experience, that very real challenges to the Gospel's proclamation exist in our world. As evangelical Christians we encounter them, sometimes daily. In fact, a number of these challenges may affect our own way of thinking about the Gospel of Jesus Christ more than we realize or would care to acknowledge.

1. *The Challenge of Religious Intolerance.* Religious intolerance is manifested when political states or peoples disdain or do not allow the free and open proclamation of the Gospel of Jesus Christ or of any other faith. Religious intolerance can occur not only in states where one religion dominates but also in so-called secular states where the religious rights of believers, though ostensibly protected by law, are in fact suppressed or curtailed. Many evangelical Christians live under regimes where they have become the victims of religious persecution due to the initiative of those who control the government and the military and the media to take away their civil and religious rights.

2. *The Challenge of Pluralism.* Pluralism denies that Jesus is the only way to God. A pluralist believes that there are many paths to God and that people can be saved through any ethical religion.

On those grounds, they say, we don't need to present the Gospel to Muslims or Hindus or Jews—in fact, such a thought is highly offensive. Most pluralists believe that ultimately everyone will be saved. By contrast, perhaps the one benefit of a pluralist attitude is that it can give people uncommitted to the Christian faith an openness to hearing the Gospel.

3. *The Challenge of Inclusivism.* Instead of saying there are many paths to God, inclusivists claim that there are many paths to Jesus. They hold that sincere followers of Islam, Judaism, Hinduism, Buddhism, or any other religion can only be saved by Jesus Christ, but that as long as they follow the light they have, such people do not need to hear the Gospel or call upon Jesus by name.

4. *The Challenge of an Unprincipled Ecumenism.* As noted earlier, Jesus prayed that his disciples would be united (John 17:23). For Christians to seek the unity of Christ's body is to obey his injunction to do so. Christ also indicated that the world will know who his disciples are by the way they demonstrate love to each other (John 13:35). In the last half-century major efforts have been made to reunite those who claim to be Christians but have been divided for centuries. These dialogues and joint worship encounters are often well intentioned and sometimes do create better understanding among the participants. The danger exists, however, that various parties will sacrifice the truth of the Gospel in the name of achieving "unity" even though there can be no true Christian unity unless it is based on the truth of the Gospel.

5. *The Challenge of Unwarranted Church Divisions.* By contrast, Christians can become so attached to certain secondary beliefs and church customs not related to the Gospel that they disdain having fellowship with other Christians who disagree with them on these matters. This challenge divides Christians from each other—even those who do indeed believe the Gospel of Jesus Christ. These divisions in turn can greatly hinder the work of evangelism and other forms of Christian witness. The more Christians bicker and wrangle with each other, the easier it becomes for non-Christians to dismiss the Gospel.

6. *The Challenge of Lack of Gospel Knowledge.* David Neff recently observed that many evangelicals do not have a thorough understanding of the Gospel: "No one should be an accidental evangelical—or a merely cultural one. Unfortunately, few evangelicals can actually articulate the gospel. They can lead people to Christ and help them pray the sinner's prayer, but when it comes to setting forth just how Jesus saves, most of us flounder."[2]

7. *The Challenge of Our Old Sin Natures.* Even after we become Christians, we remain sinners, still prone to wander away from God. We can begin to lose our first love for Christ. We can begin to treat the Gospel of Jesus Christ in an offhand manner. Even though we should know better, we throw ourselves into a renewed quest for material gain, reputation, and fame. As for telling other people about Christ, we are too busy and too self-absorbed to be concerned about their eternal salvation.

In response to these very real challenges—and this is by no means an exhaustive list—a growing number of evangelicals have come to the same conclusion: As a community of Christian believers we need to love Christ more; we need to depend more on the power of the Holy Spirit in living our lives; we need to be a people given to prayer; we need to demonstrate more compassion and love for our neighbors; we need a fresh understanding of the Gospel of Jesus Christ; we need to appreciate more fully that the Gospel is the power for salvation (Rom. 1:16).

If we have a renewed love for Christ and a deeper knowledge of the biblical Gospel, neither the temptation of radical pluralism, nor that of inclusivism, nor that of an unprincipled ecumenism, nor that of a falsely construed separatism will be as compelling or persuasive for us. Moreover, we ourselves will be less inclined to be intolerant when we understand that, as sinners, we are no different from anyone else who needs to be saved by God's amazing grace. We will be quite disenchanted with any initiative that attempts to force conversions upon others when we understand that unless God the Holy Spirit convicts people of their sins, they will not become disciples of Jesus Christ. And if we are being persecuted, we will understand that the Gospel of Jesus Christ gives us great hope. Nothing can in fact separate us from the love of God, even death itself (Rom. 8:35–38).

Thus it is paramount for us as evangelical Christians to come to a deeper understanding of the Gospel of Jesus Christ. But where do we turn to find a careful exposition of what the Gospel is—an exposition that is firmly rooted in Holy Scripture, God's Word?

THE NEED FOR A NEW GOSPEL STATEMENT

Within the last century, evangelicals—who derive their very name from the Evangel, or Gospel—have crafted relatively few detailed statements designed to explain what the Gospel is. They have written many fine books on the Gospel, volumes that richly deserve our careful study. But they have created few statements that have been embraced by the evangelical community at large.

Perhaps the last time Protestant Christians set forth a statement on the Gospel that did garner widespread evangelical support, especially in North America, was toward the beginning of the twentieth century. A discussion of the Gospel appeared in scattered articles contained in a series of pamphlets collectively called *The Fundamentals: A Testimony for the Truth* (1910–15). These publications represented a large evangelical initiative in which North American and British Protestants from various denominations attempted to enumerate the basic doctrines upon which Protestant Christians agreed. In doing so, they described the Gospel of Jesus Christ in some detail.

The intended audience for *The Fundamentals: A Testimony for the Truth* was nothing less than all English-speaking Protestant leaders throughout the world. The publisher of the pamphlets declared, "All English-speaking Protestant pastors, evangelists, missionaries, theological professors, theological students, Y.M.C.A. secretaries, Sunday School superintendents, religious lay workers, and editors of religious publications throughout the earth, are entitled to a free copy of each volume of 'The FUNDAMENTALS.'" Interest in this offer was substantial. Several million copies of the pamphlets were distributed to Christians in

North America, Great Britain, and elsewhere. Two wealthy businessmen subsidized the project.

After 1915, relatively few statements defining the Gospel of Jesus Christ appeared that received as wide distribution and consideration by the evangelical community as had *The Fundamentals: A Testimony for the Truth*. During the 1940s and 1950s, many evangelical parachurch organizations were created. Their statements of faith, however, tended to be relatively brief in scope and generally served as the doctrinal guidelines for their respective organizations. By contrast, *The Lausanne Covenant* (1974) and *The Manila Manifesto: An Elaboration of the Lausanne Covenant Fifteen Years Later* (1989) gained a large, appreciative international audience. Throughout the world Christians studied these documents with great benefit. Along with statements by the World Evangelical Fellowship, they seemed to fill a genuine need for written expressions that carefully articulate the Gospel of Jesus Christ.

In the 1980s and '90s, however, lengthy discussions and tense debates emerged in evangelical circles and in Christendom at large regarding the role of the doctrine of justification by faith alone in any definition of the Gospel. They revealed a pressing need for a fresh statement on the Gospel that clearly enunciates this doctrine as a central component.

Nevertheless, some of us may wonder if any such statement is really needed. After all, we believe that we personally have a fairly good grasp of what the Gospel is. If anything, we may sense with a little embarrassment that our familiarity with the Gospel has almost made it "old news" for us. But the discussions and debates of the past two decades made it abundantly clear that it is imperative for evangelical Christians to understand clearly what the Gospel of Jesus Christ is. If we are to communicate this Good News to others, it is important that we ourselves understand it well. Moreover, the apostle Paul goes so far as to say that a person is "eternally condemned" who preaches any gospel other than God's Gospel (Gal. 1:5–11). Much confusion can ensue when the Gospel is not faithfully proclaimed or when it is not communicated with clarity.

Failing to understand the Gospel, we can easily slip into listening to the siren calls of false gospels and not even realize it. Moreover, even if we are believers, we may miss out on enjoying the marvelous hope the Gospel affords. Our familiarity with the Gospel may dull our sensitivities to such a point that we no longer appreciate and stand in amazement at the unique power of the Gospel to bring about salvation and to transform lives (Rom. 1:16).

THE GOSPEL OF JESUS CHRIST: AN EVANGELICAL CELEBRATION

Sensing the need for a fresh articulation of the Gospel of Jesus Christ, a number of evangelicals determined to draft a wide-ranging statement. They included J. I. Packer, John N. Akers, Timothy George, John Ankerberg, R. C. Sproul, Harold Myra, David Neff, John Armstrong, Tom Oden, D. A. Carson, Scott Hafemann, Keith Davey, Maxie Dunnam, Erwin Lutzer, and John Woodbridge. In June 1999, *Christianity Today* published the fruit of their reflection, "The Gospel of Jesus Christ: An Evangelical Celebration." The statement has also been translated into a number of languages.

Appended to the Gospel statement are the names of some 115 evangelical leaders who have endorsed the document. They include men and women; they include Presbyterians, Methodists, Lutherans, Baptists, Pentecostals, Charismatics, and people who belong to other churches. Among the endorsers are African Americans, Asian Americans, Hispanics, and Whites. They minister as presidents of colleges and seminaries, denominational leaders, pastors, evangelists, professors, television and radio executives, publishers, and leaders in parachurch organizations. A few of the signatories are Europeans, including Dr. John Stott from England and Dr. Henri Blocher from France.

Since its appearance in July 1999, another eighty-five evangelical leaders have endorsed the Gospel statement, among them Dr. Billy Graham. At the back of this book you have the opportunity to add your signature as well.

Those who drafted "The Gospel of Jesus Christ: An Evangelical Celebration" hoped that the statement would not only foster unity among evangelical believers but also help us all to understand the Gospel better, including one of its central components, the doctrine of justification by faith alone. The children of the Protestant Reformation for centuries have affirmed this as the doctrine upon which the church of Jesus Christ either stands or falls. We are justified in God's sight through faith alone in Christ alone. Ephesians 2:8–9 states, "For it is by grace you have been saved, through faith—and this not from yourselves, it is the gift of God—not of works, so that no one can boast." The doctrine of justification by faith alone is not merely a theological construct of theologians; it is a biblical teaching that gives all glory to Christ for our salvation.

In his introduction to the Statement, Neff highlights the critical significance of the doctrine of justification by faith alone: "Last year, two evangelical theologians had a bright idea. Wouldn't it wonderful, they said, if evangelicals could achieve a broad consensus on the gospel and join in a common statement? These theologians felt the pinch of recent tense discussions over how to define the doctrine of justification, a key element of the gospel."

The favorable reaction of so many leaders in the evangelical community to the Statement suggests that a broad consensus on the doctrine of justification by faith alone does in fact exist among evangelical Christians. They say with conviction and joy about the Gospel of Jesus Christ: "This We Believe."

As Joseph Stowell observes in this volume, the commitment of evangelicals to the truth of the Gospel of Jesus Christ forms the basis of their unity with each other. Evangelicals belong to a large, international, and multiethnic family of Christians who affirm and celebrate the Gospel of Jesus Christ. Together we proclaim it is God's Good News for the World.

THE PURPOSE OF THIS BOOK

The purpose of this book is to help us all understand the Gospel of Jesus Christ better. Whether we are pastors or laypersons, educators or homemakers, businesspeople or farmers, nurses or teachers, single or married, there is hardly anything in life more important for us to grasp than how God has graciously provided for our salvation in Christ Jesus.

Each chapter, written by a leading evangelical Christian, unpacks a key theme related to the Gospel and refers to discussions of this theme in the Statement. In this way the book serves as a commentary of sorts on the Gospel statement. The Statement itself can be easily consulted at the back of the book.

You will also find in each chapter a brief story about how the Gospel transformed someone's life.

The chapters follow a certain progression of thought. Ravi Zacharias opens the discussion by responding to a very important question, often on the minds of many moderns: Is there any meaning to life? J. I. Packer explains that for us to grasp the Good News of Jesus Christ, we must first understand the "bad news" about who we are: We really are born rebels. Kevin Vanhoozer helps us to understand who Jesus Christ is according to the witness of the biblical writers. His discussion should bring us an even greater sense of how majestic and loving Jesus Christ is, our wonderful Savior and Lord, whom we worship and serve. Then Scott Hafemann explains why it was necessary for Christ to die on the cross.

Tom Oden provides compelling evidence that Jesus Christ did, in fact, triumph over death through the resurrection. He also makes the intriguing proposal that if we viewed the resurrection of Christ the way the first-century Christians did, it would transform the way we live out our faith. Ajith Fernando addresses head-on the important question, What difference does it make that a person is a Christian or not, anyway? He argues that Christianity is the only world religion that gives its followers true love, joy, and peace. The question he tackles is an especially significant one for him, a citizen of Sri Lanka, a nation in which evangelicals represent a very small percentage of the population. Maxie Dunnam explains that the believer is not alone in attempting to live the Christian life; the Holy Spirit empowers believers and provides all the resources needed to face the temptations and trials of life. Joni Eareckson Tada gives us a wonderful description of what heaven is like and how our hope of heaven should influence the way we live now.

Tite Tiénou answers the vexing criticism suggested by some that Christianity is a "Western religion" and therefore should not be proclaimed throughout the entire world as Christ commanded. Tiénou is an African Christian leader who has personally had to wrestle with this criticism raised in many quarters of the world. Lee Strobel offers very practical advice about how we might more effectively tell others of the Good News of Jesus Christ. His chapter constitutes a extraordinary mini-manual on evangelism. Joseph Stowell helps us understand that we belong to a wonderful family of believers who affirm the truth of the Gospel of Jesus Christ. He rightfully proposes that evangelical unity can only be based on this truth.

Finally, Timothy George demonstrates that the Gospel of Jesus Christ as expressed in John 3:16 gives world history its ultimate meaning. In some ways, George's closing chapter serves as a matching bookend for Ravi Zacharias's opening chapter; both chapters give a resounding affirmative answer to the question, Is there any meaning to life? This meaning is found only in the Gospel of Jesus Christ, the Good News for the world.

It is our hope that after you have reflected upon the Statement and have read this book, you will have gained a more profound love for Jesus Christ and his Gospel. You will be stirred afresh by the marvelous hope the Gospel of Jesus Christ affords. You will gain a renewed appreciation of the power of the Gospel to change lives (Rom. 1:16). You will know more about how you can experience the power of the Holy Spirit in living the Christian life. You will sense that you are not alone but belong to a large international family of like-minded believers who are our brothers and sisters in Christ.[3]

In a word, this book is intended to encourage, comfort, and instruct each one of us as we seek to follow Christ as Lord and Savior. May we recommit ourselves to sharing the Good News of Jesus Christ with our neighbors and friends. May we pray and work for the unity of Christian believers—a unity based on the truth of the Gospel. And may we love, care for, and pray for our brothers and sisters throughout the world—many of whom are suffering under persecution as faithful followers of Jesus Christ.

A POSTSCRIPT

How might this book serve as a resource in helping all of us gain a better understanding of the Gospel?

1. Pastors, elders, and other leaders of churches may wish to study this resource book together, reviewing in particular "The Gospel of Jesus Christ: An Evangelical Celebration."
2. The leaders of parachurch organizations might wish to assign this resource book as a part of a staff training program.
3. Members of Sunday school classes and Bible study groups might wish to use this resource book on the Gospel together. The twelve chapters constitute a three-month curriculum. The study questions at the end of each of the twelve chapters can facilitate the group's discussion.
4. Individual Christians may wish to reflect on this book in personal devotions or with a prayer partner.
5. The leadership of churches and parachurch ministries might wish to reflect on their own statements of faith in light of "The Gospel of Jesus Christ: An Evangelical Celebration."

The editors would like to express a word of appreciation to those who made this book possible. Whatever merits the book might possess, the distinguished authors of the twelve chapters deserve the credit. All of the authors have full schedules in writing and speaking, yet they sacrificially and humbly gave of themselves to their writings tasks. They accepted difficult writing deadlines with equanimity and grace. It has been a pleasure to work with these evangelical Christians who are so committed to Christ and desirous that the Good News of salvation be proclaimed throughout the entire world.

The editorial staff at Zondervan also deserves our sincere thanks. Each member of this staff evidenced superb skills. Each has the very same commitment to Christ as the authors and the same desire that this book might advance the proclamation of the Gospel throughout the world.

To these Christian colleagues and to those who drafted "The Gospel of Jesus Christ: An Evangelical Celebration," we express our heartfelt thanks.

We close by citing the last paragraphs of the Statement:

> Centuries ago it was truly said that in things necessary there must be unity, in things less than necessary there must be liberty, and in all things there must be charity. We see all these Gospel truths as necessary.
>
> Now to God, the Author of the truth and grace of this Gospel, through Jesus Christ, its subject and our Lord, be praise and glory for ever and ever. Amen.

Notes

1. Patrick Johnstone, *Operation World: The Day-to-Day Guide to Praying for the World* (Grand Rapids: Zondervan, 1993), pp. 25–26.

2. "A Call to Evangelical Unity," *Christianity Today* (June 14, 1999): 49.

3. It is important to keep in mind that the signatories have endorsed the Statement, "The Gospel of Jesus Christ: An Evangelical Celebration," not the chapters of this book. The editors have sought to ensure that these chapters accurately reflect the meaning and the implications of the Statement. But since the contributors, like the other signatories, come from various theological and denominational traditions, they may express themselves on secondary matters in ways that others might not. So to endorse the Statement is not necessarily to endorse every jot and tittle in this book.

This Gospel sets forth Jesus Christ as the living Savior, Master, Life, and Hope of all who put their trust in him. It tells us that the eternal destiny of all people depends on whether they are savingly related to Jesus Christ.

This Gospel is the only Gospel: there is no other; and to change its substance is to pervert and indeed destroy it. This Gospel is so simple that small children can understand it, and it is so profound that studies by the wisest theologians will never exhaust its riches.

■

We affirm that the Gospel entrusted to the church is, in the first instance, God's Gospel (Mark 1:14; Rom. 1:1). God is its author, and he reveals it to us in and by his Word. Its authority and truth rest on him alone.

We deny that the truth or authority of the Gospel derives from any human insight or invention (Gal. 1:1–11). We also deny that the truth or authority of the Gospel rests on the authority of any particular church or human institution.

—*The Gospel of Jesus Christ:*
An Evangelical Celebration

1

DOES MY LIFE HAVE ANY MEANING?

Ravi Zacharias

The quest for meaning is as old as the hills. One of the most familiar stories in Greek mythology is that of Sisyphus. Poor Sisyphus reaped the displeasure of the gods when he disclosed to mere mortals secrets that were known only within celestial ranks. His sentence consisted in having to roll a massive stone to the top of a hill, watch it roll down again, and repeat the exercise endlessly. His was a life consigned to futility.

All kinds of intriguing suggestions have been made by philosophers to rescue Sisyphus. "If only Sisyphus could have changed the way he viewed his task, so that he enjoyed rolling stones," opined one. "Could he not have rolled up a different stone each time, so that someone else could have built a monument with it?" asked another. In proposing such options, these thinkers not only miss the point of the predicament, but more seriously, they completely miss the very essence of meaninglessness.

We can readily discern the reason behind the futility that holds Sisyphus in its grasp. But as times have changed and possibilities abound, one would think we have come a long way from Sisyphus's malady. Instead, we deal with the same problem, only now, not in mythological terms as much as in the stark reality of our busy and varied lives.

MATERIALISM'S DESPAIR

Life magazine some years ago published an entire book on how individuals have coped with this quest for meaning. The publication is a fascinating cross section of words and pictures—from philosophers to drug addicts, from painters to plumbers. Here is one from José Martinez, a taxi driver in New York, who provides the sound bite of despair:

> We're here to die, just live and die. I live driving a cab. I do some fishing, take my girl out, pay taxes, do a little reading, then get ready to drop dead. Life is a big fake! You're rich or you're poor. You're here, you're gone. You're like the wind. After you're gone, other people will come. It's too late to make it better. Everyone's fed up, can't believe in nothing no more. People have no pride. People have no fear! People only care about one thing and that's money. We're gonna destroy ourselves, nothing we can do about it. The only cure for the world's illness is nuclear war—wipe everything out and start over. We've become like a cornered animal, fighting for survival. Life is nothing.[1]

There is a haunting candor behind this man's admission. But fearful of seeing ourselves reflected in his portrait, we rationalize his predicament: "Of course a man struggling to make a living, harried by those in control of his life, is bound to seem hopeless as well. If he were given unbridled freedom with no monetary constraints, meaninglessness would vanish." We may not word it in such a way but quietly assume that it is so. As we unpack that assumption, we get to the core of what meaninglessness is all about and why it is endemic to the human situation.

PLEASURE'S CONCESSION

No piece of ancient literature was more forthright and more penetrating of this struggle than the book of Ecclesiastes, credited to the pen of Solomon. His opening lines charge into his deduction—"Meaningless! Meaningless! Everything is meaningless!" Then he takes a regressive journey, cataloguing his path to that cynicism—wisdom, pleasure, work, material gain, and much else. He comes away empty.

> I denied myself nothing my eyes desired;
> I refused my heart no pleasure.
> My heart took delight in all my work,
> and this was the reward for all my labor.
> Yet when I surveyed all that my hands had done
> and what I had toiled to achieve,
> everything was meaningless, a chasing after the wind;
> nothing was gained under the sun.
>
> *ECCLESIASTES 2:10–11*

This was no Sisyphus speaking. At Solomon's command, others rolled stones up steep hills so that he could build his stables, palaces, and temples. He was a man who boasted capacities of unparalleled intellect and imagination that made him the envy of many, and who presided over the most pompous court of his time. In the end, he groaned that "under the sun" there was a monotony, a circularity, and a fatality to all human endeavor.

This assessment by Solomon presents a most startling, almost fearsome reality: Meaninglessness does not come from being weary of pain but from being weary of pleasure. Solomon is not the only one surrounded with wealth and success who has talked of such disappointment at the end of the road. That refrain is repeated with constancy. A modern-day writer, Jack Higgins, was asked at the pinnacle of his success what he now knows that he wished he had known as a younger man. "I wish I had known that when you get to the top, there is nothing there." So it is not the condemnation of Sisyphus that restricts meaninglessness to the ranks of the monotonous. The condition is universal and cuts across cultures, wealth, and generations.

THE NATURALIST'S ANSWER

In recent times scientists have entered into the fray. Some in their ranks have castigated philosophers for raising the problem in the first place and creating a need that ought never to have been manufactured. As naturalists, they contend that scientific laws are adequate to account for everything we experience. Their response to the philosopher's questions staggers the imagination. Here, for example, is the suggestion of Harvard paleontologist Stephen Jay Gould:

> The human species has inhabited this planet for only 250,000 years or so—roughly .0015 percent of the history of life, the last inch of the cosmic mile. The world fared perfectly well without us for all but the last moment of earthly time—and this fact makes our appearance look more like an accidental afterthought than the culmination of a prefigured plan.
>
> Moreover, and more important, the pathways that have led to our evolution are quirky, improbable, unrepeatable and utterly unpredictable. Human evolution is not random; it makes sense and can be explained after the fact. But wind back life's tape to the dawn of time and let it play again—and you will never get humans a second time. . . . We cannot read the meaning of life passively in the facts of nature. We must construct these answers ourselves—from our own wisdom and ethical sense. There is no other way.[2]

The naturalist's contribution is to assert that the search for meaning itself is pointless because it creates the possibility of metaphysical certainty, when in truth the empirical world does not need such assurances.

But what Gould correctly establishes is that the "what" of life and the "why" of life are inextricably connected. For a philosophy that defines life apart from God there is a plethora of options, each in one way or another forfeiting the right to judge anyone else's choice. G. K. Chesterton's reminder to them is appropriate: "The tragedy of disbelieving in God is not that a person ends up believing in nothing; alas! it is much worse. He may end up believing in anything." By contrast, where God is espoused, life is then intrinsically sacred—based on who he is and why he has made us in the first place. This divergence of options gives us our entry point into the subject: *What gives life meaning?*

A WORD TO THE NATURALIST

Michael Polanyi was professor of physical chemistry and social studies at the University of Manchester, a fellow of Merton College at Oxford, and a fellow of the Royal Society of England. In his book *Meaning*, Polanyi cautioned that if scientists wrongly apply their role, they are in danger of destroying the meaningfulness of life by reducing it to sheer matter, to say nothing of the reduction of their own discipline. Naturalists would do well to remember his caution.

When science overplays its hand, it picks its own pockets. As the sharp edges of life stab us from infancy to maturity, the "whys" of life proliferate and seek coherent answers. In the sense that Polanyi warns us, Stephen Hawking reinforces this concern at the end of his book, *A Brief History of Time*. Hawking says in his conclusion, after discussing the "what" of life: "If we find the answer to [the question of why], . . . then we would know the mind of God."[3]

FOUR COMPONENTS OF MEANING

It is the mind of God to which we turn in seeking an answer to meaning. The Gospel of Jesus Christ deals precisely with the question "why"—the why of creation, and the why of our existence. Jesus says, "I have come that they may have life, and have it to the full" (John 10:10). He tells his disciples that he wanted their joy to be full. All who came to him—the wealthy and the poor, the young and the old—drew life and joy from him. How did he give life meaning?

We can take many approaches in coming to the answer. I shall take an indirect route, which you can attribute to my Indian heritage. The shortest route is not always the best route because you miss many of the needed lessons along the way. I have to wonder if that is why the Lord took his people through a forty-year journey in the desert when it could have been accomplished in a few weeks.

For our purposes, let us divide life into four stages—childhood, adolescence, young adulthood, and maturity—and in that context demonstrate and explore how, at each stage, meaning is pursued, attained, and sometimes lost. At the end, we will see God's answer to it all.

1. The Romance of Enchantment—Wonder

The first stage we will consider is the world of a child. I am deeply indebted here to the writings of G. K. Chesterton, who unabashedly proclaimed that he learned more about life by observing children in a nursery than he ever did by reflecting upon the writings of any of the philosophers.

FINDING THE ANSWER

As a reporter and legal affairs editor for the *Chicago Tribune*, Lee Strobel was used to asking questions. But with regard to matters of religion and God, he figured he already had all the answers: Evolution adequately explained how life began, and God—if he existed—was merely a product of wishful thinking, of ancient mythology, of primitive superstition.

Then one day in 1979 his wife became a Christian. Wham! As Lee tells it, "I braced for the worst, feeling like the victim of a bait-and-switch scam. I had married one Leslie—the fun Leslie, the carefree Leslie, the risk-taking Leslie—and now I feared she was going to turn into some sort of sexually repressed prude who would trade our upwardly mobile lifestyle for all-night prayer vigils and volunteer work in grimy soup kitchens.

"Instead I was pleasantly surprised—even fascinated—by the fundamental changes in her character, her integrity, and her personal confidence."

Thus Lee began asking some hard questions and "launched an all-out investigation into the facts surrounding the case for Christianity." He probed

What is it about a child that fascinates us? More to the issue, what is it that fascinates a child? The answer to both questions is the same. Is it not that sense of wonder that pervades much of what the child sees and experiences? Listen to young fathers or mothers who have just welcomed a little one into their arms and their home—they themselves are starry-eyed, enveloped in the wonder of this lovely bundle of life that has immeasurably enriched their lives.

My wife and I had an unforgettable experience several years ago when I was speaking in the Middle East. Our journey took us by taxi from Jordan to Israel by way of the West Bank, crossing over at the Allenby Bridge. Once on Israeli soil, we were taken into a highly secured immigration building for routine but rigorous questioning, which was to precede our procurement of a visitor's visa. My wife, our small daughter Sarah, and I stood in one of the lines, having been warned to expect an emotionally taxing day. The room was full of machine-gun-clutching soldiers. There were sandbags piled against every wall. A sense of unease pervaded the room.

history, archaeology, and ancient literature and, most importantly, "picked apart the Bible verse by verse." The result: "Over time the evidence of the world—of history, of science, of philosophy, of psychology—began to point toward the unthinkable."

The skeptic became a believer. The questioner became a follower. He placed his faith in Jesus Christ as Lord and Savior. He became a spokesman for the Gospel that he had at one time dismissed as myth. In time he became a teaching pastor at Willow Creek Community Church near Chicago. Today he is a pastor at Saddleback Community Church in Orange County, California.

For Lee Strobel, the Gospel is no longer a myth or the object of scorn. It is "the power of God for the salvation of everyone who believes: first for the Jew, then for the Gentile" (Rom. 1:16).

Based on Lee Strobel, *The Case for Christ: A Journalist's Personal Investigation of the Evidence for Jesus* (Grand Rapids: Zondervan, 1998), pp. 13–14.

Finally it was our turn to be interrogated. Unknown to me, as she surveyed the room, Sarah had locked eyes with a young Israeli soldier who was staring back at her in "eye-to-eye combat." Suddenly and strangely there was a moment of silence in the room, broken by the squeaky little voice of my daughter asking the soldier, "Excuse me, do you have any bubble gum?"

Words alone cannot fully express to you what that little voice and plea did for everyone in the room, where hitherto the weapons of war and the world of "adult ideas" had held everyone at bay. Those who understood English could not repress a smile, and those who did not understand English knew a soldier's heart had been irresistibly touched. All eyes were now on him.

The soldier paused for a moment, then carefully handed his machine gun to a colleague. He came over to where we were standing, looked endearingly at Sarah, and picked her up in his arms. He took her into a back room and returned a few minutes later. On one arm he carried her; with the other he carried three glasses of lemonade on a tray—one for Sarah, one for my wife, and one for me. Our interrogation was short. In fact, the young soldier brought his jeep to the door and drove us to the taxi stand, sending us on our way to Jericho. I have often remarked that Sarah earned her year's keep with one little question voiced at the right time.

The incredible power of a child! The wonder-filled face of a two-year-old girl changed the feel in the room from fear to fondness. The very strength of that child's influence was only buttressed by the fact that she was not even aware of the power she wielded or of what she had accomplished.

But as a child gets older, that world of wonder begins to erode. The world becomes commonplace, and the harsh reality of conflicts, wars, and evil invades. The second stage has arisen. The question moves from a sense of wonder to the knowledge of the truth. One cannot live in a world of fairy tales at this stage. The harder questions of life surface: What is true? What is good? What is evil?

Nevertheless, wonder is a necessary component of meaning at every stage in life. But how does one find that wonder when fantasy is shattered before reality? May I suggest that wonder is not found from the pen of an author writing fantasy or otherwise. It is not even in an argument, nor is it in mere dogma. There is a clue to meaning in our experiences with children; that clue is in relationships. Look into the eyes of that soldier clasping that child. Look into the face of a mother nursing her infant. Look at the tears of a loved one weeping at the pain of another. Life's most tender and wonderful meaning comes not in the stories of "wonderland" but by way of precious relationships. That is our first clue.

In the Gospel of Jesus Christ, God offers us the ultimate relationship with himself. At the heart of the Gospel message is the offer of Christ to come and dwell in us in fellowship—making us his children and extending to us his care. The answer to the search for wonder lies in a relationship with Christ. But is this, too, mere fantasy? No. Jesus Christ went beyond fantasy: He pointed beyond the fantastic to the fantastically true. How did he do this? That takes us to the next stage.

2. Truth—An Endangered Species

In the childhood years, wonder can be attained by dabbling in a world of fantasy. That is both the glory and the fragility of childhood. But as the years pass, wonder is eroded in the face of reality and in the recognition that life may not be lived in a fairy-tale world. A displacement is brought about by the ever-increasing demand of the mind, not just for the fantastic but for the true. The search for truth then becomes all-pervasive, drawing implications for the essence and destiny of life itself. Even if not overtly admitted, the search for truth is nevertheless hauntingly present, propelled by the need for incontrovertible answers to four inescapable questions, those dealing with origin, meaning, morality, and destiny—connecting the what and the why. No thinking person can avoid this search, and it can only end when one is convinced that the answers espoused are true. Aristotle was right when he said that all philosophy begins with wonder; but the journey, I suggest, can only progress through truth.

And so we move away from the world of imagination in a child to the cerebral world of knowledge and truth.

Judging Our Judgments

The Scriptures give us a fascinating discussion between the Roman governor Pontius Pilate and Jesus. We read in John 18 that Jesus has been brought to him by the Jewish high priests, who wanted to execute Jesus because of his claim to be equal with God. Pilate asked Jesus, "Are you a king?" We can well imagine a sardonic grin planted on the face of this nervous puppet of Caesar's as he inquired into the kingship of this Jewish carpenter. Jesus responded with a question: "Are you asking this on your own, or has someone else set you up?" Pilate was somewhat exasperated by this seeming insolence. "Look," he answered, "I did not bring you here—your own people have done that."

Then Jesus answered, "My kingdom is not of this world. If it were, my servants would fight to prevent my arrest by the Jews. But now my kingdom is from another place."

Pilate said, "Ah! So you are a king."

The response of Jesus discloses Pilate's real predicament: "You are right in saying I am a king. In fact, for this reason I was born, and for this I came into the world, to testify to the truth. Everyone on the side of truth listens to me."

Pilate muttered, "What is truth?" and walked away.

The answer of Jesus is both subtle and daring. The fundamental problem Jesus was exposing to Pilate and to the world is not the paucity of available truth; it is more often the hypocrisy of our search. Truthfulness in the heart, said Jesus, precedes truth in the objective realm. Intent is prior to content. The most provocative statement Jesus made during that penetrating conversation was that the truthfulness or falsity of an individual's heart was revealed by that person's response to him. The implication was uncompromising. He was, and is, the truth. What you do with him defines the truthfulness of your search.

Was this statement made in a vacuum? Not by any stretch of imagination. From Jesus' birth to his death; from the way he lived to what he taught; from the wealth of prophecy to the completion of fulfillment; from the historicity of the Scriptures to the transformation in lives; by his death and his resurrection, it may be safely said—whether we are skeptics, like the historian W. E. H. Lecky, or we are among the devout who follow him: "No one ever spoke like him or lived like him." But if the heart is not truthful, then the very Truth of Christ is missed.

When we miss seeing who he is, it is because we get tripped up by the power of preconceived notions. Jon Krakauer, in his book *Into Thin Air*, tells a gripping story. His book recounts the ill-fated ascent of Mount Everest in 1996, in which many lives were lost, including those of the most adept leaders. At one point he recounts an episode with Andy Harris, one of the expedition guides, who had been exhausted by his conquest of the summit. On his descent, Harris started to run out of oxygen when he came across a cache of oxygen canisters. But, though starved for oxygen, he argued with his fellow climbers that all the canisters were empty. Those to whom he was speaking shouted back that these canisters were indeed full—they themselves had left them there for just such a time as this. But Harris was beguiled by a brain devoid of oxygen and made the false judgment that that which he held in his hand could not help him.[4]

What a parable of life that is. Similarly, Pilate was standing face-to-face with the truth, but snared by the disorientation of power, he walked away from the source of all life.

Personal, Not Merely Propositional

In this response of Jesus to Pilate we see how the message is unique to help us break free from the asphyxiation of other pursuits that leave us lost. Just as wonder is found in a person, so the Scriptures claim and prove that truth is fully embodied in a person, Jesus Christ. It is not so much that he *has* the answers to life's questions as much as that he *is* the answer. Again, we find the truth not merely in abstractions or in creedal affirmations but in knowing him. When the apostle Thomas asked Jesus to show him the way to God, Jesus answered, "I am the way and the truth and the life. No one comes to the Father except through me" (John 14:6).

Two obvious deductions follow from this assertion that Jesus made: First, that truth is absolute, and second, that truth is knowable. In fact, immediately preceding this conversation with Thomas, Jesus talked about the reality of heaven and said, "If it were not so, I would have told you" (John 14:2). Everything Jesus affirms about reality corresponds to reality. Everything he denies about reality is because that denial corresponds to reality.[5]

Jesus' absolute claim that he is the way, the truth, and the life means categorically that anything that contradicts what he says is by definition false. As we study his claims and his teaching, we find a message that beautifully unfolds, encompassing the breadth of human need and the depth of human intellect. It is the beauty of Jesus' life that children could understand him, yet the staunchest of skeptics such as Thomas would ultimately bend that knee and call him Lord.

3. Love's Labor Won

I have so far presented two essential components for meaning—the pursuit of wonder and the knowledge of truth—and have suggested that they are both fulfilled in a person. The third component essential to meaning is love. From the wonder of childhood to the search for truth in adolescence, we come to the consummation of love in young adulthood. Christopher Morley said, "If we all discovered that we had only five minutes left to say all that we wanted to say, every telephone booth would be occupied by people calling other people to stammer that we love them."[6]

On love and marriage, G. K. Chesterton made this poignant observation: "They have invented a new phrase that is a black-and-white contradiction in two words—'free love.' As if a lover had been, or ever could be, free. It is the nature of love to bind itself."[7]

The statement that, for me, captures the concept of love so clearly and yet seems totally foreign to our "disposable" society is that "it is the nature of love to bind itself." Realistically, what passes for love today would be more aptly described as self-gratification, or indulgence.

How strange that we call the sexual act "making love" when in actuality, if that act is without commitment, it is a literal and figurative denuding of love in which the individual is degraded to an object. Love is not love when it has been manufactured for the moment. Love is the posture of the soul, and its entailments are binding. When love is shallow, the heart is empty, but when the sacrifice of love is understood, one can drink deeply from its cup and be completely fulfilled. The more we consume love selfishly, the more wretched and impoverished we become.

But here, once more, the message of Christ stands supremely magnificent. At the heart of the Gospel is a Savior who loves us and offered himself for us. Even Mahatma Gandhi, a Hindu, stated that the cross of Jesus constantly showed itself as an unparalleled expression of God's grace. Dr. E. Stanley Jones, a famed and noted missionary to India, used to tell the story of a man, a devout Hindu government official, to whom he was trying to explain the concept of the Cross. The man kept reiterating to Dr. Jones that he could not possibly make sense of the crucifixion of Jesus Christ and the offer of salvation by virtue of the cross. Their conversations on this subject were circular and seemingly unsolvable to his satisfaction.

One day, through a series of circumstances, the man involved himself in an extramarital affair that tormented his conscience. He could live with himself no longer, and finally, looking into the eyes of his devoted wife, he told her the heartrending story of his betrayal. The hours and days of anguish and pain became weeks of heaviness in her heart. Yet, as she weathered the early shock, she confessed to him not only her deep sense of hurt but also the promise of her undying commitment and love.

Suddenly, almost like a flash of lightning illuminating the night sky, the man found himself muttering, "Now I know what it means to see love crucified by sin." He bent his knee in repentance to the Christ who went to the cross for him, binding his heart with a new commitment to his Lord and to his wife.

But there is something more, and here we get to the crux of meaning. In Christian terms, love does not stand merely as an emotion or even as an expression. In a relationship with God, it ultimately flowers into worship. All earthly relationships as we know them will someday end. It is in worship alone that wonder and truth coalesce and our hearts become enriched by his love. The enrichment that results from worship feeds all other relationships and helps us to hold sacred our commitments.

D. H. Lawrence was right when he said the deepest hunger of the human heart goes beyond love. The name Jesus gave to that "beyond" is worship. And Thomas Wolfe was right that there is a sense of cosmic loneliness apart from God. In Christ that loneliness is conquered as the hungers of the human heart are met and the struggles of the intellect are answered.

How is that so? one might ask.

Archbishop William Temple defined worship in these terms:

> Worship is the submission of all of our nature to God. It is the quickening of conscience by His holiness, nourishment of mind by His truth, purifying of imagination by His beauty, opening of the heart to His love, and submission of will to His purpose. All this gathered up in adoration is the greatest of all expressions of which we are capable.[8]

The reason life is bereft of meaning is because of the essential fragmentation that is derived if life is nothing more than matter. But if our lives are designed for the supreme purpose of worship, then the sacred binds our lives and fuses every activity with meaning, even as it enables us to resist that which desacralizes life. It is not accidental that in one of the most notable of all of Jesus' conversations—the one he had with the woman at the well—the conversation began with thirsts of life and ended with the fulfillment of worship.

4. Crossing the Bar

Beginning with wonder in childhood, through the pursuit of truth in adolescence and the fulfillment of love in the adult years, we finally face in the end an old age that longs for security.

The question that must be answered if all other answers of Jesus are to be justified is the question of life beyond the grave.

Albert Camus said, "Death is philosophy's only problem." It is a problem indeed, and for Camus, who had no answer, meaninglessness was unshakable. By contrast, Jesus, at the graveside of a friend he loved, spoke these words: "I am the resurrection and the life. He who believes in me will live, even though he dies; and whoever lives and believes in me will never die" (John 11:25).

German Chancellor Konrad Adenauer once said to Billy Graham, as he surveyed the ruins of a post-war Germany, "Outside of the resurrection of Jesus Christ, I know of no other hope for mankind." That is because, outside of the resurrection, there is no transcending view of life. Hope ceases if there is no hope beyond the grave.

In closing, let me remind you of the four essential components to meaning in life—Wonder, Truth, Love, and Security. When one claims to have found meaning, that meaning must coalesce these four elements. And all four are found in the person of Jesus Christ, who alone is the perpetual novelty and brings life meaning by meeting the test at every stage. This is the thought reflected in the glorious words uttered by Malcolm Muggeridge upon his discovery of a personal relationship with Jesus Christ.

> I may, I suppose, regard myself as a relatively successful man. People occasionally stare at me in the streets, that's fame; I can fairly easily earn enough money to qualify for admission to the higher slopes of the Internal Revenue Service. That's success. Furnished with money and a little fame, even the elderly, if they care to, may partake of friendly diversions. That's pleasure. It might happen once in a while that something I said or wrote was sufficiently heeded for me to persuade myself that it represented a serious impact on our time. That's fulfillment. Yet, I say to you, and I beg you to believe me, multiply these tiny triumphs by millions, add them all up together, and they are nothing, less than nothing. Indeed, a positive impediment measured against one drop of that living water Christ offers to the spiritually thirsty, irrespective of who or what they are.[9]

Solomon came to the same conclusion. "Under the sun"—that is, in a closed system—all is meaningless. With the relationship God offers in the Son—opening up the eternal—wonder, truth, love, and security connect.

We have moved from the world of a child to the sunset years of life in our pursuit for meaning, and we have seen how this search for meaning fails if our lives are lived without God. Augustine said it well: "You have made us for Yourself and our hearts are restless until they find their rest in Thee." The apostle Paul triumphantly reminded us all that because of who we were, every deed could be done with purpose: "Whatever you do, do it all for the glory of God" (1 Cor. 10:31).

Those who understand this know what meaning is. Those who do not, still bear the burden of Sisyphus.

Notes

1. Quoted in David Friend, *The Meaning of Life* (Boston: Little, Brown, 1991), p. 90.
2. Stephen Jay Gould, quoted in Friend, *The Meaning of Life*, p. 33.
3. Stephen Hawking, *A Brief History of Time: From the Big Bang to Black Holes* (New York: Bantam, 1988), p. 175.
4. Jon Krakauer, *Into Thin Air: A Personal Account of the Mount Everest Disaster* (New York: Doubleday, 1998).
5. I have dealt with the subject of truth testing in greater detail in appendix 2, "The Establishment of a World View," in my book *A Shattered Visage: The Real Face of Atheism* (Grand Rapids: Baker, 1990), pp. 189ff.
6. Christopher Morley, quoted in a column by Ruth Walker in *Christian Science Monitor*, 20 November 1991.
7. G. K. Chesterton, *As I Was Saying* (Grand Rapids: Eerdmans, 1985), p. 267.
8. William Temple, quoted in David Watson, *I Believe in Evangelism* (Grand Rapids: Eerdmans, 1976), p. 157.
9. Malcolm Muggeridge, *Jesus Rediscovered* (Garden City, NY: Doubleday, 1969), p. 77.

Study Questions

1. Can you identify with Sisyphus, and if so, how?
2. Who are some examples of people who seemed to "have it all," yet suffered from emptiness?
3. Of the four components of meaning, which one have you pursued the most intensely? What were its limitations? In what ways was your pursuit successful?
4. What are some ways in which human relationships fail to provide complete meaning? What are some other avenues people seek?
5. Consider Archbishop Temple's definition of worship. In what ways have you experienced it? In what ways have you fallen short?
6. If you were to tell someone why the Christian life has meaning, what would you say?

Through the Gospel we learn that we human beings, who were made for fellowship with God, are by nature—that is, "in Adam" (1 Cor. 15:22)—dead in sin, unresponsive to and separated from our Maker. We are constantly twisting his truth, breaking his law, belittling his goals and standards, and offending his holiness by our unholiness, so that we truly are "without hope and without God in the world" (Rom. 1:18–32; 3:9–20; Eph. 2:1–3, 12).

■

We affirm that the Gospel diagnoses the universal human condition as one of sinful rebellion against God, which, if unchanged, will lead each person to eternal loss under God's condemnation.

We deny any rejection of the fallenness of human nature or any assertion of the natural goodness, or divinity, of the human race.

—*The Gospel of Jesus Christ: An Evangelical Celebration*

2

DOING IT MY WAY

ARE WE BORN REBELS?

J. I. Packer

On the night of November 14, 1940, the German Luftwaffe bombed the city of Coventry in England. At around 7:40, incendiary devices hit the beautiful St. Michael's Cathedral, which was built in 1373, and by 11:00 p.m. it was clear that nothing could be done to save the building. All that the townspeople could do was stand and watch it burn. One onlooker wrote, "The whole building was a seething mass of flame and piled up blazing beams and timbers interpenetrated and surmounted with dense bronze-coloured smoke. Through this could be seen the concentrated blaze caused by the burning organ, famous for its long history back to the time when Handel played upon it." Today all that remains of this glorious structure are the outer wall and the three-hundred-foot spire.

In many ways our present condition—the "human condition," as we grandly call it—corresponds to the ruins of a cathedral or palace or castle. The remnants of great dignity are still apparent, but the ruins are useless for their intended purpose until they undergo a rebuilding more radical than anyone contemplating the scene can imagine. Meantime, there is something tragic and deeply saddening about the ruins that sensitive persons cannot but feel. The ground plan of each decayed building gives a sense of how much majesty and structural beauty, and with it how much potential usefulness, have been lost.

That is how each human individual must appear to the eye of faith—the only difference between one and another being that some are already undergoing reconstruction through the grace of the Lord Jesus Christ while the rest, not being believers, are not yet "in the life," as Welsh Christians put it.

It needs to be said with all possible emphasis that it is only as we acknowledge the tragedy and feel the misery of our personal ruination through original sin that we shall properly value the Good News of the Savior. Only he can deliver us from the guilt and power of the sins through which our inbred sinfulness has found expression. Cornelius Plantinga Jr. writes, "For the Christian church (even in its recently popular seeker services) to ignore, euphemize, or otherwise mute the lethal reality of sin is to cut the nerve of the gospel. For the sober truth is that without full disclosure on sin, the gospel of grace becomes impertinent, unnecessary, and finally uninteresting."

BAD NEWS

The Gospel of Jesus Christ is the best news ever, following the worst news possible. The bad news is that the entire human race, from the moment of each person's conception in the womb, is offensive to God. Every action of every human being in our natural condition is so motivated and performed that in itself it cannot give God full and unmixed pleasure. The only prospect divine justice holds out is of eternal repudiation by God and separation from him. The mercy that brings sinners into God's fellowship is precisely not justice. Christians know, better than anyone, that justice from God would mean condemnation and hell for everyone.

Why is this? Because we have a proud, unbelieving, thoughtless, careless, greedy, self-serving spirit. We live to please ourselves, and in our hearts we keep God at bay. Our egocentric anti-God attitude seeks to play God, use God, fool God, and fight God at the same time. Our apathetic unconcern about love, truth, respect, honesty, integrity, and justice constantly disfigures our actual doings. In other words, we deserve condemnation because of the fact and fruit of our *original sin,* as both Catholics and Protestants, following Augustine, have conceived and labeled it.

A representative analysis of the notion is given in the ninth of the Anglican Articles of Religion (1563), under the heading "Of Original or Birth-sin."

> Original sin . . . is the fault and corruption of the Nature of every man, that naturally is ingendered of the offspring of Adam; whereby man is *very far gone from original righteousness,* and is of his own nature *inclined to evil,* so that the flesh lusteth always contrary to the spirit; and therefore *in every person born into this world, it deserveth God's wrath and damnation* . . . . And although there is no condemnation for those who believe and are baptized, yet the Apostle doth confess, that *passionate lust hath of itself the nature of sin* [italics added].

So the universal willfulness that leads us to go our own way and do our own thing is the instinct—we could even say the allergy—of original sin making itself felt.

Original sin is a mystery. That means there is more in it than our minds can grasp, or more than God has told us, or maybe both. Certainly, the folly, discontent, ingratitude, thoughtlessness, irreverence, credulity, and arrogance of the first human sin, as narrated in Genesis 3, defy rational explanation. When Paul affirms everyone's solidarity with Adam in condemnation and subjection to sin and death (see Romans 5:12, 20–21; 1 Corinthians 15:22), he does not enlarge on how this is so. We have to say of original sin, therefore, that it is a perversion in us all that none of us fully understand.

Yet when we acknowledge this mystery, it is profoundly illuminating, for unless we know about original sin we cannot properly understand any aspect of human behavior—our own or anyone else's. With that knowledge, however, we begin to understand everything human at the deepest level. Bernard Ramm writes, "Without this doctrine of sin much of human life and history remains forever opaque; with it a shaft of light is cast upon personal existence, social

AMAZED BY GRACE

We only appreciate what good news the Gospel is when we first understand the very bad news about our sins and sense how far we fall short of meeting God's standards of perfect righteousness.

John Newton understood this bad news very well. He had looked deep into his own heart and was disgusted by the raw, hideous evil he saw lurking there. As a ship's captain in the mid-1700s, he had been in the shameful business of the slave trade. He also well remembered that he had been an infidel and sexually promiscuous before his conversion. Then Newton the Slave Trader became Newton the Preacher, heralding the same Gospel he had previously scorned. Overwhelmed by the bad news of his sinfulness, he could only be thankful for the "Amazing Grace" that saved him. With this sense of deep gratitude, Newton penned these remarkable yet very simple words:

> Amazing grace! How sweet the sound,
> That saved a wretch like me!
> I once was lost, but now am found,
> Was blind, but now I see.

John Newton's "Amazing Grace" is probably the most frequently sung Christian hymn around the world. Millions of Christians see a picture of themselves in Newton's description of what he was like as an unconverted person. As scrubbed up as we may appear to others, we occasionally have glimpses of the ugliness of the sin in our own hearts. We know that without God's grace we are lost wretches. For us, too, grace is amazing. It was God's grace alone that allowed us to be found and to know Christ.

existence, and the course of history, giving clarity that nothing else in the religions of the world nor the philosophies of the world can provide." Moral and relational flaws, compounded by arrogance, envy, and irresponsibility, appear in all of us. The doctrine of original sin tells us why and explains to us that life as we live it and observe it in others is not life as our Creator meant it to be.

G. K. Chesterton was surely correct when he spoke of original sin as the one Christian truth that can be verified by observation anywhere in the world, any day of the week. Racially, something has gone ruinously wrong. All hearts are disordered, all affections are inordinate, all individuals are out of order as human beings and need to be put straight. The impulse to worship our Creator, which belonged to human nature as God made it, has become an impulse to do anything but that (see Paul on this subject, in Acts 14:15–17; 17:26–30; Romans 1:21–25).

A bishop's son is recorded as having said, "I must have a religion, and it mustn't be like Father's." In the same way, all human beings crave for someone to worship, but we seem to prefer alternative religions of human design to adoring our Creator. All religions, to be sure, embody some truth at some points. They all sense, however dimly, that human life is out of joint, and offer ways of deliverance, here and hereafter, from how things currently are. But only the Gospel of Jesus Christ identifies original sin—self-will in the heart producing perverse self-service in the life—as the deepest dimension of our human predicament.

As we face up to the Bible's teaching about sin, we do well to remind ourselves that biblical writers speak not as intellectual pundits, but as loyal trustees of God's revealed truth. The Word of God has become for them a lamp by which they see in the dark and travel safely through it (look at Psalm 119:105 for this picture). Their books narrate and analyze what has become clear to them in the limited circle of vision that the lamplight has created around them. We find them presenting God-related realities in a way calculated, not to satisfy our curiosity as secular moderns, but to make us conscious of our neediness as sinners, and to point us to the path of salvation by God's great grace.

That is how, first to last, Bible writers deal with the tragic twist in human nature that makes rebellion against God as real and natural (and for the most part as unnoticed) as breathing. Evasively and perhaps skeptically, we ask how such a thing could be. The Bible's response is to say bluntly that the fact that it *could* be is demonstrated by the fact that it *is*, and we moderns had better accept that, as all of Christendom once did.

It is ironic that while the modern West has been lurching wholesale into a new barbarism beyond our wildest nightmares (genocide, massacre, torture, systematic rape and cruelty, organized crime, and so on), psychologists, educationists, social theorists, and opinion-makers generally have been laboring to assure us that original sin was only ever a neurotic myth and that it would be very bad for us all to revert to it. To pump out such oracles in face of the above facts is perhaps the greatest example of cognitive dissonance that ever was! England's James I, who fancied himself a theologian and tried to prove that absolute monarchy is a biblical doctrine, was in his day called the wisest fool in Christendom. We modern Westerners, who fancy ourselves strategists for global community while denying original sin, may perhaps deserve to be called the wisest fools the world has yet seen.

The doctrine of original sin is in reality a declaration of tragedy in its supreme form. True tragedy is what you have when evil triumphs, wisdom fails, nobility is destroyed, and great potential is snuffed out. It turns creatures who should be as good, noble, wise, and joyful as angels into perverse beings who irrationally rebel against God's lordship. They lapse constantly into envy, hatred, arrogance, conceit, selfishness, uncharitableness, and destructiveness. They find that discontent, unfulfillment, and hopelessness are their constant companions. They learn by experience that, whatever act they may put on in company, they cannot change themselves for the better deep down. That is tragedy in real life. It is our own tragedy, yours and mine.

Theologically, what we are discussing here is the corruption and ruin of the image of God in us all, and it is important to think the matter through within this frame. That God originally made humankind in his own image as the crown of his creation—to procreate, to exercise dominion, and to enjoy the world's abundance, in grateful responsive communion with his Maker—is shown, repetitiously for emphasis, in Genesis 1:26–29. In past discussions as to what precisely constitutes the image, there have been different emphases. Some have highlighted rationality, meaning our power to think, remember, and plan. Some have pointed to relationality, meaning our power to love other people interactively, as God loves us interactively. Others have focused on rulerhood, meaning our dominion over the rest of the created order. And it has been debated whether the primary thought that the image idea expresses is of being God's deputy, ruling and managing his world, or of being holy and upright in action, as God himself is. Genesis 1:1–25 yields a basis for all these notions, so the way of wisdom is surely to combine them; from this combination of substantive, relational, and functional features the original dignity of human beings as God's image-bearers at once becomes plain.

DEAF EARS

Original sin is no laughing matter, but here is a hoary story that may help us to understand better how it affects us.

A psychiatrist once faced a man who thought he was dead. After hours of futile attempts to convince the patient that he was alive, the psychiatrist settled for what he thought was a foolproof plan. He gave the patient some medical books and asked him to read the sections showing that dead men do not bleed. The man agreed to do so. A few days later the two of them met again.

"What did you learn from the books I lent you?" the psychiatrist asked.

"I'm convinced," the patient replied. "It's perfectly clear that dead men don't bleed."

At that point the psychiatrist brought out a pin and pricked the patient, who stared in shock as the blood began to flow. "My God!" the patient cried out. "Dead men *do* bleed!"

In some ways people today are like that man—only in reverse. We too, with him, are in a fixed state of denial. We think we are alive, when in fact we are spiritually dead. There are several reasons why we refuse to accept the evidence to the contrary.

First, we do not know ourselves. Long before the time of Christ, the Greeks had latched on to the maxim, "Know yourself," as a key to wisdom. But self-knowledge as a project defeated the Greeks, and at this present time it also defeats us. For all the scraping of the inside of the psyche that modern novelists and psychotherapists do, the fact remains that such self-knowledge as each of us achieves is woefully incomplete. We know and can explain our purposes and procedures, but not our motivations, about which we constantly deceive ourselves. We think we know what is driving us to act as we do, but again and again we are wrong.

We do not and cannot know the core of our personal being, which the Jewish atheist Freud conceived of as the blind and restless *id*, and which the Bible speaks of, nonphysically, as our *heart*. "The heart has its reasons, which the reason knows nothing about," said Pascal. Woody Allen, in court in 1993 trying to explain his affair with Mia Farrow's daughter, joined hands with Pascal (unwittingly, I expect) by affirming, "The heart wants what it wants," as if that was all that could be said.

Psychotherapy can sometimes dredge up from the past memories of events that are producing complexes and oddities of action in the present, but the antipathy of our heart to God's claims is born in us, is constant, and operates deeper down than psychotherapy can go. Small wonder, then, that we, who really know so little about ourselves, do not at first recognize ourselves in the descriptions of sin-driven behavior that were given above. Few have ever had much sense of the anti-God perversity of their hearts until God's light shone into them after their conversion. "The heart is deceitful above all things and beyond cure," said Jeremiah (17:9). But the feeling common to us and to most others since history began is that we know ourselves fairly well. In reality, however, we fallen human beings hardly know ourselves at all.

Second, we lack standards for moral and spiritual self-assessment. Our era is better than any before us in assessing physical health and well-being, but we are clueless when moral and spiritual health is the agenda item. At one time the West acknowledged the Bible as defining the standards and boundaries of right conduct, so that whether or not people practiced Christian morality, at least they knew what it was. But not anymore. In today's world the Bible is dismissed, moral relativism rules, and any suggestion that there are absolutes of right and wrong is frowned on as necessarily inducing intolerance.

Our society increasingly presents a range of tribal moralities, each of which is maintained by members of its own group (religious, professional, sporting, or whatever) taking their cue from their own peers and from the group's role models. The quest for entertainment and self-indulgence largely dominates current culture, so that moral seriousness is inevitably at a discount.

There is widespread uncertainty as to what modes of self-gratification, if any, are off-limits, and what degree of responsibility, if any, we should accept for other people's welfare. Secularized self-worship, with personalized self-service, has become the religion of our time. Maintaining moral vision and moral standards in a fallen world is always difficult, and today, when postmodernist post-Christianity rides so high and society's opinion-makers spend so much time trashing the Christian heritage, it is well-nigh impossible. Small wonder, then, that in modern Western society, belief in original sin is felt to be incredible, even though what is happening around us is just what was to be expected if the doctrine is true.

Third, as a direct consequence of the two facts already discussed, we do not today think of self-centeredness as a moral flaw. "Doing it my way" is seen as a sign of individual integrity and creativity in a too-conformist world, whereas it is in reality a surface-level symptom of sin's rule in the heart. Sin, like cancer, metastasizes so that you cannot always track its course or identify it at first glance for what it is. But the I-do-it-my-way syndrome is not vital and virtuous integrity so much as it is sinful rebellion against external authority in general, which means against God's authority in particular.

Anglicans love to tell of the clergyman who mounted the pulpit to preach, tapped the microphone, heard nothing, and addressed it *sotto voce*, muttering, "Oh Lord, something's wrong with you." But the microphone was working, the congregation heard his words, and, having expected "The Lord be with you," automatically responded, "And also with you." This lighthearted story points up the heavy truth that in God's sight there is something wrong with all of us, clergy and laypeople alike and unbelievers, too. Our fallen hearts are self-asserting, God-defying, self-aggrandizing, God-marginalizing, and self-deifying. We have been invaded by the cancer called original sin, against which all Christians have to be on guard and do battle all the days of their life.

REBEL RACE

What has been said so far has sought to clear away the undergrowth in the modern mind so that we may hear what the Bible tells us about our sin and about ourselves as sinners. The Scriptures tell us that rebellion is both the essence of sin and the essence of the human condition.

1. *Sin is rebellion*. Both Old Testament Hebrew and New Testament Greek have a wide array of words for sin. All of them define sin by its relation to God and characterize human acts as sinful because of how God regards them. (*Bad, cruel, faithless, wicked, worthless, senseless* are among the terms that express the divine verdict.) Some of the words for sin express the idea of willful failure to do right, deviation from the proper path, or failing to come up to standard. Other words express the thought of becoming guilty, filthy (unclean), and unacceptable before God and exposed to his penal judgment. And some of the words express the concept of active rebellion—which, by common consent of the exegetes, is the clearest, strongest, profoundest, and most far-reaching category for sin that the Bible gives us. Elihu unfairly says of suffering Job, "To his sin he adds rebellion; scornfully he . . . multiplies his words against God" (Job 34:37). Deliberate scorn and defiance are what the Puritans called "aggravations" of sin, escalating it from bad to worse. Rebellion is sin aggravated to the limit, sin in its guiltiest and most intense mode.

The reality of rebellion in any context, human or divine, has in it five factors:

- A superior who claims authority and expects allegiance, submission, fidelity, and obedience
- A revolt—that is, a defiant refusal of compliance on a permanent basis
- A positive purpose of self-determination for the future, without regard for the rejected superior
- The supposition that this self-determination is real freedom
- A certainty of punishment should the rebellion not succeed, since from the superior's standpoint rebellion is indefensible

Old Testament Israel constantly rebelled against God and suffered his constant chastisement as a result. Again and again God sent captivity, famine, and overall impoverishment in order to bring his erring people spiritually to their senses. The opening chapter of Isaiah's prophecy, for example, presents God speaking to Israel as follows:

> "I reared children and brought them up, but they have *rebelled* against me. . . . They have forsaken the LORD; they have spurned the Holy One of Israel and turned their backs on him. Why should you be beaten any more? Why do you persist in *rebellion?*. . . Your country is desolate, your cities burned with fire. . . .
>
> If you are willing and obedient, you will eat the best from the land; but if you resist and *rebel*, you will be devoured by the sword." . . . Your rulers are *rebels*, companions of thieves; they all love bribes and chase after gifts. . . . *rebels* and sinners will both be broken, and those who forsake the LORD will perish (Isa. 1:2, 4–5, 7, 19–20, 23, 28, italics added).

The prophets describe such rebellion as covenant-breaking, blasphemy, idolatry, injustice, cruelty, crime, and apostasy, and they repeatedly declare God's displeasure and threats of his judgments against the rebels. From this standpoint, God's statements through Isaiah are typical.

In the New Testament we see covenant loyalty to God—that is, total selflessness, God-centered and others-centered—modeled perfectly by our Lord Jesus Christ, by whom we should be measuring ourselves if we want to know how God regards us. If we are not always loving God with the whole of our heart, mind, and strength, as Jesus did, nor practicing such active goodwill towards needy people as Jesus pictured in his story of the good Samaritan, then we are falling short of his standard and so are sinners. If honesty forces us to admit that the idea of living as thoroughgoing a life of worship and service as Jesus lived does not appeal to us, we thereby show that we are rebels against God in our hearts.

2. *Human life is rebellion.* Rebellion against God is the natural state and condition of the entire human race, apart from those whose hearts God has changed through regeneration and new birth. This is clearly taught in Paul's letter to the Romans.

The announced theme of Romans is the righteousness of God. As the argument shows, this is Paul's tag phrase for the whole reality of God's acting in justice, faithfulness, and love to bestow "the gift of righteousness" (pardon and acceptance) on all who put their faith in Jesus Christ (see 1:17; 3:21–26; 5:17; 10:3–4). God reveals this righteousness in the Gospel, and the Good News is that through faith in Christ we receive the promised hopes, the new life, and the power for Christian behavior that the Gospel sets forth. Those who have received the gift of righteousness from God will live, enjoying the reconciled relationship with him that starts with justification and leads to final salvation and is called eternal life (1:16–17). That is the theme that Romans expounds.

The first of the argument's well-marked sections is 1:18–3:20, which describes the universal human need of righteousness. The trenchant survey of how Gentiles and Jews actually live indicates that "wrath and anger ... trouble and distress" (2:8–9) await everyone who comes to the final judgment with nothing better than his or her own track record to plead. "Jews and Gentiles alike," writes Paul, "are all under sin. As it is written: 'There is no one righteous, not even one; there is no one who understands, no one who seeks God. All have turned away, they have together become worthless; there is no one who does good, not even one'" (3:9–12).

Again: "We know that whatever the law says, it says to those who are under the law, so that every mouth may be silenced and the whole world held accountable to God. Therefore no one will be declared righteous in his sight by observing the law; rather, through the law we become conscious of sin" (3:19–20).

It is noteworthy that in 3:9 and elsewhere, as in 5:20–21 and throughout chapters 6 and 7, sin is personified as a controlling force in human lives—a force that is irresistible until co-resurrection with Christ dethrones it. Fallen humanity's natural inability to achieve the righteousness that God calls for, whether through his written law or through our natural conscience (see 2:12–15), could hardly be indicated more clearly.

The second chunk of the argument, 3:21–5:21, proclaims the gift of righteousness. Christ's substitutionary atonement is the judicial basis for it (3:21–26), faith is the means of receiving it (chap. 4), assured hope is the fruit of it (5:1–11); Adam's sin, which created our need of it, is the counterpart to Christ's obedience, which actually secured it for us (5:12–21).

We should note that in this last paragraph the emphasis is not primarily on the fact that we all sin (that was dealt with in the first section of the letter, as we saw). The primary emphasis is on the fact that the actions of our race's two representative heads, Adam and Christ, have determined the status before God of all those whom God has set in solidarity with them. This point is sometimes missed because of Paul's grammatical flurry in 5:12. He starts, "Just as sin entered the world through one man, and death through sin, and in this way death came to all men, because all sinned—" and then he breaks off and never finishes this sentence.

It is not surprising that many have thought that his words "because all sinned" must refer to actual wrongdoings, personally committed. But that will not fit into what turns out to be the flow of thought. The meaning of "all sinned" can be clarified by the following illustration: A national president's declaration of war commits the entire nation to the combat, for he is their representative. The people will say, "*We* declared war," because they accept that the president acted on their behalf, and they are involved with him in the consequences of his declaration. Should the war be lost, it will be *we* who have lost it. Similarly, because Adam was our God-appointed representative and we are all in solidarity with him, we all share in the judicial consequences of his transgression. In other words, the condemnation that Adam brought on himself extends to the whole human race; "all sinned" refers to this penal involvement.

At the end of the paragraph, however, Paul refers again to the sinful conduct of every human being described in 1:18–3:20. He does this briefly but comprehensively, half-personifying sin as he is going to do on the grand scale in the next chapter. "Sin increased ... sin reigned in death" (5:20–21). Paul's image of sin *reigning* tells us that what we, with the historic church, have been calling original sin is an inescapable racial infection. It stems from the initial disobedience of the first human male, of whom Paul has been speaking since verse 12, and exercises an inescapable measure of control over fallen humanity.

In the third unit of Romans, 6:1–8:39, the focus is on the life of righteousness. Paul expounds the image of sin reigning in a way that involves death. From his own experience he illustrates how God's law, which forbids sin, actually stirs sin into action without giving power against it. The result is that people realize that they are slaves to sin and have been all along (see Romans 7:7–13). Paul's analysis of how God's law, which defines, detects, and condemns sin, is unable to empower us against sinning, continues to the end of chapter 7. There Paul apparently moves in his testimony from his past experience as a Jew to his present experience as a Christian.

Other passages from Paul might be deployed at this point, but space does not permit examination of these passages, nor is there need for it. It is already clear enough that natural, unregenerate human existence, according to the Bible, is a playing out of an inborn instinct for rebellion against God. So now we can move on to draw some threads together and conclude.

EVANGELICALS AND SIN

Since our account of original sin aims to confirm as authentic Christianity what the evangelical declaration of the Gospel of

Christ says about humankind, the following observations are now appropriate.

First, biblically and theologically, evangelicals are right to affirm that human beings are born rebels against God by reason of the heritage of original sin that is integral to our makeup. In other words, we are right to highlight our fallenness and to oppose any position that states or insinuates that we are not so bad after all.

Second, what has been written so far has centered of necessity on the spiritual morbid pathology of fallen human nature. Nothing has been said about either the fundamental goodness of God's creation or about what Calvin called the "common" grace of God. Common grace is the kindly providence whereby God restrains sin from corrupting any person, community, or aspect of life to the point where it is truly as bad as it could be. He bestows on Christians and non-Christians alike culturally significant abilities in arts, literature, science, technology, politics, intellectual enquiry, medical development, and so on. All truth, all goodness, and all that is of civilizing value comes from God, who providentially reverses to some degree some of the effects of our fallenness. He creates a situation in which, though everybody's heart is bad and we all have it in us to be degenerate and devilish, the world yet has its quota of responsible citizens, wise and patient parents, peace-loving rulers, gifted artists, and "good pagans" who faithfully follow non-saving religious faiths. Thus, to use Pascal's terms, human beings are the glory as well as the scum of the universe. The scum aspect—cruelty and crime, treachery and robbery, pride, envy, and the rest—is to be explained by original sin, as we have seen. The glory aspect is to be explained by common grace.

Third, the in-house differences of evangelical opinion regarding sin have deliberately not been discussed in this essay. But evangelicals are at one on our actual lostness by nature and our inability to save ourselves without Christ. We all affirm our need of justification and regeneration. What has been written in the foregoing pages limits itself to basic realities on which, as this writer understands the matter, evangelicals are agreed, and which themselves belong to mainstream historic Christianity in all its forms.

Fourth, our purpose in taking the above long look at sin in human life has been to show the *realism* of the Gospel diagnosis of our need, and to generate *humility* as we grow in knowledge of God and of ourselves. The more we know of God as he is revealed in his Word and works, the more we shall know ourselves through realizing the contrast between him and us. If we have before our minds his holiness as embodied in his law and expressed in his judgments and in the incarnate life of his Son, we shall become increasingly aware of our own unholiness. If we have before our minds his redeeming love in the Gospel, we shall become increasingly aware of our own lovelessness. And that is how it is meant to be. Knowledge of God must bring us lower and lower as the sinfulness that is in us becomes more and more obvious to us. And this sinfulness must ever be highlighted so that the great grace of our Lord Jesus Christ will be appreciated.

Sin makes an ugly and nauseating study. But if it leads us to acknowledge that God knows us better than we know ourselves and causes us to humble ourselves, then it is worthwhile. If it motivates us to lean harder on Christ, to live a life of grateful praise for salvation, and to dedicate ourselves to him as his disciples, then our ugly study will guide us along life-changing paths to a very joyful outcome. May all readers of this chapter find it to be so.

Study Questions

1. What is the Bible's definition of sin?
2. In what ways does our sinful nature influence what we do and think?
3. How do some moderns attempt to gloss over the existence of sin?
4. What is common grace?
5. Why does our knowledge of the "bad news" about sin help us understand better the Good News of Jesus Christ?

The Gospel of Jesus Christ is news, good news: the best and most important news that any human being ever hears. . . .

This Gospel identifies Jesus Christ, the Messiah of Israel, as the Son of God and God the Son, the second Person of the Holy Trinity, whose incarnation, ministry, death, resurrection, and ascension fulfilled the Father's saving will. His death for sins and his resurrection from the dead were promised beforehand by the prophets and attested by eyewitnesses.

■

We affirm that Jesus Christ is God incarnate (John 1:14). The virgin-born descendant of David (Rom. 1:3), he had a true human nature, was subject to the Law of God (Gal. 4:5), and was like us at all points, except without sin (Heb. 2:17; 7:26–28). We affirm that faith in the true humanity of Christ is essential to faith in the Gospel. We deny that anyone who rejects the humanity of Christ, his incarnation, or his sinlessness, or who maintains that these truths are not essential to the Gospel, will be saved (1 John 4:2–3).

—*The Gospel of Jesus Christ: An Evangelical Celebration*

3

JESUS CHRIST

WHO DO WE SAY THAT HE IS?

Kevin J. Vanhoozer

All the armies that ever marched,
all the navies that ever sailed
all the parliaments that ever sat,
all the kings that ever reigned,
put together, have not affected the life of man on earth
as much as that One Solitary Life.

—*Anonymous*

The poem, of course, is about Jesus — like so many other poems, not to mention paintings, sculptures, cantatas, hymns, and films. Jesus is the subject of Broadway musicals and of academic treatises, of high and low culture, of East and West. The birth of Jesus is celebrated yearly around the globe. The new millennium, too, marks the arrival of the baby in the stall. Why is his birth—not to mention the rest of his life and death—of millennial significance? Why do many artists and filmmakers, philosophers and historians, believers and unbelievers continue to be fascinated with a figure whose "career," in the eyes of the world, was altogether unremarkable? Who is this Jesus?

The true identity of Jesus of Nazareth has been a subject of controversy from the start:

> When Jesus came to the region of Caesarea Philippi, he asked his disciples, "Who do people say the Son of Man is?"
>
> They replied, "Some say John the Baptist; others say Elijah; and still others, Jeremiah or one of the prophets."
>
> "But what about you?" he asked. "Who do you say I am?"
>
> Simon Peter answered, "You are the Christ, the Son of the living God" (Matt. 16:13–16).

The disciples answered Jesus with a good deal of pastoral tact. They omitted other things that people were saying about Jesus, namely, that he was a blasphemer, a false prophet, and a madman.

Jesus' question to his disciples is likewise directed to us: Who do *we* say that he is? Jesus' own straw poll has been brought up-to-date by George Gallup, who polled North Americans as to their opinion of Jesus Christ. The vast majority of those who responded affirmed that Jesus lived. Beyond this, opinions varied. Some believed that Jesus was "divine" in the sense that he was uniquely called by God to reveal God's purpose to the world. About ten percent believed that Jesus was divine in the sense that he embodied the highest human values. Others acknowledged Jesus as an important religious teacher but did not think he was divine. Finally, some forty percent affirmed that Jesus was divine in the sense that he was God living among men and women.

Of course, we cannot decide who Jesus really was simply by taking a vote. In his book *Jesus Through the Centuries*, Jaroslav Pelikan shows that each age tends to create Christ in its own image.[1] Indeed, judging from the many cinematic interpretations of Jesus Christ, each *decade* tends to have its own view of what Jesus was like. Just contrast the movie *King of Kings* with the films *Jesus of Nazareth* and *Jesus of Montreal* and the musical-turned-into-film *Jesus Christ Superstar*. It is important in this day and time to recover Jesus Christ as a non-Western, Near Eastern figure rather than the blue-eyed, fair-headed figure created by Hollywood. It is most important not to create false images of Jesus or to make "Jesus Christ" into our own image. False images of Jesus are no better than idols, and idols cannot save. Christians are called to be true witnesses to Jesus Christ, so it is important that what we say and think about Jesus corresponds to who he really was.

THE CHRISTMAS CLUE TO JESUS' IDENTITY

> And is it true? And is it true,
> This most tremendous tale of all,
> Seen in a stained-glass window's hue,
> A baby in an ox's stall?
>
> —*JOHN BETJEMAN,*
> *"CHRISTMAS"*

Good news is always welcome. The good news at the core of Christian faith, however, is something quite specific. Christians celebrate not just any gospel, but the Gospel "of Jesus Christ." The message of the Gospel is bound up with Christmas joy, with the birth of Jesus, and with his name: "Immanuel," that is, "God with us" (Matt. 1:23). To understand the Good News, therefore, we have to know something about the identity of Jesus Christ, because the Good News concerns not only what God did through him but also who he was. Christians believe that all our joys ultimately derive from the good news of what God was and is doing in this one man.

In a *Time* article entitled "Who Was Jesus Christ?" Peter Stuhlmacher rightly comments, "The biblical texts as they stand are the best hypothesis we have until now to explain what really happened."[2] Who Jesus is can be seen in the accounts of his birth, his life, his death, and his resurrection. Therefore, instead of looking to Gallup polls, contemporary films, or the fickle opinions of each generation, we should seek the responses of people found in the New Testament texts. One of our goals is to see how his own followers would answer the question: "Who is Jesus Christ?" We will also consider the responses of several of the great church councils. Then we will look at the responses of some modern scholars.

But first, it is important for us to discern who Jesus Christ said he was.

JESUS RESPONDS: "I AM"

Whose idea was it to interpret the life of Jesus of Nazareth as the fulfillment of Old Testament prophecies and promises? The evidence, I believe, points clearly to Jesus himself.

H. R. Macintosh, a Scottish theologian, makes a startling comment in his book *The Person of Jesus Christ:* "The self-consciousness of Jesus . . . is the greatest fact in history."[3] What we find reported in the Gospels is correct: Jesus explained his identity to his disciples from Scripture, "beginning with Moses and all the Prophets" (Luke 24:27). Jesus understood himself to be the beloved Son of God, chosen by God to bring about the kingdom of God and the forgiveness of sins. Our understanding of who Jesus was must correspond to Jesus' own self-understanding. If we do not confess Jesus as the Christ, then either he was deluded about his identity or we are. Three strands of evidence yield important clues as to what Jesus thought about himself.

The "I Am" Sayings. Jesus' "I am" sayings represent an amazing line of evidence. Jesus identifies himself as the bread of life (John 6:35), the light of the world (John 8:12), the resurrection and the life (John 11:25), and as the way, the truth, and the life—the only means of access to God the Father (John 14:6).

Jesus made an even more astounding claim in a discussion with the Jews. He declared himself equal with God so unmistakably that his listeners picked up stones to throw at him: "I tell you the truth, . . . before Abraham was born, I am!" (John 8:58). This particular "I am" saying recalls the famous words of God to Moses out of the burning bush: "I AM WHO I AM" (Ex. 3:14).

"Son of Man." Jesus refers to himself on some fifty occasions as the "Son of Man." Interestingly, no one else ever calls Jesus by that title. That alone gives it the ring of authenticity.

What does it mean? In Jesus' day, the title could be used simply to refer to a human being. Readers of the Old Testament, however, could hardly fail to catch the allusion to Daniel 7:13–14, which speak of a "son of man" coming in the clouds to receive an eternal kingdom. This use of the term came to be linked with a messiah figure and thus with the hope of Israel. The curious thing about Jesus' use of the title, however, is that he linked it not only with the theme of future glory but also with the theme of suffering and death. In so doing, Jesus was teaching his disciples something new about the long-awaited Messiah, namely, that his suffering would precede his glory (e.g., Luke 9:22).

The Parables. The parables make up the third clue to the identity of Jesus Christ. Jesus used the parables—simple stories—to teach people that the kingdom is "like" what *happens* in the story. According to the parables, the kingdom of God both comes and grows in surprising, unexpected ways. Jesus' parables teach that the kingdom of God is in some sense *already here*. This was difficult for the disciples to understand: Wasn't Israel still under Roman rule?

This mystery is linked with another. Jesus preached about the kingdom of God. Yet shortly after Jesus' resurrection, Peter, Paul, and all the others began to preach about Jesus Christ. What happened? Did the disciples exchange the Gospel of Jesus Christ for another gospel? Not at all. What the parables show is that Jesus identified himself with the coming of the kingdom of God. In the parable of the sower, Jesus explains that he is the Sower and his words are the seed. Something new and wonderful has begun with the ministry of Jesus Christ. A seed has been planted, a seed that will grow at an absurdly quick rate. And yet the kingdom of God is as hidden in Jesus as it is in his parables.

Confirmations of Jesus' Identity. Jesus identifies himself in the closest possible terms with the kingdom and the saving purpose of God. Three factors support Jesus' view of himself: (1) the voice of God at Jesus' baptism declares, "This is my Son, whom I love;

with him I am well pleased" (Matt. 3:17); (2) the power of God enables Jesus to do miracles: "If I drive out demons by the finger of God, then the kingdom of God has come to you" (Luke 11:20); and (3) the victory of God over sin and death, achieved through resurrection, confirms that Jesus is who he said he is: "God has raised this Jesus to life" (Acts 2:32). More than any other factor, Jesus is who he said he is because he was resurrected from the dead (see chap. 5, "Did Jesus Christ Really Rise from the Dead?").

The "finality" that Jesus claims for himself follows from the finality—the utter decisiveness—of his life's history: "No one has ever gone into heaven except the one who came from heaven—the Son of Man" (John 3:13); "no one comes to the Father except through me" (John 14:6). Peter's sermon in Acts 4:12 reflects Jesus' own exclusivistic claim: "Salvation is found in no one else, for there is no other name under heaven given to men by which we must be saved."

MARK RESPONDS: "JESUS IS THE SON OF GOD"

In the Gospels we find four portraits of the one person Jesus Christ. They show why he is the only mediator between man and God. Each of these faith portraits, while true to who Jesus really was, makes an indispensable contribution to our understanding of his identity.

Mark's Gospel, probably the first to be written, opens with these words: "The beginning of the gospel about Jesus Christ, the Son of God" (Mark 1:1). Mark's narrative moves along at a quick pace, relating briefly what Jesus said and did and then focusing on the way various characters decide for or against Jesus. Many characters—including evil spirits (1:24; 3:11), the Jewish high priest (14:61), and a Roman centurion (15:39)—all identify Jesus as the Son of God. How much more should the disciples (and Mark's readers!) make a similar faith decision.

The title "Son of God" refers to Jesus' special intimacy with God, his "Abba" ("daddy"—see Mark 14:36). It also points to Jesus' special responsibility to complete the work his Father gave him to do (John 17:4). What is most important, it emphasizes Jesus' unique nature in being the "one and only" Son of God (John 3:16). Elsewhere in the Bible, "Son of God" is used to refer to angels, to the nation of Israel, or to the Davidic king. But nowhere else does the Bible speak of someone being God's "one and only Son." Being the one and only ("begotten," KJV) Son of God means that Jesus, unlike the rest of us, is not adopted into the family of God but is rather the eternal Son of God, the second person of the Trinity.

JOHN RESPONDS: "JESUS IS THE WORD"

John's Gospel begins "from above," with an account of Jesus' heavenly preexistence. Unlike Mark, where all the action is "on the ground," the Fourth Gospel paints a heavenly backdrop for everything that Jesus says and does. John structures his Gospel around a series of Jesus' speeches, framed by narratives that tell of the "signs" or miracles that Jesus did that corroborate who he was. Jesus not only claimed to be "the bread of life" (John 6:35), but also showed what he meant by multiplying the loaves and feeding the five thousand. The miracle, as a sign, corroborated his teaching. Everything Jesus said and did, in other words, revealed who he is. Perhaps that is why John's Gospel introduces Jesus as the "Word" of God.

John declares that Jesus was "the Word" that was "with God" and "was God" (John 1:1). This Word existed before everything else, and everything else was made "through" the Word. It is this same Word that "became flesh and made his dwelling among us" (1:14). The Word thus replaced the temple as the "dwelling place" of God, the place where God's glory is to be seen. The temple was the place to go and meet God, the place to go to have one's sins forgiven.

This same Word, which existed before creation and which is now the dwelling place of the glory of God, is identified with Jesus Christ in John 1:17. Jesus Christ is therefore able to be and do all that the temple did for Israel in the Old Testament. In all that he does and says, Jesus makes known God the Father (John 1:18). Who do we say that he is? He is God's Word to the world. His words and deeds are God's own communication. His words and deeds are those of God himself.

MATTHEW RESPONDS: "JESUS IS THE CHRIST"

Matthew's portrait of Jesus highlights the fact that he is the "Christ," or "Messiah," foretold in the Old Testament Scriptures. Matthew is particularly concerned to help readers see the events in Jesus' life as a fulfillment of those Scriptures. Indeed, references and allusions to the Old Testament are scattered throughout his Gospel, as is the formula "This took place to fulfill what the Lord had said through the prophet . . ." (e.g., Matt. 1:22; 2:15; 27:9). Matthew presents Jesus Christ as a prophet greater than Moses and as the long-awaited king of the Jews.

The Greek word *christos* comes from the verb *chrio* ("to anoint with oil") and translates the Hebrew term for "Messiah," which also means "anointed." In the Old Testament, kings were anointed with oil as a sign that they had been set apart for a special divine task (e.g., 1 Sam. 10:1). Often they, like the judges (Judg. 13:25), were given the Holy Spirit to equip them for their special work (1 Sam. 10:10). To confess Jesus as "Christ" is to acknowledge that God has appointed and anointed him for a special task—specifically, to save the people from their sins (Matt. 1:21).

Matthew's portrait of Jesus as the "Messiah" includes an account of his miraculous conception. What Mary conceived was "from the Holy Spirit" (Matt. 1:20). The point of the virgin birth is to show that Jesus was anointed with the Holy Spirit in a more glorious and more permanent way than were the earlier prophets, priests, and kings whose combined work he would far surpass. Jesus is the "Christ" not because he was given the Spirit of God for a specific time only, but because the gift of the Spirit defines him in his very nature. Jesus' visible anointing with the Spirit at his baptism (Matt. 3:16) served as a public confirmation of what was already, and permanently, the case.

LUKE RESPONDS: "JESUS IS THE SERVANT OF THE LORD"

Luke's two-volume work of Luke–Acts portrays Jesus as the Christ because through his "service"—his life, his death, his resurrection—he has made possible a new outpouring of God's Spirit on the world (Pentecost). This theme comes to the fore when we read Luke–Acts together. Salvation is associated with the name of Jesus Christ alone because only the work of Jesus made possible this new coming of the Holy Spirit (the Spirit of freedom, the Spirit of new life). Luke describes how the church came into being only because the risen Christ has poured out his Spirit on his people.

Many of the sermons recorded in the book of Acts refer to Jesus as the "servant" of God (e.g., Acts 3:13; 4:27). Jesus identifies himself with the servant of the Lord when he declares in the synagogue that Isaiah 61:1–2 ("The Spirit of the Sovereign LORD is on me, because the LORD has anointed me to preach good news to the poor") was fulfilled in his own person and ministry (Luke 4:17–21). Jesus was sent into the world to be, and to do, all that Israel's prophets, priests, and kings, together with Israel's temple, could *not* do. He liberates people from sin and proclaims this freedom—forgiveness from sins—with authority.

As servant of the Lord, Jesus was not only a prophet but also a priest and the sacrifice that suffers for the sins of the world (Isa. 53:5–8; 1 Peter 2:22–25). The early church viewed the so-called Servant Songs of Isaiah—the songs put to music in Handel's *Messiah*—as crucial testimonies to the identity of Jesus Christ. The apostle Paul, too, reminds us that Jesus, "who, being in very nature God, . . . made himself nothing, taking the very nature of a servant" (Phil. 2:6–7). To name or identify Jesus Christ from the Scriptures is to understand that the Lord of the universe voluntarily took on humanity in order to become its servant.

PAUL RESPONDS: "JESUS IS LORD"

Some scholars have criticized the apostle Paul for "inventing" Christianity. They portray Paul as a Palestinian Prospero who grafted the Gnostic myth of a dying and rising god onto the historical figure of Jesus of Nazareth, thereby corrupting the "pure teaching" of Jesus about the fatherhood of God with metaphysical speculation.

"My Gospel"? It is true that Paul occasionally refers to "my gospel" (Rom. 2:16; 2 Tim. 2:8). Yet he clearly did not mean to refer to something that he had invented. On the contrary, Paul states that he did not learn the Gospel from any human source but from the revelation of Jesus Christ himself (Gal. 1:11–12; Acts 9:1–5). Paul speaks alternately of "the gospel of God" (e.g., Rom. 1:1) and "the gospel of his Son" (Rom. 1:9) as well as "the gospel of Christ"

CHILDLIKE FAITH

In the 1930s, a missionary asked an African girl about six or seven years of age a most pertinent question: "Who is Jesus Christ?" With a smile on her face, she responded cheerfully: "He is my Savior and He lives within my heart." As it happens, the missionary had previously studied at the University of Berlin with Professor Adolf von Harnack, one of the most renowned theologians and church historians of the twentieth century. The missionary recalled that one day in class Professor Harnack was addressing the same question: "Who is Jesus Christ?" Harnack replied that Christ was the greatest man who ever lived. But the liberal theologian would not acknowledge that Christ was the divine Son of God who had died on the cross for our salvation and triumphed over death through the resurrection. In one sense, the young African girl understood the Gospel far better than the brilliant professor with all his theological knowledge.

Years later, the former missionary frequently recounted the story of the great German theologian and the young African girl. He compared her simple faith in Christ with the vast knowledge of the great theologian. She provided a remarkable illustration of Jesus' teaching that unless we come to Christ with the faith of a little child, we cannot enter into the kingdom of heaven. Indeed, the Gospel is so simple that children do understand it very well. The Statement reads: "The Gospel is so simple that small children can understand it, and it is so profound that studies by the wisest theologians will never exhaust its riches."

(Rom. 15:19). The *of* could mean "from" or "about"; both senses are true. The Gospel is both *from* the Father and the Son and *about* the Father and the Son. Paul's "gospel," therefore, is the preaching of Jesus Christ, crucified and risen (1 Cor. 15:1–4).

"Lord." One of the most significant names that Paul uses to identify Jesus is "Lord." This was the term used for "God" in the Greek translation of the Old Testament (well-known in Paul's day). The name "Lord" underlines the exaltation of the risen Jesus. God has raised him from the dead, lifted him up, and exalted him. Paul prays to Christ as Lord (2 Cor. 12:8–9). He associates Jesus with God: "Grace and peace to you from God our Father and the Lord Jesus Christ" (Gal. 1:3). He links Jesus to the work of the Creator God: "There is but one God, the Father, from whom all things came and for whom we live; and there is but one Lord, Jesus Christ, through whom all things came and through whom we live" (1 Cor. 8:6). Paul's use of the term "Lord" in connection with Jesus goes far beyond what he could say of a mere human.

The origin of Paul's view of Christ dates from his encounter with him on the road to Damascus (Acts 9:1–22). It was this encounter that transformed Paul from being a persecutor of the Christian way to one of its more articulate spokesmen. Clearly, Paul underwent a dramatic reversal in his thinking about Jesus Christ. So, for that matter, did the rest of the disciples. On the day of Jesus' crucifixion, the disciples were a small, frightened band; only days later, they had a clear message and a mission. Within a generation the Gospel would reach Rome; within three centuries it would conquer the empire. Martin Hengel, a German New Testament scholar, rightly calls our attention to this amazing turnaround: "More happened [in Christology] in this period of less than two decades than in the whole of the next seven centuries."[4] Naming Jesus "the Christ" is nothing short of the "Big Bang" of Christian faith.

Paul clearly perceived the connection between the Gospel and the person of Jesus Christ. He never met the earthly Jesus, but he did know the living Christ. To be a Christian is to be "in Christ"—a phrase that occurs some two hundred times in Paul's writings. Of course, one can only be "in Christ" if Christ is still alive. For Paul, Jesus was the one on whom *all* the ages turn. The contrast Paul draws is not simply that between B.C. and A.D. but between "this age" and "the age to come."

Paul taught that Jesus, through his death and resurrection, ushered in a new world order—not a new political regime but a new kind of power: the Holy Spirit. By raising Jesus from the dead, God made him a "life-giving spirit" (1 Cor. 15:45). Paul came to see that Jesus is the one through whom God fulfills his promise to Abraham, that through his seed all nations would be blessed.

THE GREAT CHURCH COUNCILS RESPOND

Each new generation needs to confront and to answer Jesus' question for itself: "Who do you say that I am?" Guidance is available for doing this, not only from the Scriptures, which must remain the final judge of all our answers but also from the best Christian thinking from previous generations. It is especially important to pay attention to the early church creeds that have for centuries defined "orthodoxy"—that is, right opinion and right thinking about the identity of Jesus Christ. The great achievement of the church fathers, summed up by the Council of Nicea (A.D. 325) and the Council of Chalcedon (A.D. 451), was to pull all the biblical material together into creeds in order to define, in the clearest possible terms, the relation of Jesus, the Son of God, to God the Father.

The church fathers believed that right doctrine was linked to right worship. Their agonizing over what to say concerning the nature of Jesus Christ stemmed from their desire to honor Jesus' own statement: "The true worshipers will worship the Father in spirit and truth, for they are the kind of worshipers the Father seeks" (John 4:23).

Parameters were necessary because some people were saying *false* things—heresies—about Jesus, even in the church. And errors in identifying Jesus Christ ultimately lead to a loss of the Gospel itself. The Ebionites denied the divinity of Jesus Christ in order to safeguard Jewish monotheism. The Docetists, by contrast, denied the humanity of Christ. Both of these heresies had very bad entailments. Unless God became human in order to save humanity, the Gospel is ultimately meaningless. Why? Humanity cannot save itself. If Christ was not truly man, he could not be our representative or substitute. But if he were not God, his death could have no saving effect.

Jesus was sent by the Father to undertake a mission (John 3:16). The baby in the ox's stall was God's missionary to the world. No one else in the whole of human history has had such a God-appointed, God-driven mission. Jesus Christ *is* God's mission to humanity. The Son of Man was sent into the world in order to bring men and women back to God. His mission is mediation. This is precisely why we cannot separate his person from his work: he could not complete his mission-mediation if he were not both God and man.

The Council of Nicea Responds: "Jesus is the same substance as the Father." It took some four hundred years for the early church to agree about Jesus Christ's relation to God. On the one hand, the evidence from Scripture for Jesus' deity was compelling. The book of Hebrews, for example, is an extended treatise on the superiority of Jesus Christ. He is higher than earthly things (priests, temples) and heavenly things (angels) alike. He is "the exact representation of [God's] being" (Heb. 1:3). He is worshiped by angels (1:6) and is the object of human faith as well (12:2). Moreover, the Son is called "God" while at the same time the Father remains God to his Son (1:8–9).

On the other hand, how could the one true God have a son? Would not there then be *two* gods? Such was the faulty reasoning of Arius, who, out of a misplaced zeal for monotheism (belief in one God), declared that the Son was not an eternally existing person but rather the first creature that God made. That meant, for Arius, that the Son had a beginning in time. The bishop of Alexandria, Athanasius, argued against Arius that the Father and the Son share the same divine nature and yet God is nevertheless one. To say that the Son was a creature is to ignore the fact that he is the "only begotten" of the Father (KJV). What is begotten is of the same nature as the begetter (e.g., parent-child), whereas what is made does not share the maker's nature (e.g., carpenter-table).

The church eventually saw that Athanasius had rightly grasped the implications of the New Testament testimony about Jesus

Christ. Accordingly, the Council of Nicea affirmed that the Son was *homoousios* ("of the same substance") as the Father. The same goes for the Spirit. The doctrine of the Trinity therefore states that God is three persons—Father, Son, Spirit—with one nature.

The Council of Chalcedon Responds: "Jesus is one person with two natures." Nicea identified "Christ" as the second person of the Trinity. But what is the relation of the eternal Son of God to the man Jesus? This was the question that was eventually addressed by the Council of Chalcedon. Once again, the testimony of Scripture led the participants to affirm both the "true humanity" and the "true divinity" of Jesus Christ. At the same time, the council affirmed that "Jesus Christ" refers to only one person, namely, the eternal Son of God. The doctrine of the "Incarnation" states that the eternal Son of God, the second person of the Trinity, entered into human history and lived a fully human life. "Jesus Christ" is not a human person with a particularly close relation to God but rather a divine person who took on the condition of humanity, with all its problems and its possibilities.

Who does Chalcedon say that he is? He is the Son of God, one person with two natures. He is God living and dying as one of us. Chalcedon teaches us to appreciate just what the name "Immanuel" ("God with us") really means. When Jesus says "I," the one speaking is the second person of the Trinity.

THE RESPONSE OF SOME MODERN SCHOLARS AND SKEPTICS

The question of Jesus' true identity is approached differently in the modern world. For many modern scholars, the burning question is not the question of Jesus' nature but the question of Jesus' history. Is the Christ of *faith* (the Christ of the New Testament and of church tradition) really the same as the Jesus of *history?* Many modern scholars tend to rely a great deal on their own powers of reasoning and historical investigation. They think that faith leads away from understanding instead of toward it. Their aim is to sift through the biblical evidence critically (that is, suspiciously) in order to discover what *actually* happened.

This skeptical approach has dominated the study of the Bible for much of the last two centuries. The tide is now beginning to turn, however. It is becoming clear that the attempt to "know" Jesus by distrusting the primary evidence about him—the apostolic testimony—stems from intellectual pride and produces very meager results. Not everyone has seen the light. The so-called Jesus seminar is a group of academics who meet twice a year to determine what Jesus was "really" like. They are interested in the historical Jesus, not the Christ of faith. They subject the New Testament texts to critical scrutiny and vote on what they think Jesus really said and did as opposed to what the early church allegedly invented about him.

The main problem with this approach is these scholars' assumption that the best way to find the "real Jesus" is to bypass the Jesus described by the apostolic witness. But to seek to understand Jesus apart from these faith portraits is to know not more but *less*. A "critical reason seeking understanding" approach that distrusts the biblical testimony to Jesus Christ does not stand a chance of discovering his true identity.

WHO DO *YOU* SAY JESUS IS?

Each person has to confront Jesus' question, "Who do *you* say that I am?" To answer this question is to come face-to-face with Jesus Christ. The good news is that in the face of Jesus Christ we see the very face of God, the one who has decided to be with us and for us in spite of our sin.

In the account of the Transfiguration we read that Jesus' face "shone like the sun" (Matt. 17:2) with the glory of God. It is the same face that John sees in his vision of the end time (Rev. 1:16). At the very end of Revelation we read of the saints that "they will see his face, and his name will be on their foreheads" (Rev. 22:4). The Pharisees bound the law to their foreheads, but this is not the way to heaven. No, Christians bear the name of Christ. They know that life is to be had only in this name, a name that identifies Jesus as the Christ. The Gospel concerns the name and face of "Immanuel," God with us, who invites us to share his life.

The Gospel declares that God has smiled on us in Jesus Christ. The hope of the Gospel lies in this face-to-face relationship with the God who is love: "For God, who said, 'Let light shine out of darkness,' made his light shine in our hearts to give the light of the knowledge of the glory of God in the face of Christ" (2 Cor. 4:6).

And is it true that God is love? Yes, that is the meaning of the baby in the ox's stall. God is here for us. Jesus Christ is the Good News of what God has done to save us. He is God's Gospel to the world. This Gospel anticipates a world far different from C. S. Lewis's Narnia, where it is "always winter, and never Christmas." The promise of the Gospel is that it is "*always* Christmas." To be "in Christ" is to enjoy each morning as a Christmas morning with the family of God, celebrating the gift of God around the tree of life.

Notes

1. Jaroslav Pelikan, *Jesus Through the Centuries: His Place in the History of Culture* (New Haven: Yale University Press, 1999).
2. *Time*, August 15, 1988.
3. H. R. Macintosh, *The Person of Jesus Christ* (Edinburgh: T. & T. Clerk, 1913), p. 2.
4. Martin Hengel, *The Son of God: The Origin of Christology and the History of Hellenistic-Jewish Religion* (Philadelphia: Fortress Press, 1976), p. 2.

Study Questions

1. Why is the Gospel told as the story of Jesus Christ?
2. Who started the idea that Jesus is the Christ? Explain.
3. What do the many titles and "I am" sayings of Jesus tell us about his identity?
4. How do the four Gospel writers explain the identity of Jesus?
5. What does it mean to say that, in the case of Jesus Christ, the man is the message?

Salvation in its full sense is from the guilt of sin in the past, the power of sin in the present, and the presence of sin in the future. . . .

Sinners receive through faith in Christ alone "the gift of righteousness" (Rom. 1:17; 5:17; Phil. 3:9) and thus become "the righteousness of God" in him who was "made sin" for them (2 Cor. 5:21).

■

We affirm that the atonement of Christ by which, in his obedience, he offered a perfect sacrifice, propitiating the Father by paying for our sins and satisfying divine justice on our behalf according to God's eternal plan, is an essential element of the Gospel.

We deny that any view of the Atonement that rejects the substitutionary satisfaction of divine justice, accomplished vicariously for believers, is compatible with the teaching of the Gospel.

—*The Gospel of Jesus Christ: An Evangelical Celebration*

4

AM I NOT GOOD ENOUGH?

WHY JESUS HAD TO DIE FOR MY SINS

Scott J. Hafemann

Lightning bolts flashed around him. The thunder roared. The skies looked ominous. As the storm's fury intensified, the young German feared that he would die. The full force of nature's fury suddenly overtook him as he walked through the open field. Or was it God using nature's awesome power to judge him for his evil heart? Fearful, the young German swore an oath to Saint Anne. Should he survive the assault of the fiery bolts around him, he would give his life to God and enter the monastic life. The young man survived. The year was 1505. His name was Martin Luther. And true to his promise, Luther joined the monastery to prove his sincerity to God. Yet the young monk's intense search to find peace with God through his relentless and often extreme religious devotion left him empty.

Young Luther worried about his sins. He understood well that God in Christ is a righteous judge who punishes evil. To placate God's anger, Luther tried to be the best monk he could. To counter his sin, he served God. Yet he remained deeply troubled by his guilt and by the unrelenting power of sin in his life. He had no peace, no sense that God had forgiven him, no surety for his future.

But God was gracious. Driven by his despair, and through his passion-filled study of the Bible, Luther came to understand that Christ, our judge, is also a loving savior, who through his own death on the cross had paid the full penalty for our sins—past, present, and future. Rather than attempting to make up for his sins by trying harder for God, Luther began to see that sinners, helpless to rescue themselves, can and will be justified in God's sight only by trusting in Christ alone to save them.

It was this biblical truth that set Luther free and reformed the church. Many of Luther's contemporaries understood that Christ is our judge. God used Luther to make it clear that this same Christ is our savior.

In today's world, Luther's experience seems strange. We have dismissed the twin realities of God's wrath and love that drove Luther to the monastery, and then in the monastery drove him to Christ. Yet, no matter who we are or where we live or what we think about life, God remains the sovereign Lord of the universe, and Jesus stands as our judge.

Although dismissed by the world at large, this fact is more important than any other single reality in human history. Although mankind is in rebellion against God now, God, in Christ, will have the last word, "when the Lord Jesus is revealed from heaven in blazing fire with his powerful angels" (2 Thess. 1:7). At that time, God, in Christ, "will punish those who do not know God and do not obey the gospel of our Lord Jesus. They will be punished with everlasting destruction and shut out from the presence of the Lord and from the majesty of his power on the day he comes to be glorified in his holy people and to be marveled at among all those who have believed" (2 Thess. 1:8–10; cf. 2 Cor. 5:10).

These are strong words. I do not quote them lightly, but with a sense of their weight and warning. Like Luther, we must face them. The clear, cold fact of God's judgment runs through the center of the universe. God is God. Jesus is our judge. But it is the reality of God's wrath against a world that stands condemned for its idolatry (Isa. 42:8; Rom. 3:9–18) and is already experiencing God's judgment for suppressing the truth of his existence and power (Rom. 1:18–32), that makes the reality of the Gospel so breathtaking: "Here is a trustworthy saying that deserves full acceptance: Christ Jesus came into the world to save sinners" (1 Tim. 1:15). Jesus, the Judge, is also Jesus the Savior. This is the heart of the Gospel.[1] When we begin to understand this, we too, like Luther, begin to understand the Gospel.

THE REASON FOR GOD'S JUDGMENT

Such strong words of judgment, and therefore the Gospel itself, seem quite out of place in our day and age of easy belief. For most of the world, God seems no more significant than a good-luck charm. And the world's religions have made him the servant of their personal or political agendas. However, as we understand the truth of God's existence, and the true, biblical character of his all-sufficient sovereignty, purity, and love, the reason for God's judgment becomes clear.

Instead of seeking first God's kingdom and his righteousness, as Jesus commanded (Matt. 6:33), all of us have pursued the health and wealth, pleasure and prestige that this world has to offer. Jesus' command to seek first God's righteousness has become undesirable in a world in which "holiness" has become a matter of individual tastes and relativistic values.

We seem oblivious to the fact that our love affair with the world is hatred toward God (James 4:4). Further, "if anyone loves the world, the love of the Father is not in him. For everything in the world—the cravings of sinful man, the lust of his eyes and the boasting of what he has and does—comes not from the Father but from the world" (1 John 2:15–16).

To cast God away for the temporary trinkets of this life, as if he were a secondhand piece of jewelry, is deeply dishonoring to the sovereign character of the Creator, who himself alone can satisfy the deepest longings of our hearts (Ps. 16). At the center of our sin is our nonchalant neglect of God, as if we were the creators and rulers of our own lives, doing with them as we please. In short, "all have sinned and fall short of the glory of God" (Rom. 3:23). Our failure to honor God is an intolerable situation for the Creator and Savior of mankind, who will not share the rightful glory of his sovereignty with anyone or anything else (Ex. 9:16).[2]

BLESSED ARE THE PERSECUTED

Joon Gon Kim was studying for the ministry when the Korean War began in 1950. Seeking safety from the Communist invaders, Kim and his family fled to his father's house on an island off the southwestern coast. But there was no escape. Communist partisans began to seize property and kill resisters, eventually leaving dead one-tenth of the island's twenty thousand inhabitants.

One night the Kims, along with sixty others, were taken away, his wife and his father were killed, and he himself was beaten and left for dead. After repeated beatings, he managed to escape and rushed home to get his three-year-old daughter, who had been left behind during the bloody rampage. But his ordeal was not over. Once a soldier was about to cut Kim's throat, only to stop when a Communist woman shouted that he was not to shed blood in her house. Another time, he was put into a sack to be thrown from a cliff into the sea—but at that moment, the soldiers were given new orders and promptly left.

"All during this persecution, I was not at peace with God," Kim recalled. "Then I recalled my Savior—God heard my crying. As I looked upon my Savior

Yet, blind to God, all we are left with is a futile drive to meet our unmet craving for God by means of the second-rate pleasures of this world. Like a fish in water, we are unaware of the very thing to which we owe our every breath, namely God himself. And like an addict in denial, we gorge ourselves on the very things that destroy us, namely the false gods that we have made out of ourselves and the other created things of this world.

But the desire and attempt to find our happiness, identity, contentment, or security in anything or anyone apart from God is to worship a false god. The first of the Ten Commandments ("You shall have no other gods before me") and the last ("You shall not covet . . . anything that belongs to your neighbor," Ex. 20:3, 17) are, in reality, the same commandment. Covetousness is idolatry. And so we can be sure that "no immoral, impure or greedy per-

on the cross, I renewed my fellowship with Him." Peace and joy replaced his fear and hatred for the Communists. He prayed for those who had murdered his family. "I learned that day, in the midst of human tragedy, to confess fear as sin. Then I could experience God's cleansing and forgiveness."

Once his strength returned, he took his daughter to visit the home of his enemy. Shaken by Kim's boldness, the man invited him in. "As I spoke to him of salvation through Christ, he wept over his sins," Kim recalled. "We prayed together, and this man later became a faithful witness among the Communists." This was the experience that confirmed for Kim his calling to proclaim the Gospel. And when the United Nations forces retook the island, he intervened to help spare the lives of the Communists who had killed his family.

After study in the United States, Kim returned to Korea and there founded the first overseas ministry of Campus Crusade for Christ. Today there are Christians all over the world who trace their spiritual origin to the ministry of Joon Gon Kim.

—Adapted from "Dr. Joon Gon Kim: Heart and Seoul,"
in *More Than Conquerors*, ed. John D. Woodbridge
(Chicago: Moody Press, 1992), pp. 186–90.

son—such a man is an idolater—has any inheritance in the kingdom of Christ and of God. Let no one deceive you with empty words, for because of such things God's wrath comes on those who are disobedient" (Eph. 5:5–6).

Because we worship ourselves and the world God has made, we stand condemned by God and under his wrath already as we await the final judgment to come. God cannot pretend that we have not been living lives of rebellion against him, nor can he simply wink at our acts of pride, hatred, selfishness, self-rule, greed, and godlessness. And left to us, there is no way out of our adulterous affair with the idols of this world.

Even our best efforts at self-improvement simply reveal how far away we are from depending on God for "life and breath and everything else" (Acts 17:25), thereby exhibiting the very heart of sin itself. God cannot deny himself as the one and only true God who is worthy of all our worship and dependence. He maintains his glory by judging all those who have "fallen short" of his glory by disregarding him, distrusting his Word, and disobeying his commandments (Gen. 2:17).[3] For God simply to look the other way when people dishonor him would be for God to cease to be God. To be righteous, God must display and maintain his own glory in the world.

OUR NEED FOR GOD'S MERCY

Those who realize that their lives are an ugly, inescapable distortion of what God intended them to be and experience real remorse over it no longer downsize the gravity of their sins by comparing themselves with others or by offering God pitiful excuses for their actions. Nor do they attempt to escape God's judgment by vowing to "try harder" next time.

Our sinful nature as rebels makes a mockery of all such strategies of self-help and self-justification. The first step is to see our need for God's mercy by seeing our own ugliness, plain and simple. We must be like William Carey, the shoemaker-turned-pioneer-missionary whose forty years of service in India (1794–1834) made him "the father of modern missions." As a young man he came to the place where he had a "crisis of faith" that "arose from a dual awareness: the gravity of his sinfulness and his inability to save himself." At the end of his life—during which he founded a college and translated the entire Bible into Bengali, Oriya, Marathi, Hindi, Assamese, and Sanskrit, and parts of it into twenty-nine other languages—the epitaph he requested for his gravestone reveals that he had never forgotten the answer to his crisis:

WILLIAM CAREY
Born August 17th 1761
Died June, 1834
A wretched, poor and helpless worm,
On Thy kind arms I fall.

The experience of William Carey makes it clear that repentant sinners will throw themselves on the mercy of God as their only hope. As Israel's King David said when he was confronted with his adultery and murder,

> Have mercy on me, O God,
> according to your unfailing love;
> According to your great compassion
> blot out my transgressions.
> Wash away all my iniquity
> and cleanse me from my sin.
> For I know my transgressions,
> and my sin is always before me.
> Against you, you only, have I sinned
> and done what is evil in your sight,
> so that you are proved right when you speak
> and justified when you judge.
> Surely I was sinful at birth,
> sinful from the time my mother conceived me....
> Hide your face from my sins
> and blot out all my iniquity.
> Create in me a pure heart, O God,
> and renew a steadfast spirit within me.
>
> (Ps. 51:1–2, 10)

To see God's holiness is to see our own sin and to recognize that all our sins against others are, in reality, sins against God (Ps. 51:4). We must realize God's righteous judgment against us and cry out for mercy and restoration (vv. 1, 10). All of us have David's sinful heart, regardless of how well we keep it under wraps. (Jesus taught that those who lust are already adulterers, and those who lose their temper are murderers!—Matthew 5:22, 28) We all share in David's need for forgiveness and renewal. Yet David also knows that God would be justified to ignore our prayer for mercy altogether and punish us for our sin instead (Ps. 51:4). All we deserve from God is his judgment.

But David prays anyway, because he knows that God is a God of "unfailing love" (v. 1). David knows that God delights to forgive those who, because they know of God's "great compassion" (v. 1), simply and wholly trust him to do so. When we throw ourselves on God's mercy in the confidence that he will respond with forgiveness and renewal, we honor God greatly. Doing good to his people, despite their sin, not only reveals the magnificence of God's character but also brings forth praise from his people themselves. As David himself put it later in the psalm, "Save me from bloodguilt, O God, the God who saves me, and my tongue will sing of your *righteousness*. O Lord, open my lips, and my mouth will declare your *praise*" (vv. 14–15, italics added).

Sinners come to God knowing that although there is no reason *in them* that God should be merciful, God has every reason *in himself* to show mercy. "I, even I, am he who blots out your transgressions, for my own sake, and remembers your sins no more" (Isa. 43:25). God reveals his glory when he judges, but the greatest display of God's glorious righteousness is to show mercy to those who call on him to do so, even though they deserve only condemnation (1 Sam. 12:22).[4] At his very core, God is love (1 John 4:8).

So as David's prayer makes clear, the almost unbelievable thing about God is that the barrier to our forgiveness is not our sin, no matter how deep and ugly and godless it may be. God's infinite love is larger than even our greatest rebellion—even if we have rejected Jesus three times in the past (John 18:15–27; 21:15–19). The only "unforgivable sin" is the persistent refusal to come to God with a broken spirit over our sin in the first place. Such a lack of remorse shows that one has "blasphemed" against the Holy Spirit's work of softening the heart and leading us to repentance (Matt. 12:31–32). Since what we are asking God for is *mercy* and *forgiveness*, there is nothing we can do anyway to earn or deserve it. Mercy, by definition, is undeserved and unwarranted.

To offer God our works while at the same time pleading for him to blot out our iniquity would be a contradiction in terms, showing that we really do not understand either who we are in our sin or who God is in his righteousness. Being sinful to the core of our being, all we bring to God is our need, trusting that he will love us, have compassion on us, "blot out our iniquity," and re-create in us a pure heart.

Thus, in commenting on David's experience and insight, the apostle Paul observes that David pronounces a blessing on "the man to whom God credits righteousness *apart from works:* 'Blessed are they whose transgressions are *forgiven*, whose *sins* are covered. Blessed is the man whose *sin* the Lord will never count against him'" (Rom. 4:6–8, quoting Ps. 32:1–2, italics added). God's mercy and the hope of sinners come together in our reception of unmerited forgiveness.

The real barrier to our forgiveness, therefore, is not our sin, but the very fact that we are asking *God* to do the forgiving, because in the end, sin is ultimately against God's character itself. Since to maintain his justice as God he must judge all sin, on what basis can God forgive any sin without compromising his own justice and integrity?

The story is told about a judge whose daughter was brought into the courtroom for breaking the law. Because the judge was both just and loved his daughter, he faced a dilemma: If he simply forgave his daughter, the judge would compromise his justice. But if he passed judgment on his daughter, he would compromise his love for her.

What did he do? First, he declared that his daughter was guilty and ordered that a fine be paid. Then he took off his robes, stepped down from the bench, and paid the fine himself.

In the Gospel we see the glory of God as judge on the disrobed face of Christ (2 Cor. 4:4, 6). As the judge of the world, Christ first came as its savior in order to make it possible by his own death for God to save sinners without sacrificing his own righteous character.

THE HEART OF THE GOSPEL

That is why the central point and climax of the Bible is a message about Jesus of Nazareth, who lived and ministered in Palestine in the first decades of the first century. The heart of Jesus' message was his announcement and demonstration that the long-awaited kingdom of God was now being established through his ministry. This could only mean that Jesus was Israel's "messiah," that is, the one "anointed" to be her final king and deliverer (Matt. 16:13–20).[5]

Since the coming of God's kingdom meant the judgment of the wicked, the vindication of the righteous, and the establishment of God's righteous reign on earth, Jesus called people to repent and trust in the Good News of the breaking in of God's rule over his people (Mark 1:14–15).[6] However, in a shocking turn of events, Jesus also declared that he had not come to establish a political kingdom of national liberation for Israel, but to die for his people's sins as the suffering servant proclaimed by Isaiah (Isa. 52:13–53:12).[7] In Jesus' own words, "the Son of Man did not come to be served but to serve, and to give his life as a ransom for many" (Mark 10:45).

Only at his return would Jesus judge the world and establish the kingdom in all its fullness (cf. Mark 8:34–38; 14:62; Matt. 16:27; 24:30–31; 25:31–46; 26:62–64). The kingdom of God was here, but it was not here in all its fullness, and the suffering and death of the Messiah himself had established it. The pathway to glory was to be his own death on a Roman cross (Mark 10:32–34; Luke 9:51).

Though a "stumbling block to Jews and foolishness to Gentiles" (1 Cor. 1:23), the judgment of God that Israel had expected the Messiah to bring upon the wicked (Matt. 3:1–12; Luke 3:1–18) fell on Jesus himself. Though sinless and innocent, Jesus was crucified by the Romans for the sake of political expediency, having been rejected by Israel's leadership because of his criticism of their character and authority (Mark 3:6).[8] In accordance with Deuteronomy 21:23, the Jews consequently interpreted Jesus' death as a sign that he had been cursed by God for his attempt to lead the people astray as a messianic pretender.

Indeed, had the cross been the end of Jesus' life, the only conclusion would have been that he was a false messiah, killed and cursed by God for his presumption, blasphemy, and false witness.

Yet none of this was a mistake. Jesus did not die because he got in over his head, got carried away by the fickle enthusiasm of the crowds, misinterpreted God's will, or underestimated the political climate of the day. The events of Jesus' life went according to God's plan and purpose as announced in the Scriptures (Luke 24:13–48; Rom. 1:2–4). It became increasingly clear that Jesus was more than Israel's messiah; he was also God's divine, preexistent Son (Mark 1:1; 2:1–12; 4:35–41).[9]

As the final and ultimate certification of Jesus' claims to be Israel's king, and as the vindication of his identity as God's Son, the divine savior of the world, God raised Jesus from the dead and seated him at his right hand in glory. He will return one day to save his people and to judge the living and the dead (Acts 2:22–36; 1 Thess. 1:10). As a result, Peter declared to the Jews on the Day of Pentecost, just before he offered them forgiveness in the name of Jesus Christ, "Therefore let all Israel be assured of this: God has made this Jesus, whom you crucified, both Lord and Christ" (Acts 2:36).

Jesus' resurrection makes it clear that on the cross he was not being cursed by God for his own sins, but for the sins of his people, regardless of whether they are Jews or Gentiles (1 John 2:2; 4:10). The earliest formulation we have of the Gospel, quoted by Paul in 1 Corinthians 15:3–5, can consequently summarize the Gospel with five brief statements:

> that Christ died for our sins according to the Scriptures,
> that he was buried,
> that he was raised on the third day according to the Scriptures,
> that he appeared to Peter,
> and then to the Twelve.

THE GREAT EXCHANGE

In Charles Dickens's book *A Tale of Two Cities*, a man named Charles Darnay is condemned to die by the guillotine. "Alone in a cell, [he] had sustained himself with no flattering delusion since he came to it from the Tribunal. In every line of the narrative . . . he had heard his condemnation. He had fully comprehended that no personal influence could possibly save him."

As Darnay sits quietly thinking of his wife and child, he suddenly hears footsteps in the stone passage outside the door. "The key was put in the lock, and turned. . . . The door was quickly opened and closed, and there stood before him face to face, quiet, intent upon him, with the light of a smile on his features, and a cautionary finger on his lip, Sydney Carton." This man has come to trade places with Darnay. Carton is willing to go to the guillotine so that Darnay can be free to live and rejoin his family.

After the exchange has been made, and the prisoners are gathered to be taken to their execution, a little seamstress approaches him. "'Are you dying for him?' she whispered. 'And his wife and child,'" he replies.

Sidney Carton died so that another might live. But as great as his act was, it still does not compare with what Christ has done for us. While Carton acted heroically for a good man and his family, Christ died mercifully for a humanity caught in rebellion against God. As the apostle Paul put it, "You see, at just the right time, when we were still powerless, Christ died for the ungodly. Very rarely will anyone die for a righteous man, though for a good man [like Darnay] someone might possibly dare to die. But God demonstrates his own love for us in this: While we were still sinners, Christ died for us" (Rom. 5:6–8).

Jesus' death, as a sacrificial offering made to God in our place, "atones" or makes up for our sin by receiving the punishment that would otherwise be ours. Jesus, in his sinlessness as a man and in his identity as the divine Son of God, was able to pay the penalty for the sins of all humanity. "For Christ died for sins once for all, the righteous for the unrighteous, to bring you to God" (1 Peter 3:18).

Because of Christ's sacrificial death in our place, we are reconciled with God as new creatures in Christ (2 Cor. 5:17–21), since "God was reconciling the world to himself in Christ, not counting men's sins against them" (v. 19). "You see, at just the right time, when we were still powerless, Christ died for the ungodly.... when we were God's enemies, we were reconciled to him through the death of his Son" (Rom. 5:6, 10; cf. Col. 1:20, 22).

The death of Christ is the means by which God fulfills the need for atonement prefigured in the sacrifices of the old covenant (see, for example, 1 Cor. 6:11; 11:23–26; 15:3–5; Rom. 3:25–26, against the backdrop of Lev. 4:13–24; 10:17). In Christ, "we have redemption through his blood, the forgiveness of sins" (Eph. 1:7). As our great high priest, Jesus not only mediates the offering before God but is himself the offering (Heb. 9:26–28). His death pays the penalty for our sin in our place. Accordingly, the Statement declares, "We deny that any view of the Atonement that rejects the substitutionary satisfaction of divine justice, accomplished vicariously for believers, is compatible with the teaching of the Gospel."

Moreover, as sinners we were in bondage to the power of sin and Satan and were enslaved to a hostile "slaveholder" who kept us separated from our true master, God (Eph. 2:1–3; Rom. 6). Hence, Jesus' death is also understood in the New Testament to be a price paid in order to ransom us from our slavery to sin (Mark 8:36–37; 10:45; 14:24 against the backdrop of Isa. 53:4–8, 10–12). To set us free from both the consequences and dominion of sin over us, God buys us back with the life and death of his only Son (Acts 20:28; Gal. 3:13–14; 4:4–5; 1 Cor. 1:30). Christ's death not only pays the penalty for our sin but also frees us from the rule of sin in our lives (1 Peter 2:24, quoting Isa. 53:5).

THE POWER OF THE GOSPEL

For these reasons, the apostle Paul declares in Romans 1:16 that the Gospel "is the *power* of God" that brings about the salvation of everyone who entrusts their lives to Christ. The power of the Gospel is brought about by the divine act of deliverance in Christ from both the penalty and the power of sin. In Romans 1:17 Paul points out that the Gospel is the power of God precisely because it declares how God reveals his righteousness when he saves sinners.

God cannot act in any way that would compromise his justice. In establishing his reign on earth through the death and resurrection of

Christ, God made it possible to forgive sinners and welcome them into his kingdom while at the same time remaining righteous. So the Gospel is the vehicle through which God's righteousness is unleashed just as much in his mercy toward sinners as it is in his wrath against sin.

Now we know what David, the Old Testament prophets, and even angels longed to learn, since "now a righteousness from God . . . has been made known, to which the Law and the Prophets testify" (Rom. 3:21). As John Piper puts it, "The wisdom of God has ordained a way for the love of God to deliver us from the wrath of God without compromising the justice of God."[10] This righteousness is outlined in the important paragraph of Romans 3:21–26. Here Paul tells us that God's righteousness comes as both the gift of Jesus' death for our sin and the power of Jesus' death over our sin. That is why the Statement declares, "We affirm that the righteousness of Christ by which we are justified is properly his own, which he achieved apart from us, in and by his perfect obedience. This righteousness is counted, reckoned, or imputed to us by the forensic (that is, legal) declaration of God, as the sole ground of our justification." At the same time, we also set forth that "The Father sent the Son to free us from the dominion of sin and Satan. . . . Jesus paid our penalty in our place on his cross. . . . The Bible describes this mighty substitutionary transaction as the achieving of ransom, reconciliation, redemption, propitiation, and conquest of evil powers (Matt. 20:28; 2 Cor. 5:18–21; Rom. 3:23–25; John 12:31; Col. 2:15)."

In Romans 3:25 the apostle Paul tells us that Jesus' sacrificial death for sinners and for sin establishes him as the new "mercy seat" for God's people. The mercy seat was the plate of gold placed over the ark of the covenant as the place of atonement within Israel's temple. There, within the "holy of holies," God made himself known during Israel's history under the old covenant (Rom. 3:25; Ex. 25:17–22; 31:7; Lev. 16:2–15; Num. 7:89). As the new mercy seat, Jesus is both the place of atonement and also the one who makes God known in his righteousness.

There is, however, an important difference. The Exodus from Egypt led to the creation of the Tent of Meeting, the veil of Moses, and the temple. Due to Israel's hardened, rebellious nature, God's glory had to be separated from them in order to make it possible for God to continue in the midst of a hard-hearted people without destroying them (Ex. 32:9–10). In the "second exodus" now brought about by Christ, his sacrificial death cleans us up in God's sight so that his presence may dwell among us and his Spirit live within us without destroying us.[11] As the mercy seat, Jesus, by his Spirit, dwells within us, revealing God's glory. By faith in Christ, we become God's temple. The preamble to the Statement summarizes it this way: "All who are justified experience reconciliation with the Father, full remission of sins, transition from the kingdom of darkness to the kingdom of light, the reality of being a new creature in Christ, and the fellowship of the Holy Spirit. They enjoy access to the Father with all the peace and joy that this brings."

So the Gospel is also God's justifying word about himself, since under the old covenant, with its symbolic sacrificial system, it appeared as if God was ignoring the sins of those who simply trusted in him for forgiveness (Rom. 3:25). Now, in the shadow of the cross, it is possible to see that Jesus is the reason that God could justify the ungodly, like Abraham and David (cf. Rom. 4:1–8), without compromising his own integrity. When God forgave his people in the past, he did so looking forward to the cross of Christ as the basis of and revelation of that divine righteousness which makes forgiveness possible. The death of Jesus demonstrated with finality God's "justice at the present time, so as to be just and the one who justifies those who have faith in Jesus" (Rom. 3:26).

But that is not all that the prophets and angels longed to learn. The "justification" language itself makes clear that God's "justification of the ungodly" on the basis of Christ's death is a divine declaration of our righteous standing before God's court of judgment, with God himself as judge. As such, our justification is a legal act of acquittal, which declares us to be righteous and sets us free from the condemnation that would have been ours (Phil. 3:9; Rom. 3:22; 5:16–17; 8:33).

Of course, in ourselves we are guilty. Here too, then, the reason for our being considered innocent in God's sight is the great exchange that takes place between Christ and us. Viewing us in Christ, God considers, or "reckons," us from the first moment we trust him to be perfectly righteous as if we had never sinned. Because of the death of the sinless Christ who took on our sin, we may take on his righteousness in a great exchange of his perfection for our guilt. From our very first moment of trusting in Christ as our Savior and Lord, we are declared "not guilty" and treated as "just" or "innocent," even though we deserve death. In theological language, "we are justified by faith alone through Christ alone."

We must always affirm, as in the Statement, "that the biblical doctrine of justification by faith alone in Christ alone is essential to the Gospel (Rom. 3:28; 4:5; Gal. 2:16)." God declares us just, forgives our sins, and adopts us as his children, by his grace alone and through faith alone, because of Christ alone, while we are still sinners (Rom. 5:6–8).

In the words of the Statement, "As our sins were reckoned to Christ, so Christ's righteousness is reckoned to us. This is justification by the imputation of Christ's righteousness. All we bring to the transaction is our need of it. Our faith in the God who bestows it, the Father, the Son, and the Holy Spirit, is itself the fruit of God's grace. Faith links us savingly to Jesus, but inasmuch as it involves an acknowledgment that we have no merit of our own, it is confessedly not a meritorious work." For this reason, "We deny that any works we perform at any stage of our existence add to the merit of Christ or earn for us any merit that contributes in any way to the ground of our justification (Gal. 2:16; Eph. 2:8–9; Titus 3:5)."

THE "PROBLEM" WITH US

A man who had fallen off a cliff was hanging desperately to a small branch, hoping that he would not fall to his death on the rocks below. In fear and anguish he cried out, "Can someone up there help me?" To his surprise, a voice from heaven replied, "I'll help you. If you let go of the branch, I will catch you." The man thought about this for a minute and then cried in a louder voice,

"Can anyone *else* up there help me?" Even in the most dire circumstances, our natural desire is to cling to our own sources of security and "branches" of self-reliance.

The Gospel is clear that there is nothing we can do to be saved—except trust in Christ. Like the man hanging on the branch, we must let go of our efforts to save ourselves. This is great news to those of us who have suffered under the attempt to earn God's favor by working hard for him. But it is terrible news to those who still take pride in steering their "own" course, determining their "own" destiny, and taking credit for their "own" accomplishments. The good news of the Gospel is bad news for mankind's sinful propensity to think that their problem is simply a failure to fulfill their human potential. After all, when it comes to dealing with God, we are quick to justify ourselves by comparing ourselves to others. We find deceptive comfort in thinking that, although we are not all that we should be, we are at least not as bad as other people. Add to this our ethnic pride and sense of self-worth, and it is a deadly mix.

The Bible makes it clear that the life, death, and resurrection of Jesus Christ are the *only* basis upon which God can forgive us and reconcile us to himself and still remain righteous. Jesus is the *only* way of salvation for the entire human race. We cannot save ourselves in *any way*. Like David, the only thing we bring with us when we confess our sins, is our sin. We seek forgiveness for our lives, not a paycheck (Rom. 4:4–5).

In our coming to God with nothing but our sin, our faith is a trusting in *God* to work for us, not an attempt to show God how sincere we are. Our faith glorifies *God*, being the expression of the fact that we are fully persuaded that *God* is willing and able to do what *he* has promised, even if this means God must give life not merely to a dead womb but to a spiritually dead heart and, one day, to a physically dead body (Rom. 4:17, 21, 23–25). Such faith overturns our sin and makes us righteous in God's sight, since it honors him as the one whose word can be trusted and whose presence is to be valued more than the rewards of this world. This is why when we trust in God because of what he has already done for us, our faith is credited to us as righteousness (Rom. 4:5, 22–23).

Our active dependence on God must therefore not be perverted into a "work" that we think earns God's blessings or forces his hand. Faith is not a bargaining chip but our dependence on God to do what he has already promised in Christ. When it comes to getting right with God, we must resist our natural inclination to think God is calling us to cooperate with his plan of salvation by matching his work with our own, by meeting God halfway, or by showing God how sincere we are through our efforts at self-reformation.

We do not trust God so that Christ might die and be raised from the dead for us. We trust God because Christ has *already* died and been raised from the dead (Rom. 4:24–25). For when we trust God *alone* because of what he *alone* has already done for us in Christ, God *alone* gets the glory. The giver gets the glory.

That is why Paul emphasizes that our salvation, including our faith, is a gift. It is not something God owes us because we have earned it by our own works, lest we think that we have some ground for boasting before God (Rom. 4:2–4; Eph. 2:8–9). By "works" in this negative sense, Paul means thinking that God saves us based on some attitude or activity or ethnic heritage or anything else we might think makes us deserving of God's love.

God will not share his glory with his creatures. Even our "good works" as a new creation in Christ "God prepared in advance for us to do" and brought them into being through the death of Christ (Eph. 2:10; 2 Cor. 5:17–21). "And he died for all, that those who live should no longer live for themselves but for him who died for them and was raised again" (2 Cor. 5:15). That is why the *gift* of salvation is only given to the person "who does not work but trusts God who justifies the wicked." Only those who realize that they do not earn or deserve their salvation in any way have a faith that glorifies God and is therefore "credited as righteousness" (Rom. 4:5). For this reason, Abraham is the father of all those who trust in God alone without attempting to earn God's blessing, since he trusted God *before* he was circumcised (Rom. 4:9–17; Gal. 2:16–17; 3:8, 11).

THE PROMISE OF GOD

The great news of the Gospel is that in and through the death and resurrection of Christ, *God* forgives us for our lives of self-serving independence and delivers us from its consequences. In Christ, God does for us what we cannot do for ourselves: He redeems us from our sin and rescues us from living for ourselves, thereby saving us from his judgment.

Our response is to trust him to do so. When trusted, the death and resurrection of Jesus secure for us all the promises of God, past, present, and future. As the Statement says, "Salvation in its full sense is from the guilt of sin in the past, the power of sin in the present, and the presence of sin in the future." In all three cases we are justified by faith alone, as we trust in the fact that "he who did not spare his own Son, but gave him up for us all—how will he not also, along with him, graciously give us all things" (Rom. 8:32).

Therefore we live by faith in God's promise that no accuser can condemn us on the day of judgment. After all, God is the one who predestines, calls, justifies, and glorifies, and Christ is the one who intercedes for us (Rom. 8:31, 33–34). In the present we must place our hope on the fact that no earthly circumstance or heavenly power—not even death itself—can separate us from the love of God in Christ (Rom. 8:35–39).

Notes

1. It is a humbling honor to contribute to this statement of the Gospel, and also to recognize that virtually nothing in this essay is really original. Every statement could be footnoted to what my friends and teachers have taught me. In addition, John Woodbridge and Jack Kuhatschek provided the illustrations throughout the essay. *Sola fide; sola gloria.*

2. See also Psalm 81:8–10; Isaiah 43:11; 46:9–10; 48:11; Romans 11:33–36.

3. See also Deuteronomy 27:15–26; Isaiah 5:13–17; Romans 2:5–24; 6:23; Revelation 20:11–15.

4. See also Psalms 31:1–5; 79:9; 143:11; Jeremiah 14:7–21; Daniel 9:16–18; 1 John 1:9.

5. See also Matthew 23:10; 26:63–64; Luke 23:2; John 20:31.

6. See also Matthew 4:12–17; Luke 4:14–21, 43; cf. Isaiah 52:7; 61:1.

7. See also Mark 8:27–33; Matthew 20:28; 26:47–56; John 18:33–37.

8. See also Mark 12:13; 15:16–20, 25–32; Matthew 26:1–5; 27:15–26; John 8:31–47.

9. See also Matthew 28:19; John 1:1–18; 5:18; 8:58; 10:22–42; 17:5; 20:28; Romans 9:5; Colossians 1:15–20; Titus 2:13; Hebrews 1:8–9; 2 Peter 1:1.

10. John Piper, *Desiring God: Meditations of a Christian Hedonist* (Sisters, OR: Multnomah Books, 1996), p. 59.

11. On this, compare Exodus 33:3, 5 and 34:29–35 with 1 Corinthians 3:16; 2 Corinthians 3:7–11, 18; 6:16; Ephesians 2:11–22; Hebrews 7:18–19; James 4:8–10.

Study Questions

1. How is Jesus the Judge and the Savior at one and the same time, or to put it another way, how is the Gospel simultaneously the vehicle for both God's righteousness and God's mercy?
2. Explain why "our love affair with the world is hatred toward God."
3. Why is neglect of God as harmful as rebellion toward God?
4. What are the dangers in self-reliance and self-improvement?
5. Describe a time when you were like the man hanging by a small branch from a cliff.
6. What is God's promise for the past, the present, and the future?

This Gospel further proclaims the bodily resurrection, ascension, and enthronement of Jesus as evidence of the efficacy of his once-for-all sacrifice for us, of the reality of his present personal ministry to us, and of the certainty of his future return to glorify us (1 Cor. 15; Heb. 1:1–4; 2:1–18; 4:14–16; 7:1–10:25). In the life of faith as the Gospel presents it, believers are united with their risen Lord, communing with him, and looking to him in repentance and hope for empowering through the Holy Spirit, so that henceforth they may not sin but serve him truly.

■

We affirm that the bodily resurrection of Christ from the dead is essential to the biblical Gospel (1 Cor. 15:14).

We deny the validity of any so-called gospel that denies the historical reality of the bodily resurrection of Christ.

—*The Gospel of Jesus Christ: An Evangelical Celebration*

5

DID JESUS CHRIST REALLY RISE FROM THE DEAD?

Thomas C. Oden

Anyone who has bid a sad farewell to a departed loved one at a graveside knows that death is a formidable foe. Yet, for Christians facing death, there is hope for life beyond the grave. This hope comes from the belief that Jesus Christ overcame death and its sting. Christ did this through his triumphant resurrection. Through Christ's victory over death, his followers have the hope of resurrection to eternal life in heaven. Christ's resurrection and our own, therefore, are inseparably related. His makes our resurrection possible.

The apostle Paul repeatedly speaks of this hope. If Christ had not risen from the grave, then the apostle's own preaching would have been vain and the Christian faith proven phony. Christians would be left in their sins. Those who had died in Christ would have perished. For Paul, the conclusion was simple: no resurrection, no hope. Christians would be of all people the most miserable and pitiable (1 Cor. 15:14–19). But according to Paul, the glorious truth is that Christ has indeed risen from the grave and has triumphed over death. He is alive. Consequently, all who are in Christ shall be made alive. Moreover, death itself shall be destroyed (1 Cor. 15:20–26). No Christian thinks Christ is now dead.

For this reason Christians do not grieve the death of their believing loved ones in the same way as those who mourn with "no hope" (1 Thess. 4:13). For if Christians believe that Jesus Christ died and rose again from the dead, then they can have confidence that their loved ones as well will rise again from the dead in the Last Day. The Statement confesses, "At death, Christ takes the believer to himself (Phil. 1:21) for unimaginable joy in the ceaseless worship of God (Rev. 22:1–5)."

And lest anyone question the reality of Christ's resurrection, the apostle Paul provided evidence that Christ has risen. Paul reported that eyewitnesses had seen Christ after the resurrection. They included Peter, the other disciples, and more than five hundred people at one time, some of whom were still living in Paul's day and could be questioned about what they saw (1 Cor. 15:4–7). Paul also viewed himself as an eyewitness. He placed the resurrection of Jesus Christ at the very heart of the Gospel.

Affirmation 10 of the Statement reads, "We affirm that the bodily resurrection of Christ from the dead is essential to the biblical Gospel (1 Cor. 15:14)." The denial states, "We deny the validity of any so-called gospel that denies the historical reality of the bodily resurrection of Christ."

Many well-crafted books have been written in which the resurrection of Jesus Christ is discussed at length. Here we will consider only two issues, but they are very important ones: (1) How might we respond to people who doubt that the resurrection actually took place? Obviously, a belief in the resurrection of Christ weaves constantly into the texture of the life of faith. But the New Testament is intent on laying out compelling evidence that supports the reality of Christ's bodily resurrection; (2) Why did the resurrection of Christ carry such overwhelming significance for the early Christians? A response to this question may help us gain a better understanding of the central role the resurrection of Christ plays in the Christian faith today.

IS THERE EVIDENCE THAT THE RESURRECTION REALLY HAPPENED?

Many of our friends and associates may have honest questions about whether or not Christ did in fact rise from the dead. Other people may approach the resurrection narratives with a hardened predisposition not to believe them. The latter would be like the Athenians who first heard of the resurrection from Paul: "When they heard about the resurrection of the dead, some of them sneered" (Acts 17:32).

If a person has decided that resurrection cannot occur and that no evidence could ever convince him or her to the contrary, then it should at least be pointed out that a prevailing predisposition to rule out evidence is at work, shaped by a reductive naturalism that refuses to consider some events as real. If the case against Christianity is so strong, why should they not be open to weighing the evidence for the resurrection on its own merits?

But what is the nature of the evidence regarding a resurrection? It is too much to ask of this evidence that it be historically validated in the manner of a laboratory experiment. The standards for verifying the truthfulness of an experiment in the natural sciences are hardly comparable to the evidence used in historical science. In history, events cannot be repeated in the same way that experiments can be. But in the discipline of history, a careful, modest presentation of evidence can nonetheless be quite persuasive to an open-minded person. Historians are prone to argue frequently for the "truthfulness" of an event with far less evidence from eyewitnesses than from those who testified that Christ was risen from the dead.

Martin Luther summarized the various types of testimony: "The resurrection of the Lord Christ is made certain (1) by the testimony of His adversaries, (2) by the testimony of His friends, (3) by the testimony of the Lord Himself, and (4) by the testimony of dear prophets and of Holy Scripture."[1]

In what follows, we will consider a few of the more serious objections to the reality of the bodily resurrection of Christ by examining the testimony and actions of Christ's adversaries and the testimony and actions of his friends and disciples. We will also see as evidence the changed lives of the disciples.

Objection One: Christ Did Not Really Die (The Swoon Theory)

Some skeptics have argued that Christ swooned or fainted on the cross and did not really die. Obviously, if he did not die, then he did not rise from the dead. But the evidence of Christ's death seemed sufficient to his enemies and to civil officials. The centurion reportedly assured Pilate that Jesus was dead, in effect officially verifying the death (Mark 15:44–45). The reason the soldiers did not break Jesus' legs, as would have been customary, is that they "found that he was already dead" (John 19:33). It was after this that "one of the soldiers pierced Jesus' side with a spear" (v. 34). Joseph of Arimathea "asked Pilate for the body.... With Pilate's permission, he came and took the body away" (v. 38). Joseph was accompanied by Nicodemus. If Jesus were not dead, no one would have described him as "the body."

Jesus' body was put through a complex burial process: "Taking Jesus' body, the two of them wrapped it, with the spices, in strips of linen ... in accordance with Jewish burial customs." And there was "in the garden a new tomb" in which Jesus was laid (John 19:40–42).

Hence, it is implausible to imagine that Jesus did not really die in the crucifixion. Moreover, it is unlikely that the disciples would or could have covertly removed the body from the tomb, because a specific plan had been initiated by Pilate to prevent just that. Pilate had ordered his guards to "'make the tomb as secure as you know how.' So they went and made the tomb secure by putting a seal on the stone and posting the guard" (Matt. 27:65–66).

Objection Two: Someone Stole the Body (The Theft Theory)

If the authorities themselves had removed the body or they had secretly asked the guards to do so, then they would have had at their disposal the means of silencing the earliest proclaimers of resurrection—and they would have had sufficient motive to do so. The authorities could have simply displayed the body. Case closed—no resurrection. The vitality of the Christian faith would have quickly dissipated. But the authorities did not have the body. The tomb was empty.

Careful unpacking of the evidence presented by John 20:1–9 yields the remarkable conclusion: Jesus' body was not in the tomb. What's more, the grave clothes were precisely in the place and in the exact form in which he had been laid. The narrative bears peculiar marks of a direct eyewitness account in its precision and detail. John reached the tomb first and looked in, but Peter entered it first. Then John entered the tomb and saw something that immediately convinced him that Jesus had risen.

The account is precise: He "went inside. He saw and believed" (John 20:8). But exactly what evidence did he see that elicited instant belief? Not just the absence of the body, but the particular way the grave clothes were lying, precisely as they would have been as if on the body but now collapsed without the body and left in an undisturbed condition. Joseph and Nicodemus had wound the linen around the body, inserting spices in the folds, and used a separate linen for the head (John 19:40).

It is astonishing that we have this very precise description of such a crucial moment by an eyewitness: The linen cloths also, which had enveloped Jesus and which he left behind when he rose, were early regarded as silent witnesses. Three centuries later, Cyril of Jerusalem was confident that the specific location of this sepulchre had been correctly remembered and identified, "the spot itself, still to be seen" (namely, the site of the Church of the Holy Sepulchre, the very place where Cyril was offering his catechetical lectures).[2]

Objection Three: The Disciples Made Up the Story of a Risen Christ (The Projection Theory)

The least plausible of all explanations of the resurrection was that it was generated out of the despairing imagination of the disciples. The core of this hypothesis, called the projection theory, is found in Hegel, anticipating Freudian views of wish projection: "The need for religion finds its satisfaction in the risen Jesus."[3] The projection theory requires that there be a strong disposition on the part of the disciples in a particular, predisposing direction to believe that Christ was risen from the dead.

NO PIT SO DEEP

Corrie ten Boom passed the first fifty years of her life in quiet spiritual devotion and cheerful domestic activity with her extended family in the town of Haarlem in the Netherlands. Having given her life to Jesus at the age of five, she was always active in religious service such as starting a Christian "Girl Scout" movement, called "The Triangle Girls," and a club for mentally retarded children.

And then the war came. Corrie and her family hid Jews in their home until one day in February 1944 they were betrayed to the Nazis. Corrie, her sister Betsie, and other members of her family were taken away to prison or to concentration camps, from which few of them ever returned.

In the dreaded Ravensbruck camp in Germany, Corrie and Betsie took every opportunity to tell others about God. They had been able to smuggle in a Bible, so they held daily Bible studies. Frail and seven years older than Corrie, Betsie became ill, but her faith remained strong. She said, "Corrie, when the new year comes, we will both be free. God has given me a vision. We must go around the world and tell everyone who will listen the truth that we have discovered here, that there is no pit so deep the love of God is not deeper still."

With the new year, they were indeed both free. Betsie died in Ravensbruck. Corrie was released from the camp, as she put it later, "by a clerical error of man and a miracle of God." She returned to the Netherlands and eventually embarked on a ministry that took her to sixty-four countries in thirty-three years and endeared her to millions of people around the world through her testimony to the grace and faithfulness of God.

—Adapted from Pamela Rosewell,
The Five Silent Years of Corrie ten Boom
(Grand Rapids: Zondervan, 1986), pp. 10–11.

The texts indicate the opposite tendency, as Thomas Aquinas pointed out: "Because their hearts were not disposed so as to accept readily the faith in the Resurrection. Then He says Himself [Luke 24:25]: 'O foolish and slow of heart to believe'; and [Mark 16:14]: 'He upbraided them for their incredulity.'"[4]

No sequel to Christ's death was expected. The body was received by friends and bound in linen. There seems to be no doubt that Jesus was dead and buried. The tomb was sealed. Burial rites began Friday and were still continuing on Sunday ("after the Sabbath, at dawn"—Matt. 28:1) when the women came to the sepulchre. If large numbers of disciples had been expecting some sequel to his death, there surely would have been some indication that they were eagerly awaiting it.

Rather, the women came to the tomb for the express purpose of proceeding with the burial. They did not come expecting to find the tomb empty. If they had been expecting the resurrection, they surely would not have done as the text of Mark indicates: "Trembling and bewildered, the women went out and fled from the tomb. They said nothing to anyone, because they were afraid" (Mark 16:8).

The disciples were hard to convince. When the appearances were first reported, those who witnessed them had an exceptionally difficult time persuading anyone that they were true: "They did not believe it" (Mark 16:11). Luke's account states the point more strongly: "But they did not believe the women, because their words seemed to them like nonsense" (Luke 24:11). Subsequently, "Jesus himself stood among them and said to them, 'Peace be with you,'" and "they were startled and frightened" (Luke 24:36–37). Jesus "rebuked them for their lack of faith and *their stubborn refusal to believe those who had seen him* after he had arisen" (Mark 16:14, italics added). That hardly sounds as if the disciples were predisposed to expect a resurrection so intensely that they fabricated it from whole cloth.

Thomas even more stubbornly refused to credit the reports: "Unless I see the nail marks in his hands and put my finger where the nails were, and put my hand into his side, I will not believe it" (John 20:25). Far from being portrayed as intensely expecting the resurrection, the disciples were portrayed as stubbornly resistant, cautious, and skeptical. Jesus indicated their resistance when he described them as "slow of heart to believe" (Luke 24:25).

The only remaining option is that the account is true. According to Thomas Aquinas's analysis, Jesus sufficiently manifested the truth of his resurrection by showing that he had (1) a physical body after death (by eating); (2) an emotive life capable of interpersonal relationships (by greeting and talking with others); (3) an intellectual life (by dialogue and discoursing on Scripture); and (4) the divine nature (by working the miracle of the draft of fishes, and by ascending). Each of these testimonies, or proofs, "was sufficient to its own class": so as to maintain a correspondence between the testimony of human observers and testimony of Scriptures.[5]

The Changed Lives of the Disciples

The radically changed behavior of the disciples after the resurrection is the best evidence of the resurrection. The disciples did not intend or propose that we look at their behavior—all they wanted us to do is look at the evidence on which they based their testimony. But their behavior itself becomes an overriding argument for the authenticity of their testimony.

Their lives were completely reversed by the resurrection. They were different people after the resurrection. They had left the burial with a deep sense of loss, facing the collapse of what they had hoped would be the decisive event in Israel's history. Suddenly the people we see portrayed in Acts were willing to risk "their lives for the name of our Lord Jesus Christ" (Acts 15:26), who were proceeding to "turn the world upside down" to attest the living Lord (Acts 17:6 KJV). Their behavioral change was instantaneous, radical, and continuing.

Even today, the primary evidence for the resurrection remains: changed lives, walking testimonies, people willing to proclaim the Good News the world over. The argument is powerfully stated by Daniel Whitby, an Anglican divine of the seventeenth century:

> It is highly unlikely to think that a poor ignorant young man, of lowest birth and breeding of a most despised nation, and hated by

> that nation to the death because, having pretended that He was a prophet sent from God, and after this His death, was only avowed to be so by twelve fishermen, who only pretended with loud boasts of miracles, false as God is true, to testify to His Resurrection through a greater falsehood? Were they promising to all that would believe it nothing besides this power of working miracles but death and miseries at present, which their experience proved to be true? I say, it is prodigious to think that He and His disciples should with no other charms work such a lasting faith in all the wisest part of men, that neither time nor vice, though most concerned to do so, should ever be able to deface it.[6]

In a word, some hypothesis is necessary to make plausible the transformation of the disciples from grieving followers of a crucified messiah to those whose resurrection preaching turned the world upside down. That change could not have happened, according to the church's testimony, without the risen Lord. There would have been no community to remember the cross had there not been those whose lives were transformed by their meeting with the risen Lord.

It is only a living Christ, thought Athanasius, who could empower the risk-laden witness of martyrs who did not flinch from torture. The demonstration of Jesus' resurrection lies in factually embodied evidence—that of people whose lives have been decisively changed by the One who is alive. Christ's death increased his influence. The works of costly witness and service are not "of one dead, but of one that lives."[7] It is only a living Christ that can account for those Christians today who take up their cross daily and follow the Savior even if that may mean losing their own lives.

THE RESURRECTION NARRATIVES AS TESTIMONY TO CHRIST'S RESURRECTION

Jesus' resurrection is not considered myth or symbol in the New Testament documents but rather a fact attested by credible witnesses: "God has raised this Jesus to life, and we are all witnesses of the fact" (Acts 2:32).

The church did not receive its life from a moral teacher whose body was decomposing in the grave, but from one whose incomparable power made him known to his disciples as "the risen Lord."

It was not the case that the resurrection narratives were contrived and foisted upon the remembering community some months or years after Jesus' death. The resurrection testimony could not have exercised the power that it did in the lives of the disciples if it were not rooted in an actual occurrence immediately attested. Its truth value for its attesters depended entirely upon the authenticity of its historical occurrence.

The resurrection provided evidence to the disciples that Jesus is the Christ, as Tertullian affirms.[8] A major reason for writing the Gospels was to summon up this evidence (John 20:31). The Gospel Paul proclaimed far and wide was summarized simply as "the good news about Jesus and the resurrection" (Acts 17:18). The apostles thought that those who rejected the resurrection were thereby rejecting the whole revelation of the Son of God.[9]

No aspect of Jesus' ministry was more minutely recorded than his resurrection. The evidence for the resurrection appears to have been assiduously collected, transmitted, and embedded in the essential proclamation of salvation attested by the earliest Christian communities. The Gospel narratives seem to be saying to us that if we cannot credit the last validating episode of his life, we are not likely to grasp anything else said about him.[10]

Paul argued that there were many eyewitnesses who could attest that they had seen the risen Christ. For him, the resurrection was at the heart of the Gospel message. It was the source of the Christian's hope that death had been vanquished by Jesus Christ, the Lord and Savior of the world.

THE MEANING OF THE RESURRECTION FOR EARLY CHRISTIANS

In his *First Apology*, Justin Martyr, who lived in the second century, argued ironically that persecutors could kill Christians but could not hurt them. To the modern mind this claim seems to make no sense whatever. Most of us identify killing with an extreme form of hurting someone. But so powerful was the belief in the resurrection of Christ among the early Christians that many did not fear what happened to their bodies. They did not fear death. Had not Paul said, "For me, to live is Christ and to die is gain" (Phil. 1:21)? The resurrection of Christ had transformed their basic way of thinking about their physical existence.

To grasp what the resurrection meant to the early followers of Jesus, it is necessary to review what was the prevailing idea of general resurrection among Jews in the period preceding Jesus. Everyone knew exactly what resurrection meant: the anticipated end of history. The general resurrection was seen specifically as the event that was expected to happen at the end of time. The dead would rise and be judged. A powerful hope intensified in the century prior to Jesus that the end time would occur soon. At the end of history the will of God would be fully, finally, and clearly revealed. End-time communities such as those on the Dead Sea were intently readying themselves for the end of history, which for all Jews meant the resurrection of the just and the unjust.

The underlying assumption in these communities was that the meaning of history would be fully known only at its end. If God makes himself known in history, then it is evident that we do not know the whole story until the last day. So we do not learn the will of God merely by looking at a phase or segment of the historical process anymore than we understand a novel only by reading up to the middle chapter. We grasp the full meaning only by reading the whole, as concluded by its last page.

Similarly, the meaning of our own personal history is not fully revealed as long as we are still living. Something decisive might happen at some future date that would change substantially the meaning of our present existence, such as a heroic act or religious conversion or complete cynicism. So it seemed to Jewish prophetic consciousness that the meaning of history could finally be revealed only at its end. And what was to happen at the end? Resurrection. The dead would rise for final judgment.

We may debate details of what the text says occurred after Jesus' crucifixion. But one thing is absolutely clear: All who beheld it called it "resurrection." Of that there can be no doubt. Among early Christians a consensus emerged that all who encountered Christ after the crucifixion were experiencing something real, the correct term for which was "resurrection." This meant that they had experienced and tasted the firstfruits of the expected event at the end time of judgment and redemption.

Now suppose a general resurrection was expected at the end time, and call it Event Z. Suppose there was a widely held consensus prior to Jesus about what Event Z would look like and what would happen. Then Jesus came, lived, and died. After his death, a series of occurrences took place that observers unanimously called resurrection and identified as the end-time Event Z, and this event transformed all their previous ideas of resurrection.

The significance of this is stunning: The events surrounding Jesus' death were experienced as the fulfillment of history, the decisive event of the last days, and the decisive anticipation of the final event of history that reveals God's will once for all. So even though history continued to occur after Jesus died and rose again, there was a sense in which the early Christians understood that through their meeting with this risen Lord they were already in touch with the end time, and therefore with the very meaning of universal history!

This empowered the early Christian community with incredible courage in the face of seemingly impossible obstacles and terrifying threats. Why? Because their trust was not in this broken world but in the risen Christ present to them as they sat together "at the Lord's Table" or faced the wild animals of the Roman Coliseum.

Christians understood their lives as fundamentally altered in relation to the resurrection. They concluded that in Jesus' resurrection the end is already present! They understood this in a personal sense. Thus the will of God is finally revealed. So to be "in Christ" is already to share in the events of the last days. This conclusion made sense in the light of Jewish prophetic expectations. So the Statement declares, "His death for sins and his resurrection from the dead were promised beforehand by the prophets and attested by eyewitnesses."

This is why we today must learn to think historically in the Hebraic sense if we are to grasp the full meaning of this central proclamation of Christianity. Seen in this frame of reference, Christ's resurrection is so decisive that all other events pale in comparison. It discloses nothing less than the final revelation of the will of God in history.

If we are searching for the center point of Christian experience and testimony, we find it here. Only if the Lord lives now is it possible to have a personal meeting with him. The resurrection, therefore, should not be seen only as an idea or past event but as that which permits an experience of present personal encounter with the living Lord. This is why a personal meeting with the risen Christ has been a very significant feature of Christian teaching from its inception. Something so decisive happened for human history in the resurrection of Jesus that it does not and cannot fit into our ordinary categories of understanding.

We cannot rule out the resurrection of Jesus (as Ernst Troeltsch's law of analogy did) simply on the grounds that nothing like this ever happened to us before. How could it! Nineteenth-century German liberals argued that since there is nothing to compare it with, it cannot be credited as a fact in time. This was half right—there is nothing to compare it with — but it was and remains a fact in time. The central event of which Christianity speaks is, like all truly significant personal meetings, an event without analogy.

Classical Christianity is saturated with this language about resurrection—both Christ's and ours. When the apostles began to try to express what had happened to them, they did not begin with a system of metaphysics or ethical injunctions or scientific data. Rather, they began with experiential testimony of an interpersonal meeting with the risen Christ that "made all things new." All other forms of knowing were seen in relation to their being known in this way by God.

Once that point is grasped, everything else in Christianity falls into place. Human encounter is seen in relation to the divine human encounter. Our walk through daily life is understood as "participating in Christ." Pastoral care becomes an active sharing in the life of the risen Christ. Preaching is the announcement of the coming of the risen Christ into ordinary human life. The Lord's Supper is the presence of Christ experienced through the elements of bread and wine as an end-time banquet. The moral life is grasped essentially as the sharing of the love of God in and for the world.

The resurrection of Jesus Christ, then, came to pervade the thinking of the early Christians. It meant many things for them, a number of which we will consider here:

1. The resurrection meant liberation from the power of sin and death. The early Christians understood themselves to be liberated persons: freed by the risen Christ from the power of sin and death. They were liberated to serve the next one who appears to them at hand—the "neighbor." They were called by God to the life of responsible freedom in the world.

> So if the Son sets you free, you will be free indeed (John 8:36).
> Therefore, brothers, we are not children of the slave woman, but of the free woman. It is for freedom that Christ has set us free. Stand firm, then, and do not let yourselves be burdened again by a yoke of slavery (Gal. 4:31–5:1).
> The law of the Spirit of life set me free from the law of sin and death (Rom. 8:2).
> Live as free men, but do not use your freedom as a cover-up for evil; live as servants of God (1 Peter 2:16).

The Statement declares, "In the life of faith as the Gospel presents it, believers are united with their risen Lord, communing with him, and looking to him in repentance and hope for empowering through the Holy Spirit, so that henceforth they may not sin but serve him truly."

2. For the early Christians, the resurrection signified a seal and confirmation of Christ's saving activity on the cross. The redemptive value of his death for others was attested to and ratified by his actual bodily resurrection. Luke wrote, "After his suffering, he showed himself to these men and gave many convincing proofs that he was alive. He appeared to them over a period of forty days and spoke about the kingdom of God" (Acts 1:3). Thereafter Christians have sought to "know Christ and the power of his resurrection and the fellowship of sharing in his sufferings, becoming like him in his death, and so, somehow, to attain to the resurrection from the dead" (Phil. 3:10).

3. The resurrection transformed the early Christians' view of the Sabbath. Sabbath observance for Christians took place on Sunday, resurrection day, the eighth day, as a continuing, weekly testimony of the church to the centrality of the resurrection. On that new day that changes the meaning of all other days, Christians celebrate the Lord's Supper as meeting with the risen Lord. The resurrection is not celebrated on Easter alone, but on every Lord's Day. The phrase "the first day of the week" was not found in Jewish tradition, but the Gospel writers frequently employed it (Matt. 28:1; Mark 16:2, 9; Luke 24:1; John 20:1, 19; see Acts 20:7; 1 Cor. 16:2).

4. In the minds of early Christians, the resurrection became linked to Christ's death. Indeed, they viewed Christ's death and resurrection as a single event or complex of events rather than two separable events. For "he was delivered over to death for our sins and was raised to life for our justification" (Rom. 4:25). The cross "contains in itself the mystery of Easter," wrote Leo the Great.[11] Cyril of Jerusalem understood that one sees Jesus' death most clearly through the lens of the resurrection: "I confess the Cross, because I know of the Resurrection."[12] Hence the preamble to the Statement declares, "This Gospel declares the only way to know God in peace, love, and joy is through the reconciling death of Jesus Christ the risen Lord."

5. The resurrection helped the early Christians understand the meaning of the whole of history. In Jesus' resurrection the disciples understood themselves to be hearing the final word that history was already beginning to speak. To anyone who earnestly shared the apocalyptic hope in the general resurrection, the resurrection of Jesus would have revealed the meaning of universal history. It glimpsed the end of history. The meaning of the whole was made known through the lens of this one end-time event.[13]

The moment the disciples were met by the risen Jesus, they understood that they were already standing at the beginning of the end time, the last days, the general resurrection. The event communicated to them its own message. It stood as confirmation of the meaning of Jesus' earthly ministry and atoning death.

In an instant it became clear to them that the end had indeed appeared and begun and that Jesus was the "firstfruits of those who have fallen asleep" (1 Cor. 15:20). This recognition was not a matter of gradual or lengthy development. The central teaching of Christology was fully formed in a single instant when the disciples and others met the risen Christ. His divinity was implied by his resurrection. If risen, then Son of Man, Son of God.

6. The resurrection ratified Jesus' messianic teaching for the early Christians. Jesus had explained "plainly" to his disciples in advance that "the Son of Man must suffer many things and be rejected by the elders, chief priests and teachers of the law, and that he must be killed and after three days rise again" (Mark 8:31).

The resurrection made it clear that Jesus' sacrificial offering of himself for others had been accepted. His atonement for humanity was received by God, and humanity brought near to God. The resurrection confirmed the atoning value of his death.

Jesus' resurrection therefore vindicated the Father's sending of the Son and the Son's suffering death. The resurrection stands as the key to the Christian understanding of suffering, for it is God the Son who comes to share our human suffering and the triune God who vindicates that mission.

Moreover, through the resurrection Christ became exalted as messianic king. From the tomb he arose to give his disciples the Great Commission, wherein the legitimate authority of the resurrected Lord became clear: "All authority in heaven and on earth has been given to me. Therefore go . . ." (Matt. 28:18).

As his death culminated Jesus' humble *descent* (from preexistent glory through incarnation to birth, ministry, death and burial, and descent), so his resurrection began his glorious *ascent* (from the empty tomb, resurrected, ascended to heaven, to intercede and sit at the right hand of God). His life and death embodied the full measure of obedience to the Father (actively through his life, passively through his death).

Jesus rose "on the third day."[14] This phrase of the creed reminds us that redemption of the world was a datable event, an occurrence in history, not merely an abstract idea.

7. *To return to our starting point, the early Christians believed that Christ's triumphant resurrection made their own possible.* They could face death with hope. This gave them great comfort and great courage as they underwent persecution. They attempted to live a life hidden in Christ—born from above by the power of the Spirit, embodying and declaring the Good News, going about doing good, willing to die for the truth, living in newness of life and in hope of the resurrection to eternal life.

The apostle Paul tersely summarized the Christians' relationship with their Lord and Savior:

> We were therefore buried with him through baptism into death in order that, just as Christ was raised from the dead through the glory of the Father, we too may live a new life. If we have been united with him like this in his death, we will certainly also be united with him in his resurrection. For we know that our old self was crucified with him so that the body of sin might be done away with, that we should no longer be slaves to sin—because anyone who has died has been freed from sin. Now if we died with Christ, we believe that we will also live with him (Rom. 6:4–8).

The Statement confesses, "This Gospel further proclaims the bodily resurrection, ascension, and enthronement of Jesus as evidence of the efficacy of his once-for-all sacrifice for us, of the reality of his present personal ministry to us, and of the certainty of his future return to glorify us (1 Cor. 15; Heb. 1:1–4, 2:1–18, 4:14–16, 7:1–10:25)."

The resurrection of Jesus Christ liberated many early Christians to serve their Master with great freedom, power, and joy. The same has been true for countless millions of Christians from the first century to our own day. Together we proclaim: "Christ is risen. He is risen indeed!"

Notes

Portions of this chapter (on pages 103–10 and 114–117) are adapted from Thomas Oden, *The Word of Life: Systematic Theology, Volume 2* (San Francisco: Harper & Row, 1992), pp. 451–64, 483–500. Used by permission.

Portions of this chapter (on pages 111–14) are adapted from Thomas Oden, *After Modernity—What?* (Grand Rapids: Zondervan, 1990), pp.133–36.

1. Martin Luther, *What Luther Says* (St. Louis: Concordia, 1959), I:181.
2. Cyril of Jerusalem, *Catech. Lect.* XIV, Fathers of the Church, vol. 64, p. 46.
3. Friedrich Hegel, *The Spirit of Christianity, On Christianity: Early Theological Writings*, p. 292.
4. Thomas Aquinas, *Summa Theologica*, 1LI, C255.6, II, p. 2322 of the Benzinger edition.
5. Ibid., Q55.6, II, p. 2323.
6. Adapted from Daniel Whitby, *Logos tes pisteos*, p. 400, Anglicanism, p. 272.
7. Athanasius, *Incarnation of the Word* 30, Nicene and Post-Nicene Fathers 2 IV, p. 52.
8. Tertullian, *Against Marcion* V.9–10, Ante-Nicene Fathers III, pp. 447–52.
9. Tertullian, *On the Resurrection of the Flesh*, ANF III, pp. 545–94.
10. Augustine, *City of God* XXII.12–22, Nicene and Post-Nicene Fathers 1 II, pp. 493–501.
11. *Sermon* LXXI.1, NPNF 2 XII, p. 182.
12. *Catech. Lect.* XIII, Fathers of the Church 61, p. 6.
13. Wolfhart Pannenberg, *Jesus God and Man* (Philadelphia: Westminster, 1968), pp. 53–88.
14. *Tertia dei*; Creed of 150 Fathers, Creeds of the Churches, II, p. 58.

Study Questions

1. Which, if any, of the objections to the resurrection of Jesus have you encountered from other people, and how did you respond?

2. What did Justin Martyr mean by saying that persecution could kill Christians but not harm them?
3. Why is the resurrection of Jesus Christ not just the key event of history but also the "anticipated end of history"?
4. The resurrection is explained as being important to the early Christians in seven ways. Which of these means the most to you?
5. What does it mean to you that an encounter with the risen Christ makes "all things new"?

All who are justified experience reconciliation with the Father, full remission of sins, transition from the kingdom of darkness to the kingdom of light, the reality of being a new creature in Christ, and the fellowship of the Holy Spirit. They enjoy access to the Father with all the peace and joy that this brings.

The Gospel requires of all believers worship, which means constant praise and giving of thanks to God, submission to all that he has revealed in his written word, prayerful dependence on him, and vigilance lest his truth be even inadvertently compromised or obscured.

■

We affirm that saving faith includes mental assent to the content of the Gospel, acknowledgment of our own sin and need, and personal trust and reliance upon Christ and his work.

We deny that saving faith includes only mental acceptance of the Gospel, and that justification is secured by a mere outward profession of faith. We further deny that any element of saving faith is a meritorious work or earns salvation for us.

—*The Gospel of Jesus Christ: An Evangelical Celebration*

6

BEING A CHRISTIAN

WHAT DIFFERENCE DOES IT MAKE?

Ajith Fernando

Mahatma Gandhi rejected the Christian idea of salvation by grace through the work of Christ, claiming that it was an irresponsible doctrine that opened the door to moral laxity. He would cite examples of people who were morally lax in their behavior while claiming to receive God's forgiveness and thereby enjoy his salvation. Buddhist missionary societies in my country, Sri Lanka, are sending missionaries to the West in the conviction that the "Christian" West needs the discipline of Buddhism to stem its destructive trend of moral degradation.

These criticisms present a major challenge to our claim that Christianity is unique. People ask, "If Christianity is unable to really effect a change in the lives of its adherents, then how could it be all that great?" When we say that Christianity is the truth, postmodern people (who are not much interested in objective truth) simply respond that this does not interest them. What they want to know is whether Christianity really gives what they consider an "authentic experience."

Yet, all through its history Christians have claimed that Christianity is the answer to the problem of human sin and unrighteousness because it provides a way to overcome sin and live righteous lives. During a conference in Peru, the other two visiting preachers and I were each given a bodyguard because a terrorist group was targeting foreigners. Toward the end of the conference I was trying to persuade my bodyguard, Salomon, to receive God's salvation. He told me that would be impossible for him because he was too great a sinner. I pointed him to 1 Timothy 1:15: "Here is a trustworthy saying that deserves full acceptance: Christ Jesus came into the world to save sinners—of whom I am the worst." He was very impressed with that verse, for he said that he was the worst of sinners. I told him that, if it were so, then this verse refers to him. But subsequently he lost hope, saying that he was too accustomed to a life of sin to be able to live a Christian life. I pointed him to Philippians 4:13: "I can do everything through him who gives me strength." Again he took heart. By the end of the day, one of the other preachers in our team had led Salomon and another bodyguard to Christ.

Can we give irreligious people like Salomon the assurance that God can do the seemingly impossible work of completely transforming their lives? Salomon's life after his conversion showed that God could do this. And the Bible clearly claims that God can do it. It is my task here to demonstrate in what way the Gospel changes a person so that we could assert that Christ is indeed unique, not only because he is the Truth, but also because he can do a work in our lives that no other "savior" can.

A RELATIONSHIP WITH GOD

In our natural state we are sinners who fall short of the glory of God (Rom. 3:23). But through Christ's work we receive forgiveness (Acts 2:38; 13:38), which frees us from the burden of guilt (Heb. 9:14) that ruins any hope of our being truly satisfied.

Whereas we were sinners condemned to die (Rom. 6:23), now we receive the gift of eternal life (e.g., John 3:15–16, 36; 4:14). So marked is the change that takes place at conversion that Jesus described it as crossing over from death to life (John 5:24).

With our guilt taken away, we can be reconciled to God and thus relate to him personally (Rom. 5:10; 2 Cor. 5:19). The apostle Paul describes this reconciliation in these words: "Remember that at that time you were separate from Christ, excluded from citizenship in Israel and foreigners to the covenants of the promise, without hope and without God in the world. But now in Christ Jesus you who once were far away have been brought near through the blood of Christ" (Eph. 2:12–13). Jesus said that the resulting relationship with God ("knowing God") is the most important aspect of eternal life (John 17:3). God provides the deepest fulfillment that anyone could have as our loneliness is banished and a friendship is established with God.

Human beings are made to find their deepest fulfillment through relationships of love. This is why so many of the popular songs of any given era are love songs. Because music is the language of joy and because love is the most joyous experience on earth, people often express love through songs. But human love always falls short of complete fulfillment, because humans are fallible. So we must never expect from people what only God can give—complete fulfillment.

Why is it, then, that many Christians are not experiencing deep fulfillment in Christ? The fulfillment that comes from our relationship with God entails some of the same principles necessary for complete enjoyment of any interpersonal relationship. For example, if we do not trust God to be with us and look after us as he has promised (Deut. 31:6, 8; Josh. 1:5; Heb. 13:5), we will struggle with loneliness, doubt, and anxiety when problems come our way. And this will take away our joy. True enjoyment from relationships comes when they are cultivated. Our relationship with God is often compared with the relationship between husband and wife. Isaiah 54:5 says, "For your Maker is your husband—the LORD Almighty is his name." If a married couple do not spend time conversing with each other, they will not really enjoy their relationship. In the same way, if we do not spend time with God in what we call the spiritual disciplines (reading the Bible, meditation, prayer, and worship) we will not experience the fullness of which the Bible speaks.

Today followers of New Age movements and Eastern religions are testifying to sublime spiritual experiences through spiritual exercises, which, they claim, are more fulfilling than what Christians experience. When people exercise the spiritual part of their personalities, they free themselves from the bondage of life in a rushed and competitive society. Therefore they will experience refreshment and serenity. Nor should we be surprised by these testimonies. Even these experiences, however, will fall short of the fulfillment that comes through deepening our relationship with God. David said, "You have made known to me the path of life; you will fill me with joy in your presence, with eternal pleasures at your right hand" (Ps. 16:11). These pleasures are open only to those who spend time at the "right hand" of God.

When the Indian evangelist Sadhu Sundar Singh was a youth, he experienced great heights of spiritual ecstasy through practicing Hindu and Sikh spiritual disciplines. But these experiences would end in frustration when he returned from the "mountaintop" to day-to-day life on earth. He finally surrendered to Jesus Christ, whom he had been opposing through various anti-Christian activities. He became one of the great Indian evangelists of the twentieth century—and also enjoyed wonderfully ecstatic experiences with God through the Christian spiritual disciplines. He once said, "Without Christ I am like a fish out of water. With Christ I am in an ocean of love." He discovered that Christ fulfilled the aspirations he had tried to fulfill through Hindu and Sikh disciplines.

Christian spiritual disciplines, however, do not aim to establish a relationship with God as some non-Christian disciplines do. We cannot find God by our own efforts at reaching out to him through spiritual exercises. We are too sinful to be able to do that (Rom. 3:23). But God has reached out and initiated a relationship with us by offering his unmerited favor (grace) through what Christ has done (Rom. 5:8). Here, then, is one of the most basic differences that being a Christian makes: It opens the door to a relationship with God that in turn opens the door to life's most fulfilling experiences.

This relationship that God establishes with us does not end with this life. It is everlasting in duration, and that is why it is called eternal life. The Buddhists are not impressed with this idea because, according to their understanding, all of life entails suffering and frustration. So eternal life would mean eternal suffering and frustration! But for the Christian, the next life is a consummation of all that is good in this life, without the pain and suffering that we experience today. Paul refers to this as "glory," and says, "I consider that our present sufferings are not worth comparing with the glory that will be revealed in us" (Rom. 8:18). He says that we are "groaning" at present, eagerly waiting for the day when we fully experience the results of becoming children of God (Rom. 8:23). So death has lost its terror for us (1 Cor. 15:54–55). As Dietrich Bonhoeffer said, "Death is the supreme festival on the road to freedom."

LOVE AND JOY

While many characteristic experiences ensue from entering into a relationship with God, two of the most commonly mentioned in the Bible are love and joy. If we enter into a love relationship with God, love will become a very important feature of Christian experience. Love is such an important aspect of God's nature that John says, "God is love" (1 John 4:8, 16). Therefore, if our relationship with God is the most important thing about our lives, it is not surprising to find Paul saying that our lives are controlled by God's love. He says, "Christ's love compels us" (2 Cor. 5:14). Love now becomes our aim in life (1 Cor. 14:1) and the best mark by which to identify a Christian (1 Cor. 13:1–7).

Yet this love is not something that we ourselves produce through our efforts. It is something that God has freely given us. Paul says, "God has poured out his love into our hearts by the Holy Spirit, whom he has given us" (Rom. 5:5). Here, then, is another major difference that Christ makes in those who receive his salvation: They become people whose lives are filled and characterized by love.

We have already said how love is closely related to joy. One of the key results of a love relationship is joy. So when Paul wants to describe the fruit of the work of God's Spirit in our lives, the first two qualities he mentions are love and joy (Gal. 5:22). When we realize that God loves us so much as to send Jesus to die for us, and that he forgives all our sin, freeing us from the burden of

A WORK OF MERCY

Pandita Ramabai was born into a Hindu family of the highest caste of Brahmins in southern India. She became a leading Hindu teacher of the Sanskrit language. (Pandita is the feminine form of pandit, meaning teacher.) In 1883, after seeing some "works of mercy" by Christian women trying to care for prostitutes, she wrote, "I began to think that there was a real difference between Hinduism and Christianity. I asked the Sister who instructed me what was it that made the Christians care for, and reclaim, the 'fallen women.' She read the story of Christ meeting the Samaritan woman, and His wonderful discourse on the nature of true worship, and explained it to me. She spoke of the Infinite Love of Christ for sinners.... I realized, after reading the 4th Chapter of St. John's Gospel, that Christ was truly the Divine Savior He claimed to be, and no one but He could transform and uplift the downtrodden womanhood of India and of every land."

That very same year, Ramabai confessed Christ as her Lord and Savior and was baptized. She worked and fought for the care of widows, established homes and schools for boys and girls, and arranged for the translation of the Bible. She sometimes faced opposition from high-caste Hindus because of her evangelistic efforts. She often put her life at risk in caring for the ill and the starving during times of severe famine. And she was rejected by the Brahmins when she married a man of a lower caste. Yet, through her sacrificial ministry, which spanned more than forty years, thousands of people came to know Christ as Lord and Savior.

Adapted from "Pandita Ramabai: Mission to Hindu Women," in *Ambassadors for Christ,* ed. John D. Woodbridge (Chicago: Moody Press, 1994), pp. 167–73.

guilt and accepting us as his children, we are amazed (1 John 3:1). When we experience the thrill of having this love "poured out into our hearts," our joy peaks.

A fairly new Christian was giving his testimony at a meeting, and it went smoothly until he came to describing God's love. He wanted to find a word that adequately described this amazing thing he had experienced. Finally he blurted out, "The staggerating love of God." There is no word called "staggerating" in the English language, but his joy over God's love was so intense that he needed to coin a word to express his feelings. St. Francis of Assisi said, "Let us leave sadness to the devil and his angels. As for us, what can we be but rejoicing and glad."

Problems may come and cause us temporary fear and anxiety, but we reckon that God is with us (Ps. 23:4) and is greater than the problems (Ps. 46), and therefore he will turn them into something good (Rom. 8:28). Then the joy returns with great depth, for we realize that even problems cannot remove this joy. This is why the Bible often talks about rejoicing amid suffering (Rom. 5:3–5; Col. 1:24; James 1:2–4). The Bible describes such joy that is not diminished by circumstances "the joy of the Lord" or "the joy of God" (Rom. 5:11; Phil. 3:1; 4:4, 10).

Of course, if we block the love of God through disobedience or through refusing to believe that God is looking after us, this joy will leave us. Some, perhaps because they have faced serious rejection in life, may find it difficult to believe that God would love them and wholeheartedly accept them as his children. We have the responsibility to lead such people to the healing of their wounds that will free them to accept God's love. Often such healing grace is mediated through an accepting community or a capable counselor. So several factors can cause the anomalous, though all too common, incidences of Christians who are unhappy and discontented, even as they claim to believe in God and obey him.

There is a general recognition among people everywhere of the fact that love is "the greatest thing in the world." There is also a deep desire in people to be truly happy, which really lies at the root of the human quest for love. Blinded as they are by sin, people are looking for love and happiness in the wrong places. They may find love and happiness that temporarily still the yearnings of their hearts. But for true fulfillment they must come to the One who made them. And in Christ, our Creator has provided an answer to human need. Surely only that can adequately fulfill the deepest aspirations within the human heart.

HOLINESS

We have said that because God is love and has a relationship with us, love and joy characterize the Christian life. But God is also holy and pure. Therefore those who have a relationship with God should also be holy and pure. We cannot keep on doing the sinful things that we did before we became Christians. This idea is expressed so many times in the Epistles that it should be considered a basic aspect of Christianity. Peter says, "As obedient children, do not conform to the evil desires you had when you lived in ignorance" (1 Peter 1:14). Then he gives the reason that holiness must characterize Christians: "But just as he who called you is holy, so be holy in all you do; for it is written: 'Be holy, because I am holy'" (vv. 15–16). In a recent study I found that about 1,400 of the total of 2,005 verses in Paul's epistles have something to say about holiness, godliness, or Christian character. Obviously, this is a key aspect of Christian teaching and should figure heavily in Christian instruction and preaching.

In the Bible, sin is never an acceptable practice for Christians. John puts it bluntly: "No one who is born of God practices sin, because His seed abides in him; and he cannot sin, because he is born of God" (1 John 3:9 NASB; see also 2:1; 3:6). That John does not mean absolute sinless perfection here is indicated by the fact that he had earlier suggested that it is wrong for Christians to claim to be without sin and that he prescribed a way of recovery for Christians who do commit sin (1 John 1:7–9; 2:1–2). Perhaps most interpreters are right in their suggestion that in the earlier passages Paul is talking about habitual sin (see NIV). However, we must remember that there is no excuse at all for Christians to sin.

John said, "I write this to you so that you will not sin" (1 John 2:1). That is the expected standard for Christians.

The Bible often warns people who claim to be Christians that they will not be saved in the end if their lives are characterized by sin (1 Cor. 6:9–10; Gal. 5:21; Eph. 5:5; Heb. 6:4–6). Does this mean that those who are saved can lose their salvation because they rejected the way of Christ at some time after their conversion? The church has long battled that issue, and it is an important battle for, without clarity in the matter, there could be abuses on both sides.

On the one hand, some Christians could lull people, who had once professed faith in Christ but are now living in sin, to a false sense of security by assuring them that because of that initial "decision" to receive Christ's salvation they are eternally saved despite their wickedness. This is wrong because the Bible clearly states that those who continue in sin in this way cannot enter the kingdom. A biblical way out of this dilemma is for those holding this perspective to suggest that perhaps those who behave in this way, despite their profession of faith, were never really saved; they had not exercised saving faith. Jesus said that we would recognize the genuine people of faith by their fruit (Matt. 7:16–20; John 15:8).

On the other hand, other Christians could adopt an unbiblical approach by asserting so much the possibility of falling away that they miss the tenor of Scripture, which, despite the warnings, is one of confidence in God's power to keep those whom he saved until the Last Day (John 6:38–40; 10:27–29; Rom. 8:30; Eph. 1:13–14; Phil. 1:6; 1 Peter 1:5).

Our discussion shows that for people to carry the name Christian while blatantly breaking God's laws is not biblically acceptable. Of course, we are not transformed to perfect people overnight. It is said that Martin Luther equated conversion to the time when a doctor diagnoses the cause of an illness and starts the patient on the correct course of medicine. Until then, the patient's health had been rapidly deteriorating. Complete healing does not come at the moment the correct diagnosis is made and the appropriate medicine is prescribed. It takes time for the medicine to have its full affect. But at the time the correct course of treatment starts, the patient takes a decisive turn for the better. Whereas once he was going downward toward his death, after the correct medicine begins to be administered, he begins to move in the direction of complete healing. Similarly, after our conversion, the course of our lives is changed, and from being hell-bent sinners we become pilgrims along the road to heaven. This change of our nature to conform to the likeness of Christ (Rom. 8:29) is called sanctification (Rom. 15:16; 1 Thess. 4:3; 5:23; 1 Peter 1:2).

In the next chapter of this book Maxie Dunnam shares how the Holy Spirit enables us to live holy lives. Here we would say that the Holy Spirit does not bulldoze his way through us against our wishes. We must let him change us from within (Rom. 12:1–2). First of all, we believe in his ability to change us (Rom. 6:11), and thus we approach life with this change as a goal. We make use of the means that God has provided to help us grow spiritually. We study the Word (1 Peter 2:2) and seek to obey what we know to be God's will (James 1:22–23). We pray (Matt. 26:41), we participate in worship, and we let our fellow Christians help us to be obedient to God (Heb. 10:24–25). A girl went to her pastor and confessed that although she thought she was filled with the Spirit, she saw none of the fruit of the Spirit in her life. The pastor asked her what kind of devotional life she had. "Hit and miss," she replied. "Do you have your meals that way?" asked the pastor. She replied, "I had my meals like that once and I nearly lost my health." She got the message! If she does not spend time with God, she is not going to become like Jesus (2 Cor. 3:18).

I believe that one reason why Christians do not take the call to be holy seriously enough is that our preaching and teaching have been defective. I believe that some Christians have not realized that racism and prejudice are completely incompatible with Christianity. This is why the evangelical movement has such a bad record in this regard. Perhaps our believers have not been clearly told that Christians simply must not do things like exploiting customers or employees, like lying and bribing, like disturbing neighbors, like being rude to spouses.

Today many people are coming to Christ because they realize that he can meet some need of theirs. This is a legitimate way to be attracted to Christ, as the book of Acts shows. In Acts we see that miracles got the attention of people so that they would be open to hearing the Gospel. But the Gospel that was preached in Acts included many things in addition to the fact that God meets the felt needs of people. The early Christian evangelists preached about the nature of God, about God's sovereignty over history, about the life, death, and resurrection of Jesus, about judgment and repentance. This enabled those considering Christ to see something of the whole "package" that they were accepting. They came to God with a vision of him that was not confined simply to the belief that he supplies their needs. They were made to realize that this God is holy and that he has acted to deal with the terrible thing called sin, which he intends for us to leave behind when we come to him.

Hinduism and its offspring, the New Age movements that are growing in popularity in the West, have a pantheistic understanding of the divine. That is, they believe that everything that exists is part of the divine. In such an understanding there is no idea of a Supreme God who is holy and to whom we are accountable. Therefore there isn't the corresponding incentive to holiness. If this is the environment in which we live, then it is very important for the church today to proclaim the biblical idea of a holy God.

I fear that much of the evangelistic preaching today focuses so much on the fact that Jesus meets felt needs that other important aspects of the Gospel are neglected. Therefore, often when people think about Christianity and about God, their primary focus is on how he meets needs, even though, if asked, they could recite the basics of the Gospel. Today many people have a magical approach to religion. They go to various gods, to psychic readers, to gurus (Hindu holy men/teachers), to medicine men and witches to get some favor done. They are prescribed some rules to follow, like abstaining from eating meat or giving alms to the poor or gifts to the religious group or attending a given number of worship services. This assures them that their request will be granted. The religious power or group does not ask them for total allegiance. They must simply follow the prescribed rituals and the gods will give them what they want. Many people have come to Christ with just such an understanding of God.

About 70 percent of the members of the church where I worship are converts from Buddhism. They first came to our church because a Christian friend brought them at a time of need, with the promise that the need would be prayed for in church. After this initial contact they kept coming to church and began to understand the Gospel and came to accept Christ as their Savior and join the church through baptism. Each Sunday we have a time when members can testify to God's blessings to them. One Sunday I was thinking about the fact that, like most other Sundays, the testimonies are about temporal things like healing from sickness and the provision of jobs or finances. Then a leader of the church, who is paralyzed from his waist down, testified to the wonderful grace that saved him from sin and brought him into the kingdom. I wondered whether the negative answer to hundreds of prayers for his physical healing had led him to see the much greater blessing of eternal salvation.

One who understands that the heart of salvation is deliverance from sin, which merited eternal punishment, should realize how serious sin is. It caused God to send his Son to the cross. And if not for the merits of Jesus' death, we would be headed for hell! If we realized the holiness of God and the horror of sin, we would be very careful about trifling with it (Heb. 10:26–31); with great urgency we would flee from sin and pursue the way that pleases God (2 Tim. 2:22). My point is that if people thought about God and Christianity the way the Bible describes it, they would be much more serious in their pursuit of holiness.

PEACE BECAUSE NEEDS ARE MET

While the fact that God meets our personal needs should not be allowed to eclipse the fact that he is holy and wills for us to be holy, it is indeed true that God does meet our every need. Paul said, "And my God will meet all your needs according to his glorious riches in Christ Jesus" (Phil. 4:19). This, of course, does not mean that we will not have problems. It does mean that even the problems are going to be turned into something good by God (Rom. 8:28). Therefore we can face life with confidence, knowing that God does look after us. In the Sermon on the Mount, Jesus, using some beautiful images, shows that we have no reason to be anxious or worried, because God knows what our needs are and will provide for us (Matt. 6:28–34). In this passage is Christ's famous statement: "But seek first his kingdom and his righteousness, and all these things will be given to you as well" (v. 33).

As God is committed to meeting our needs, we have been told to present these needs to him. Paul says, "Do not be anxious about anything, but in everything, by prayer and petition, with thanksgiving, present your requests to God" (Phil. 4:6). Paul presents the consequence of such trust in God in the next verse: "And the peace of God, which transcends all understanding, will guard your hearts and your minds in Christ Jesus" (v. 7). This peace surpasses in quality anything that the world can offer. Jesus said, "Peace I leave with you; my peace I give you. I do not give to you as the world gives" (John 14:27).

Earlier we said that we experience God's love through our relationship with him and that this produces joy. Now we see that we also experience a peace that dispels anxiety because we know that he cares about us (1 Peter 5:7). This represents the triad of qualities that constitute the first three features of the fruit of the Spirit: love, joy, and peace (Gal. 5:22). This threefold blessing is perhaps the greatest heritage that a Christian enjoys on earth.

PURPOSE AND SIGNIFICANCE

When we enter into a relationship with God, we also become his agents on earth. Paul goes so far as to say that we are Christ's ambassadors (2 Cor. 5:20). God entrusts each Christian with tasks to fulfill on earth. At the same time that Jesus called his first disciples to follow him, he also told them of the task he had for them: "'Come, follow me,' Jesus said, 'and I will make you fishers of men'" (Mark 1:17). The Epistles explain that this usefulness is made operative through the presentation of gifts to each believer (1 Cor. 12:4–30; Rom. 12:3–8; Eph. 4:7–13; 1 Peter 4:10–11). By the exercise of these gifts we participate in the most significant cause in the world: the cause of the kingdom of God. And this kingdom will finally conquer the world and go on for eternity (Rev. 11:15).

All success on earth is tinged with the frustration of impermanence, as the book of Ecclesiastes so vividly tell us. When I was a child, a visiting missionary wrote in my autograph book some words that had a marked influence upon my young heart: "Only one life, it will soon be past. Only what's done for Jesus will last."

Psychologists say that people who believe that what they are doing in life is significant are generally happy and contented. If so, Christians should be the happiest people in the world, for they are involved in the most significant thing anyone could be involved in. Often, for psychological and other reasons, Christians find it difficult to accept the full implications of the fact that they are children and ambassadors of the King of kings and the Lord of lords. They know in their minds that they are children of God, but that truth has not traveled down to the heart and caused the joy that it should.

Often it is through gifts God gives us that we realize our significance as children of God. I was fourteen years old when I experienced God's salvation, yet for many years I struggled with a feeling of uselessness and inferiority. Then I realized that God had called and equipped me to be a minister. Realizing the fact that God had given me something important to do helped me to experience the beauty of the fact that I am a child of God. I had always believed that in my mind, but I did not think and feel as one who believed it. Realizing my significance helped change that unscriptural attitude I had toward myself.

CONCLUSION

What an amazing combination of blessings we have considered! Every aspect of the human makeup has been touched as a result of us receiving eternal life.

- We are made for relationships of love, and God gives us a relationship with him that is deeper, more solid, and more loving than any other relationship the world can offer.

- The love we experience helps produce a joy that fulfills the yearning for pleasure that is basic to the human psyche.
- Although they may be reluctant to accept the fact, human beings can never be satisfied if they are unholy and carry a burden of guilt. Through the work of Christ we experience forgiveness, which removes guilt, and strength, which enables us to live holy lives.
- The punishment for sin is eternal death, but Christ bore that punishment on our behalf, and therefore we can experience eternal life, which consists of a new quality of life in this world and eternal glory in the next.
- While we live on earth, we are not immune to problems, but God will supply our every need so that even the problems are turned into something good.
- Because our needs are met, we have a peace that surpasses anything the world can give.
- Once we enter the family of God, we are given a role to play in fulfilling his kingdom agenda. Because this is the most important agenda in history, this role gives us a sense of significance that none can match.

No wonder Jesus described the life he gives as "life to the full" (John 10:10). No wonder Paul said, "If anyone is in Christ, he is a new creation; the old has gone, the new has come!" (2 Cor. 5:17). Every area of life has been touched by the newness of salvation!

Yet we could miss out on experiencing these great blessings through our immaturity, our unbelief, our disobedience, or our refusal to avail ourselves of the blessings freely accessible to us. If we do accept and experience these blessings, the world will have to take note, and the criticisms against Christianity, like those of Gandhi mentioned at the start of this chapter, will pale into insignificance. Jesus said, "Let your light shine before men, that they may see your good deeds and praise your Father in heaven" (Matt. 5:16).

Study Questions

1. What is the role of "religious disciplines" in the life of a Christian?
2. How would you describe your "spiritual experience" to a Buddhist or a Hindu?
3. Expand on Luther's analogy comparing spiritual health and medical treatment. How would you describe your own spiritual health?
4. Why do we sometimes fail to express peace or joy in the Christian life?
5. In what ways does God meet our spiritual needs?
6. How might we respond to Mahatma Gandhi's charge that belief in the Christian Gospel opens the door to moral laxity?

By his sanctifying grace, Christ works within us through faith, renewing our fallen nature and leading us to real maturity, that measure of development which is meant by "the fullness of Christ" (Eph. 4:13). The Gospel calls us to live as obedient servants of Christ and as his emissaries in the world, doing justice, loving mercy, and helping all in need, thus seeking to bear witness to the kingdom of Christ.

■

We affirm that saving faith results in sanctification, the transformation of life in growing conformity to Christ through the power of the Holy Spirit. Sanctification means ongoing repentance, a life of turning from sin to serve Jesus Christ in grateful reliance on him as one's Lord and Master (Gal. 5:22–25; Rom. 8:4, 13–14).
We reject any view of justification which divorces it from our sanctifying union with Christ and our increasing conformity to his image through prayer, repentance, cross-bearing, and life in the Spirit.

—*The Gospel of Jesus Christ: An Evangelical Celebration*

7

POWER FOR CHRISTIAN LIVING

AM I ON MY OWN?

One of the joys of my life is to chair the Evangelism Committee of the World Methodist Council. This gives me opportunity to travel the world and meet extraordinary Christians. One of those is Stanley Mogoba. He was the first black person to be the Presiding Bishop of the Methodist Church in Southern Africa. His story is a thrilling one.

About the time Nelson Mandela was sent to prison in South Africa, Stanley met with a group of angry students and sought to dissuade them from violent demonstration. Just for that—trying to avert violence—he was arrested and imprisoned for six years on the notorious Robin Island. Mandela was already in prison there, and the two men became friends. One day someone pushed a religious tract under the cell door. Stanley read it and, as a result, began to read the Bible. He became a Christian. Later, Stanley wrote a book, *Convicted By Hope*, in which he told of his prison experience, Christian conversion, and call to ministry. He spent his time in prison dressed in khaki shorts, sleeping on a straw mat in a cold cell, with very little food to sustain him. He had nothing to read; even the Bible a friend had given him was taken away. He had read the story of the rich young ruler and the words Jesus said to him: "Go, sell, come and follow me." Those words changed Stanley's life. He was not rich—in fact, he had nothing—but he made a response to that call. He quoted the words of Charles Wesley to describe his experience:

> Thine eye diffused a quick'ning ray:
> I woke—the dungeon flamed with light!
> My chains fell off, my heart was free,
> I rose, went forth and followed Thee.

"Extraordinary power was given me," Stanley said. "I survived hunger and beatings, and I decided to become a minister of the gospel of Jesus Christ."

Can you imagine? Not only converted in prison by reading the Bible, but called to preach—and more, receiving power that enabled him to survive until released from prison, then to become the leader of the Methodist Church in Southern Africa.

The glorious good news of the Gospel is that not only are we pardoned by grace through faith in Jesus Christ, but we are empowered by the Holy Spirit to live as "a new creation." "The old has gone, the new has come!" (2 Cor. 5:17). We are not on our own. After expressing the truth that we are justified by faith and have peace with God through Jesus Christ (Rom. 5:1), Paul states a heartening aspect of the Gospel:

> Not only so, but we also rejoice in our sufferings, because we know that suffering produces perseverance; perseverance, character; and character, hope. And hope does not disappoint us, because God has poured out his love into our hearts by the Holy Spirit, whom he has given us (Rom. 5:3–5).

So we look in this chapter at the power for Christian living that the Holy Spirit provides.

GREATER WORKS THAN THESE

The Bible is filled with all sorts of promises—God's offer of life and meaning. The New Testament is especially filled with promises, many of which come from Jesus himself.

> "Because I live, you also will live" (John 14:19).
> "Never will I leave you; never will I forsake you" (Heb 13:5).
> "Remain in me, and I will remain in you" (John 15:4).
> "Come to me, all you who are weary and burdened, and I will give you rest" (Matt. 11:28).
> "You will receive power when the Holy Spirit comes on you" (Acts 1:8).

Fantastic promises all, but none is more fantastic than this: "I tell you the truth, anyone who has faith in me will do what I have been doing. He will do even greater things than these, because I am going to the Father" (John 14:12). If this even comes close to the truth, then mustn't we confess we have never taken Jesus seriously? The least we have to confess is that we have been satisfied with far less than he promised and far less than is possible.

The setting for this promise in John's Gospel is the occasion of Jesus promising the Holy Spirit.

> "And I will ask the Father, and he will give you another Counselor to be with you forever. . . . I will not leave you as orphans; I will come to you. . . . All this I have spoken while still with you. But the Counselor, the Holy Spirit, whom the Father will send in my name, will teach you all things and will remind you of everything I have said to you" (John 14:16, 18, 25–26).

Can you imagine a more radical possibility? "He"—that is, "you"—"will do greater things than these, because I am going to the Father."

Note the phrase "going to the Father." What did Jesus say he would do when he went to the Father? A promise we have already noted: "But you will receive power when the Holy Spirit comes on you; and you will be my witnesses in Jerusalem, and in all Judea and Samaria, and to the ends of the earth" (Acts 1:8).

Jesus is faithful and keeps his promises. In John 20 we read the amazing story of the resurrection. The living Lord came to the disciples, who were frightened, cowering behind closed doors. They supposed that sooner or later the vengeful enemies of Jesus would seek them out. Jesus came to them there. His first words, "Peace be with you!" entailed far more than the familiar greeting friends share on the street. This was the gift of peace—the fruit of the salvation Jesus won on the cross. When he showed these men the nail prints in his hands and the great wound in his side, Scripture says, they were "overjoyed" (v. 20). Why were they so glad? Here was the visible evidence that this was not another Jesus who had come. The scars proved that this was the same Jesus who had been crucified. He was now the risen Christ. His word of peace was the assurance that he would be with them forever. Then Jesus commissioned these men, "As the Father has sent me, I am sending you" (v. 21). What audacity! These cowards are sent into the world as emissaries of the Father?

But there is more. Jesus knew these men could not begin this mission of healing and peace without power and energy not their own. So he breathed on them—yes, breathed on them and said, "Receive the Holy Spirit" (v. 22). As Roger Fredrikson has reminded us, "As God had breathed His life into that first man and He became a living soul, so now His Son shares the intimacy of His own life with His disciples that they may be a new humanity, created and empowered for their mission."[1] This Spirit was a gift for them to accept at that moment, a foretaste of Holy Spirit who was yet to come and remain in them permanently after Jesus returned to the Father.

We Christians need to see ourselves as post-resurrection, post-ascension followers of Jesus. We need to continually rehearse the Gospel story. This Jesus whom we have accepted as Savior and are seeking to follow as Lord was once a baby in his mother's arms. But he is not that now.

He was once a carpenter, teacher, companion, and friend—one whose healing love mercifully blessed all he touched, all he could see, and hear, and speak to—but he is not limited by time and space now.

He was a self-giving suffering servant who hung on a cross, pouring out his life and love on our behalf—but he is not hanging there now. God raised him from the dead!

But there is more. This Jesus ascended, and the curtain went up on a new act in the drama. Pentecost happened. The Spirit of the Ascended One was poured out on his followers and the church was born.

At Pentecost, the people of God became the Spirit-filled body of Christ. So the church lives and functions by the action of the Holy Spirit. All that the disciples needed, and all we need today, came to the world on the day of Pentecost. The church is powerful in her witness to the world as the believers who make up her membership are gifted and empowered by the Holy Spirit.

It is important that as the church we do not close ourselves to the empowerment of the Holy Spirit over disagreement on what gifts are available today and which may be more important. The nature of the gifts is varied, and the purpose is clear: to "build up the church" (1 Cor. 14:12). The crucial difference lies not in the signs and wonders but in the infilling of ordinary men and women with the Holy Spirit.

POSITION AND CONDITION IN HARMONY

The Holy Spirit not only gave birth to the church but is constantly available to Christ's followers, showing Christ to us, forming Christ in us, guiding us into truth, and empowering us to live a Christ-life in the world. The Statement says, "Saving faith results in sanctification, the transformation of life in growing conformity to Christ through the power of the Holy Spirit."

To be a Christian is to change. It is to become new. It is not simply a matter of choosing a new lifestyle, though there is a new style. It has to do with being a new person. New persons do not emerge full-blown. Conversion, passing from death to life, may be the miracle of the moment, but the making of a saint is the process of a lifetime. The process of saint-making is to work out in fact what is already true in principle. In position—that, is in our relation to God in Jesus Christ—we are new persons. Now our condition—the actual life we live—must be brought into harmony with our new position.

A man once said to Dwight L. Moody, "Sir, I am a self-made man." Moody replied, "You have certainly saved the Lord from a very grave responsibility." Paul contended we are new creatures in Christ Jesus (2 Cor. 5:17), "created to be like God in true righteousness and holiness" (Eph. 4:24), renewed according to the nature of him who created us (Col. 3:10). Nothing less is the aim of the Christian life. Paul uses a striking word to describe our new life in Christ: "For you died, and your life is now hidden with Christ in God" (Col. 3:3).

It is, as the Statement says, by God's "grace alone, and through faith alone, because of Christ alone" that God declares us just, remits our sins, and adopts us as his children. But this is not complete salvation. Justifying grace issues in sanctifying grace—the process of our being restored and conformed to God's image. The founder of Methodism, John Wesley, offers this distinction. Justification is "what God does for us through His Son. Sanctification is what God works in us by His Spirit."[2]

CALLED TO AND EMPOWERED FOR HOLINESS

One of the major works of the Holy Spirit is to sanctify us, to make us holy. Holiness is not an option for God's people. God speaks clearly: "I am the LORD your God; consecrate yourselves and be holy, because I am holy" (Lev. 11:44).

Paul makes plain that we have been blessed and chosen by Christ to "be holy and without blame before him in love" (Eph. 1:4 KJV). In 1 Thessalonians 4:7–8 he forged the indissoluble link between God's call to be holy and the Holy Spirit, who makes holiness possible. This is in keeping with God's Old Testament promise: "I will put my Spirit in you and move you to follow my decrees and be careful to keep my laws" (Ezek. 36:27).

God's saving activity not only forgives and frees us from previous sin but makes us capable of obedience. When we yield ourselves to the divine working of our Lord, he gives us a new heart.

He alters our nature. He subdues the old nature and breathes new life into us, making obedience possible.

Obedience is the key. While God has made provision for our holiness, he has also given us responsibility for it. Herein lies the struggle. We have deep desires to live a holy life, but we have given up on the possibility. We have struggled long and diligently with particular sins and moral weaknesses. We may have overcome blatant sins, yet we struggle with anger, pride, jealousy, lust, racism, and unconcern for the poor. If not lazy or slothful, we waste time; if not gluttonous, we eat too much; if not completely idolatrous, we often make a god out of money and material security; if not blatant liars, we slip into deceitful patterns and shade the truth; if not covetous of things, we find ourselves jealous of the position or popularity of others. We know we sin, and we come to the edge of despair: Where is the victory in Jesus others talk so glowingly about?

We have concentrated on victory to the detriment of obedience. How many times have we heard, "Just give your sins to Jesus" or "Let go and let God" or "Stop trying and start trusting"? There is a kernel of truth in all these slogans. What we do—our discipline, our "works"—has no merit for our salvation. In our "old life" of sin we struggled with temptation and destructive patterns of behavior and over and over again failed to find meaning and joy. Then the Good News—that all we need to do for salvation is to trust in Christ and rest in his finished work—delighted us and was received like a life preserver thrown to a drowning man. But after a while we begin to sense we don't have total victory. We are not yet free of sin. Careful self-examination shows we are not obedient. The truth is, we can't merely give our sins to Jesus; we must give *ourselves* to him. When we give ourselves to Jesus, he gives his Holy Spirit to us. The Spirit empowers us for obedient living, which is the dynamic of a holy life. Paul tells us, "If you live according to the sinful nature, you will die; but if by the Spirit you put to death the misdeeds of the body, you will live" (Rom. 8:13). Stating it another way, Paul says, "You died, and your life is now hidden with Christ in God.... Put to death, therefore, whatever belongs to your earthly nature: sexual immorality, impurity, lust, evil desires and greed" (Col. 3:3, 5). He could have gone on to list other sins with which we may be currently struggling.

GIVING ALL FOR OTHERS

Charlotte Diggs Moon stood only four feet, three inches tall, but her life cast a long spiritual shadow. "Lottie" grew up in a family of landed gentry in antebellum Virginia, affirmed her faith in Christ at age eighteen, became a school teacher and an excellent linguist, and then was called to join her sister, Edmonia, as a missionary in China. Edmonia had to return home because of poor health and culture shock, but Lottie stayed and spent most of the rest of her life there.

Lottie developed her own mission strategy, using an educational approach. She opened a school in the seaport city of Tengchow (now Qingdao) in Shantung (Shandong) Province in northern China, where there was a small Christian community. Amid recurring famines she expended much of her own money and energy in helping to feed the poor around her; for many years she provided for as many as fifteen destitute women at a time in her own home.

(Throughout her service Lottie used many of her own funds while continuing to appeal for funds from American Christians. In one letter published in the Southern Baptist Foreign Mission Journal in December 1887, she called for an annual Christmas offering to be taken for foreign missions. The idea caught on; eventually the annual appeal was named for her. Over the next hundred years more than one billion dollars was collected for missions through the Lottie Moon offering.)

In time, along with other missionaries, Lottie began to venture out of Tengchow into country villages. During the war between China and Japan in

Holiness is a joint venture. The Holy Spirit enables, but I must act. The Holy Spirit's refining power and my obedience in "putting to death" the old life are two sides of the same coin. The Holy Spirit provides the power for me to move from "I can't" (settling into a mediocre life void of victory) to "I can do everything through him who gives me strength." E. Stanley Jones said it best: "Unless the Holy Spirit fills, the human spirit fails." Thus, a holy life is a life of victory as we grow more and more into the likeness of Jesus.

1895, she made evangelistic excursions to 118 villages in three months. The word back in Tengchow was, "Miss Lottie Moon is out preaching in the country." Amid her evangelistic success she repeatedly encountered suspicion as a foreigner, and more than once she was called "devil woman," in part because, with her Western clothing and appearance, some were not always sure at first whether she was a man or a woman.

When she moved from Tengchow to P'ingtu (Pingdu), some 120 miles away, Lottie began to wear Chinese garb and found doors opening that had been closed to her before. As the only foreigner in P'ingtu she became something of a celebrity. The Gospel spread. One convert, Li Show-ting, became ordained as an evangelist and over the years baptized more than ten thousand new Christians. As the number of Christians grew, so did persecution. Lottie often placed herself in harm's way in order to protect others.

Eventually Lottie returned to her school in Tengchow. There, when an especially hard famine struck during the Boxer Rebellion, she went on a sympathy fast and became ill. She died on board a ship that was taking her back to America. Despite the fruits of her ministry in China, she had often written of how lonely her life had been. Yet she gave all that she had—financially, physically, and emotionally—for others for the sake of the Gospel. After her death, the church at P'ingtu wrote, "Oh, how she loved us."

—Adapted from "Lottie Moon: A Thousand Lives for China," in *Ambassadors for Christ,* ed. John D. Woodbridge (Chicago: Moody Press, 1994), pp. 56–62.

I remember a time in my life, back in the early 1960s, when I was confronted with this shocking fact: "I am as holy as I want to be." I was a young Methodist preacher in Mississippi and the organizing pastor of a congregation that had experienced amazing growth and success. Then the fellowship of the congregation was splintered by my involvement in the civil rights movement. I didn't think there was anything radical about my involvement, but many people in the congregation could not understand my commitment and participation. I couldn't understand their lack of understanding. The Gospel seemed clear to me.

The pressure, stress, and tension wore me out. I was physically, emotionally, and spiritually exhausted—ready to throw in the towel. Then I went to a weeklong conference, led by the world-famous missionary evangelist, E. Stanley Jones. I will never forget going to the altar one evening to have Brother Stanley lay hands on and pray for me. He knew my story, and as I knelt, he asked, "Do you want to be holy? Do you want to be whole?" Something extraordinary happened that night. I was filled with the Holy Spirit in a measure I had not known before. It was a signal, sanctifying experience in my life, changing forever the direction of my ministry, challenging me to allow Christ to minister through me rather than my struggling to minister for Christ.

Over the years since then, I have continued to ask myself, "Do I want to be holy?" And I have constantly reminded myself that I am as holy as I want to be. Paul calls us to be nothing less than "imitators of God" (Eph. 5:1); this is possible through the Holy Spirit.

THE GIFT OF ASSURANCE

One of the primary works of the Holy Spirit is to provide the ongoing assurance of our salvation in Jesus Christ. This was powerfully witnessed to in John Wesley's Aldersgate experience. For years he had ardently sought to be holy, but his fruitless discipline and devotion left him deeply discontented. In 1725 he made a lifelong dedication to God that was never repudiated or outgrown. But it was not life-giving. In 1727, he had another definite religious experience, which led to a kind of asceticism within the world. He became avidly devoted to the development of his interior life and rigorously disciplined in religious practice. That, too, left him lifeless, empty, uncertain, and joyless. Then came his most famous experience on May 24, 1738. He recorded that experience in his journal:

> I felt my heart strangely warmed. I felt I did trust in Christ, alone, for my salvation; and an assurance was given me that he had taken away my sins, even mine, and saved me from the law of sin and death.[3]

Note that this was not the transformation of an irreligious man into a person of faith. Nor was it the last of his "conversions." It was not even the beginning of the Methodist revival, though the revival was rooted in that experience. It was, however, the decisive turning point in Wesley's entire life and work. It was his trustful response to Christ for salvation. As Albert Outler has said, "Aldersgate was less the reconstruction of Wesley's basic doctrines of God-in-Christ than an unexpected discovery of their power and effects. And its focus was 'the internal witness of the Spirit' (as in Romans 8 and Ephesians 2:5, 8–10). Aldersgate was the work of the Holy Spirit, witnessing to Wesley that Christ had saved him, and given him the assurance of that gracious, unmerited salvation."

The Holy Spirit assures us that God is our Father and loves us. God has poured out his love into our hearts (Rom. 5:5). Romans 8:15–16 says that when we cry, "*Abba*, Father," the Holy Spirit is witnessing to our spirit that we are God's children. Few experiences can provide more power in our lives than to have the assurance of our salvation.

Think what it could do for us:

- We would be joyous in our service for God, but not driven in our works, or mistaken in the notion that our works would save us.
- We would be delivered from frantic preoccupation with taking our spiritual temperature minute by minute.
- We would be free and spontaneous in our witness, exercising patience, and understanding as well as speaking with conviction and challenge.
- We would not get overwrought with our friends about future security, for we would be assured of our present relationship with Christ—who loves us with an immeasurable love.

WALKING IN THE SPIRIT

Paul reminded the Colossians that God "has rescued us from the dominion of darkness and brought us into the kingdom of the Son he loves, in whom we have redemption, the forgiveness of sins" (Col. 1:13–14). The Holy Spirit empowers us to be obedient and keep Christ on his throne in this new kingdom into which we have been transferred by the gracious mercy of God.

In Galatians 5:13–6:10 the work of the Holy Spirit is most clearly spelled out as Christians are commanded to "walk in the Spirit" (5:16 KJV). They are promised that those who do so "will not gratify the desires of the sinful nature." Christians are "led by the Spirit," and they bear "the fruit of the Spirit . . . love, joy, peace, patience, kindness, goodness, faithfulness, gentleness and self-control" (Gal. 5:22–23). Walking in the Spirit—or, as the NIV puts it, living by the Spirit—means that the life of Christ is reproduced in the life of the believer. The Spirit enables us as Christians to be, as Luther said, "little Christs" to others.

The Holy Spirit empowers us to prevail over "unholy" spirits. There are spiritual forces that overpower us in a destructive way. The New Testament refers to these spiritual forces as demons, and there is no hesitation in Scripture to deal with Satan. Paul urged the Ephesians to put on the whole armor of God to prepare themselves for battle, "for our struggle is not against flesh and blood, but against the rulers, against the authorities, against the powers of this dark world and against the spiritual forces of evil in the heavenly realms" (Eph. 6:12). I have seen the Holy Spirit overpower these "unholy" spirits by empowering people with the very power of the living Christ. Luke tells the story of Jesus' healing of a man who was controlled by a demon (Luke 8:26–39):

> Many times [the evil spirit] had seized him, and though he was chained hand and foot and kept under guard, he had broken his chains and had been driven by the demon into solitary places. Jesus asked him, "What is your name?"
> "Legion," he replied, because many demons had gone into him (vv. 29–30).

Jesus' power prevailed over these spirits. The man was freed. When people came out to see what had happened, "they found the man from whom the demons had gone out, sitting at Jesus' feet, dressed and in his right mind" (v. 35).

The same Christ who worked in that man is at work today, overpowering "unholy spirits" and empowering people to live in freedom and joy.

BECOMING MORE THAN CONQUERORS

In preparing to leave his disciples, Jesus promised to send the Holy Spirit. In John's Gospel the Greek designation for Holy Spirit is translated variously "Comforter," "advocate" (KJV), and "Counselor" (NIV), indicating the empowering presence of the Holy Spirit.

I have seen it many times—people transformed from helpless objects of forces beyond their control into dynamic, active, decision-making persons who participate in the ministry and mission of Christ. They are in control of their lives because, by their testimony, they are controlled by the Spirit.

A friend of mine, whom we'll call Jane, is spending two years in prison. She was implicated in drug dealing by her relationship and association with her father, who was a drug lord and has been imprisoned for life. Jane insists she is innocent, and I believe her. She was converted to Christ about two years before her arrest. We have corresponded during the time of her imprisonment, and I have seen a powerful transformation. In one letter she wrote,

> The things I have learned throughout this experience I will never forget. As painful as it has been, I now see it as an important, perhaps necessary step in my breakthrough to a happier life. For one thing, I have been profoundly humbled. I see that "of myself I am nothing."
>
> So when I had finally had enough and couldn't take it any more I realized there had to be a better way—that's where God came in. The moment of surrender is not when life is over. It's when it begins. . . .

> I feel fortunate and very grateful to have gotten a second chance at life.
> I am so excited! This is the absolute best HIGH I have ever known.
> Totally awesome!!
> Thinking of you and looking at life through new eyes. . . .

How do you explain this, but by the empowerment of the Holy Spirit! The Holy Spirit gives us the power to bear the burdens of life and be "more than conquerors" (Rom. 8:37).

EMPOWERED TO FORGIVE

In her book *The Hiding Place*, Corrie ten Boom tells about the forgiving power of the Holy Spirit operating in her life. After her release from the concentration camp where her sister died, she lectured and preached all over the world about the need to forgive our enemies. Then one day she was uniquely confronted by her own message. Following one of her sermons, she was greeted by a man whom she recognized as the S.S. guard at the "shower room" at the concentration camp. Suddenly it was all there—the roomful of mocking men, the heaps of clothing, her sister Betsie's pain-blanched face.

> He came up to me as the church was emptying, beaming and bowing. "How grateful I am for your message, *fraulein*," he said. "To think that, as you say, He has washed my sins away!" His hand was thrust out to shake mine. And I, who had preached so often to the people in Bloemendaal the need to forgive, kept my hand at my side. Even as the angry, vengeful thoughts boiled through me, I saw the sin of them. Jesus Christ had died for this man; was I going to ask for more? *Lord Jesus*, I prayed, *forgive me and help me to forgive him.*
>
> I tried to smile. I struggled to raise my hand. I could not. I felt nothing, not the slightest spark of warmth or charity. And so again I breathed a silent prayer. *Jesus, I cannot forgive him. Give me your forgiveness.*

> As I took his hand, a most incredible thing happened. From my shoulder along my arm and through my hand a current seemed to pass from me to him, while into my heart sprang a love for this stranger that almost overwhelmed.
>
> And so I discovered that it is not on our forgiveness any more than on our goodness that the world's healing hinges, but on His. When He tells us to love our enemies, He gives, along with the command, the love itself.[4]

It is not easy to forgive—we know that. Corrie ten Boom confessed that empowerment beyond herself was at work. The Christ who told her to love her enemies gave love, and the Holy Spirit empowered her to put that love into practice by forgiving.

THE HOLY SPIRIT IN MISSIONS AND EVANGELISM

Pentecost was a missionary event. Because God is a missionary God, the Holy Spirit is the chief evangelist. In the historic mission of the Christian church, the Holy Spirit is the primary actor. The Manila Manifesto, produced by the Second International Congress on World Evangelization in 1989, expressed this very clearly.

> The Scriptures declare that God himself is the chief evangelist. For the Spirit of God is the Spirit of truth, love, holiness and power, and evangelism is impossible without Him. It is He who anoints the messenger, confirms the word, prepares the hearer, convicts the sinful, enlightens the blind, gives life to the dead, enables us to repent and believe, unites us to the body of Christ, assures us that we are God's children, leads us into Christ-like character and service, and sends us out in our turn to be Christ's witnesses. In all this the Holy Spirit's main preoccupation is to glorify Jesus Christ by showing Him to us and forming Him in us.[5]

Jesus made it clear he would send the Spirit to empower us for ministry (Acts 1:8). Earnest Christians will discover that we cannot keep the Spirit to ourselves. To neglect mission and ministry as individuals or congregations is to grieve, even contradict—at least to neglect—the Holy Spirit. Jesus promises the presence and power of the Spirit for local ministry "in Jerusalem," and global mission "to the ends of the earth."

Every week I pray by name for a different, specified group of students in our seminary. The week before, I write a letter to each one, giving them the opportunity to share their "praises and thanksgiving" and requests for intercession. One student recorded on the request form his praise and thanksgiving to God for the six adults who wanted to be baptized in his church sometime during the coming weeks. That hit me solidly and caused great joy to rise up within me. There are churches that go an entire year or two years or more that are unable to report an adult won to Christ on profession of faith, or an adult baptism. Yet here was a young man, from a diminished population area, who was able to bring to the altar fruits of his labor. When I talked to him about this, he responded, "The Holy Spirit is doing a great work in our church."

CHRISTIAN HOPE

Among the major works of the Spirit in the Christian community is the giving of hope. When the Holy Spirit came in vivid power at Pentecost, God's expectant people knew that the messianic age their prophets had proclaimed had dawned. They soon realized that the coming of the kingdom was only partial; final fulfillment was yet to come. The Holy Spirit is both a gift and a promise. God puts "his seal of ownership on us," giving us his Spirit "as a deposit, guaranteeing what is to come" (2 Cor. 1:22; see also 5:5).

The scriptural metaphors are inspiring and challenging. The gift of the Spirit is like the reaping of the firstfruits, with the guarantee that the rest will follow. It is like the first course of a banquet, with the entrée to follow (Heb. 6:4–5). The Holy Spirit provides the Christian community with gift and promise, experienced reality and future hope.

When I think of the hope and the triumph of the kingdom now and in the future, I remember a moving experience I had several years ago. My wife, Jerry, and I visited churches in what was then Czechoslovakia. One pastor spent more than one-half his monthly salary to buy the gasoline to come to one of our meetings at a seminary. As I looked at the pastors and laypersons, I saw in them a people who were filled with great hope. But no wonder! For decades, every church in Czechoslovakia was severely restricted by the Communist government. Christians could not evangelize. They had to be careful about how they spoke in public. They could post no public notices on their church buildings or signs outside them. They could make no public declarations. They could not even ring their church bells.

Then, in November 1989 a group of students confronted a group of young soldiers, and this proved to be the catalyst that brought a simmering revolution against the government out in the open and to full flower. Everybody took to the streets, and the old Communist regime knew that it was over.

Christians there told us the story. It was decided that on November 27 at noon, everybody in the country would walk out of homes, businesses, offices, factories, or fields. Everybody would simply walk into the streets at noon. Every bell in every church in Czechoslovakia would be rung at noon. And when that day and time came, bells that had been silent for forty-five years began to ring. It was electric. Everybody knew that something new had come.

Dr. Vilem Schneeberger, one of the pastors, said that for the first time they were able to put a sign in front of their church in Prague. On the sign were written four words: THE LAMB HAS WON. What a truth! What a victory! What hope! What a sign of the kingdom! The Lamb has won! Not the bear, but the Lamb! Not the tiger, but the Lamb! Not the lion, but the Lamb!

We can believe it. The Holy Spirit secures the hope that one day "every knee should bow . . . and every tongue confess that Jesus Christ is Lord, to the glory of God the Father" (Phil. 2:10–11). So be it! Hallelujah!

Notes

1. Roger L. Fredrikson, *The Communicators Commentary: John* (Waco, TX: Word, 1985), p. 286.

2. John Wesley, Sermon 45, "The New Birth."

3. Nehemiah Curnock, ed., *The Journal of John Wesley*, vol. 1 (London: Epworth Press, 1909–16), pp. 476–77.

4. Corrie ten Boom, *The Hiding Place* (Lincoln, VA: Chosen Books, 1974), p. 215.

5. John Stott, ed., *Making Christ Known: Historic Mission Documents from the Lausanne Movement, 1974–1989* (Grand Rapids: Eerdmans, 1996), p. 238.

Study Questions

1. What are some of the promises in the Bible applicable to Christian living?
2. What does it mean to see ourselves as "post-resurrection, post-ascension followers of Jesus"?
3. What does it mean to be a "new person" in Christ?
4. What is the role of holiness in a Christian's life?
5. In what ways does the Holy Spirit empower a Christian?

At death, Christ takes the believer to himself (Phil. 1:21) for unimaginable joy in the ceaseless worship of God (Rev. 22:1–5). . . .

Thus, while in foretaste believers enjoy salvation now, they still wait its fullness (Mark 14:61–62; Heb. 9:28).

—*The Gospel of Jesus Christ: An Evangelical Celebration*

8

IS THIS LIFE ALL THERE IS?

WHY HEAVEN IS WORTH THE WAIT

Joni Eareckson Tada

"File this, Francie, and make copies of this letter, would you?" I said to my secretary. "And, oh yes," I sighed, "would you please pull out the sofa bed one more time?"

"Are you serious? Again?"

"Again." With that, my face flushed and my eyes became damp. For the fourth time that day, I needed to be lifted out of my wheelchair and laid down. I had to undress to readjust my corset, which I wore to help improve my lung capacity. However, my shallow breathing, sweating, and rising blood pressure were signaling that something was either pinching, bruising, or sticking my paralyzed body. Francie tissued away my tears and unfolded my office sofa bed.

As she shifted my body, examining me for any telltale pressure marks or red areas, I stared vacantly at the ceiling. "I want to quit this," I mumbled.

Not finding anything wrong, she put my clothes back on and hoisted me into my chair.

"Where do I go to resign from this stupid paralysis?" I said sheepishly.

Francie shook her head and grinned. She'd heard me say that many times. As she gathered the letters off my desk, and was about to leave, she paused at the door. "I bet you can't wait for heaven. You know, like Paul said, 'We groan, longing to be clothed with a heavenly dwelling.'"

My eyes dampened again, but this time they were tears of relief and hope. "Yeah, it'll be great."

■

I still can hardly believe that I—with atrophied muscles, shriveled, bent fingers, and no feeling from the shoulders down—will one day have a new, dazzling body that's in wonderful working order and clothed in righteousness. Not to mention, I'll also have a new mind that doesn't want to resign or quit!

That's right—the spinal cord injury I have lived with since I dove into shallow water in 1967 will no longer keep me from the pleasures I have missed for so long: horseback riding, plucking guitar strings with my fingers, or simply throwing back the covers in the morning and hopping out of bed. Can you imagine the hope that heaven gives someone who is disabled, whether by cerebral palsy, brain injury, or manic depression? No other religion or philosophy promises glorified bodies, hearts, and minds. Only in the Gospel of Jesus Christ do hurting people find such incredible hope.

You may not be paralyzed with a broken neck, but you could be paralyzed by other limitations: a broken heart, a broken home, a broken reputation. Those earthly things that may be screaming for your undivided attention and hampering your happiness are a reminder that this short life can't deliver a lasting "heaven on earth." The temporal troubles we face may slam the door to sustained satisfaction in this life, but then again, they can throw windows wide open to a vibrant hope of heaven.

How real is heaven to you? In the past three decades I have contemplated heaven a lot. What I have discovered—through eyes of faith and the descriptions in God's Word—is that heaven is not a wispy, vaporous place where cherub-faced angels play harps on clouds. Nor is it a never-never land where you can't hug people because they are spacey spirit beings. No way! It's a rock-solid place with streets, gates, walls, rivers, and people who will touch and taste, move and run, laugh and sing, and never have reason to cry.

Sounds great, doesn't it?

Every time my corset wears a wound in my side or I am bedridden for days or I feel the stab of someone else's pity, I look beyond the negatives of this temporary world and envision the positives of my eternal home. And believe me, friend, the positives of heaven are plentiful and worth pondering

FREE AT LAST

For one thing, the Bible makes a distinction between our earthly and resurrection bodies. "The body that is sown is perishable, it is raised imperishable; it is sown in dishonor, it is raised in glory; it is sown in weakness, it is raised in power; it is sown a natural body; it is raised a spiritual body" (1 Cor. 15:42–44).

Trying to understand what heavenly bodies will be like is similar to expecting an acorn to understand its destiny as a majestic oak tree. My earthly body is wasting away; my resurrected body will never die. My earthly body is permanently paralyzed; my immortal body will be painless and powerful. Did you know that in the twinkling of an eye, Jesus Christ, the sinless Savior who rose from the dead, will personally transform my lowly body so that it will be like his glorious body? That is one reason why the apostle Peter tells us not to be surprised at the painful trials we suffer. "But rejoice that you participate in the sufferings of Christ, so that you may be overjoyed when his glory is revealed" (1 Peter 4:13).

Years ago, when I read verses that called me to rejoice in suffering, my first thought was, *Sure, God, I'll rejoice the day you get me out of this stupid wheelchair!* But I was thinking backward. I needed to view this life and its suffering from an eternal, end-of-time perspective. Then I could understand why the apostle Paul said, "For our light and momentary troubles are achieving for us an eternal glory that far outweighs them all" (2 Cor. 4:17). When viewed from the timelessness of eternity, our earthly troubles *are* light and momentary. Every pain and trouble will be erased and atoned for in heaven. In fact, Jesus—the "Lamb that had been slain"—will be the only One in heaven who will bear the scars of life on earth: the nail prints in his hands and feet. He willingly sacrificed his own life on the cross to pay for our sins.[1] But the grave didn't keep him down. And it won't keep me down, either. Like his risen, glorious body, mine will be an actual, literal body, bearing his likeness and perfectly suited for heaven.

Now, as much as I relish the idea of leaving my old body and wheelchair behind, there is something I look forward to even more: a completely purified heart and mind. I am sick and tired of sinning and battling the flesh. Yes, I have been cleansed by the blood of the Lamb, and I have power from the Holy Spirit to resist the devil and become more and more holy, but until I die—unless Christ returns first—I still have this old body to deal with. So I can't wait to be beautifully clothed in the perfect righteousness of Christ, without a trace of sin. Even my worship will improve. For once I won't be insincere or distracted while singing a hymn to God. No longer will I interrupt my prayer time to make next week's grocery list. With my healthy new body, sinless heart, and pure mind, I will be able to offer uninhibited praise and enjoy full fellowship with the Father and the Son. That, to me, will be the best part of heaven.

LOOKING UP

The Bible says, "We are looking forward to a new heaven and a new earth, the home of righteousness" (2 Peter 3:13). A new heaven *and* a new earth, where people are in "right standing" with God. What an astounding place it will be! The book of John's visions—Revelation—describes "the Holy City, the new Jerusalem, coming down out of heaven from God, prepared as a bride beautifully dressed for her husband" (21:2). Imagine a glittering twelve-layered celestial city made of pure, transparent gold, with jasper city walls more than two hundred feet thick and twelve foundations inlaid with precious gems. The proportions of the city are identical to King Solomon's construction of the Holy of Holies in the ancient temple in Jerusalem, where the ark of the covenant rested. The only difference is that while the original inner sanctuary was thirty feet long, thirty feet wide, and thirty feet high, the New Jerusalem is said to be about a quarter of a million times larger. There is no temple in heaven, because God himself will be its temple. Just as God's presence filled the Holy of Holies, so his glory fills heaven's Holy City.

Are these descriptions hard to picture? I used to have a tough time getting excited about the biblical descriptions of heaven. Although rainbow thrones and pearly gates sounded beautiful, they didn't seem as appealing as Pike's Peak on a cloudless day. But then I was reminded by a good friend that those symbols are simply meant to give our faith something to hold onto. Just as a sign that says "Chicago: 50 miles" isn't the city itself, our limited human language and imagination can't begin to picture all that God has in store. Yet we know that heaven will be far more glorious than the most gorgeous places in our world today. "No eye has seen, no ear has heard, no mind has conceived what God has prepared for those who love him" (1 Cor. 2:9). But look beyond the glitter and gold, because heaven is more than a place. It's God dwelling with us.

THE BRIDEGROOM COMETH

The night before he died, Jesus told his disciples, "In my Father's house are many rooms; if it were not so, I would have told you. I am going there to prepare a place for you. And if I go and prepare a place for you, I will come back and take you to be with me that you also may be where I am" (John 14:2–3). We are not home yet. Philippians 3:20 says, "Our citizenship is in heaven. And we eagerly await a Savior from there, the Lord Jesus Christ." Jesus, who now sits on the throne in heaven, is coming back soon for those who love him. We won't miss his arrival, because "the Lord himself will come down from heaven, with a loud command, with the voice of the archangel and with the trumpet call of God, and the dead in Christ will rise first. After that, we who are still alive and are left will be caught up together with them in the clouds to meet the Lord in the air. And so we will be with the Lord forever" (1 Thess. 4:16–17).

"FOR ME, TO LIVE ..."

Karen Ruth Johnson, a popular, outgoing seventeen-year-old, gave her teacher her last senior assignment at San Marino (Calif.) High School on June 5, 1959. This paper, called "A Philosophy of Life," began this way:

"My philosophy of life is based on the Holy Bible and the God that wrote it. I know that He has a plan for my life and through daily prayer and reading of His Word I will be able to see it. As far as my life work or life partner I am leaving it in His hands and am willing to do anything He says.

"I feel that this philosophy is very practical and can be applied to everyday life."

The very next day, Saturday, June 6, Karen Johnson and two other young people were killed in a head-on traffic accident near Palm Springs.

Karen's death had a lasting impact on many of her classmates and her many friends in Youth for Christ. At her funeral, one person prayed that Karen's untimely death would become a "teenage triumph." And it did. Her family published her paper "My Philosophy of Life" and told about her death in a brochure that went around the world in as many as twelve languages. It was called "A

I start feeling homesick for heaven and missing my Savior when I think about how Jesus feels about me. "The LORD will take delight in you. . . . As a bridegroom rejoices over his bride, so will your God rejoice over you" (Isa. 62:4–5). Yes, these are the words of Christ, the Bridegroom, the Lover of my soul, who is brimming over with heartfelt love for his bride, the church. In fact, Jesus gave his very life as his dowry, and the cross he endured shows me that he and his Father agreed on an exorbitant price. As the betrothed, it is our responsibility to get "fitted" for heaven and to wait for his return.

Are you "fitted" and prepared to meet the Lord? Have you abandoned yourself to holy living and cut away every sin that entangles? According to Revelation 19:7, we are on our way to embrace our Savior at the Wedding Supper of the Lamb, yet it is hard to imagine being ready to meet Jesus—especially if our own devotion to him has been inconsistent or halfhearted on

Teenage Triumph." Many people have written to Karen's parents, Edward and Joyce Johnson, to tell them that they came to saving faith in Christ through reading Karen's story. Many young men decided to go into Christian ministry as a result of it.

At age five, before the family moved from Illinois to California, Karen, full of life, was riding in the car and suddenly piped up, "Daddy, you know we have three homes."

"What do you mean, Karen?"

"We have one home in Illinois, one home in Michigan, and one home in heaven."

Karen already knew that, as she was to express it years later in her senior paper, "I know that I am on this earth to have fellowship with God and to win others to the saving knowledge of His Son, Jesus Christ. I know that after death I will go to be with Him forever.... 'For me, to live is Christ, to die is gain.'"

Adapted from "Epilogue: A Teenage Triumph"
in *More Than Conquerors*, ed. John D. Woodbridge
(Chicago: Moody Press, 1992), pp. 353–56.

earth. Won't we cower when we see our Bridegroom face-to-face?

On my own wedding day, I felt awkward as my girlfriends strained to shift my paralyzed body into a cumbersome wedding gown. No amount of corseting and binding my body gave me a perfect shape. The dress just didn't fit well. Then, as I was wheeling into the church, I glanced down and noticed that I'd accidentally run over the hem of my dress, leaving a greasy tire mark. My paralyzed hands couldn't hold the bouquet of daisies that lay off-center on my lap. And my chair, though decorated for the wedding, was still a big, clunky gray machine with belts, gears, and ball bearings. I certainly didn't feel like the picture-perfect bride in a bridal magazine.

I inched my chair closer to the last pew to catch a glimpse of Ken in front. There he was, standing tall and stately in his formal attire. I saw him looking for me, craning his neck to look up the aisle. My face flushed, and I suddenly couldn't wait to be with him. I had seen my beloved. The love in Ken's face had washed away all my feelings of unworthiness. I was his pure and perfect bride.

Our entrance into heaven may be something like that. Someday Jesus will come for me and gaze into my eyes. One look from God will change me and purify any remaining stains and smears of sin. Heaven will be an undoing of all the bad things in our lives as God wipes away every tear and closes the door on pain and disappointment. Jesus' love for us is so amazing that he will more than match our attempts at single-hearted love with his pure, radiant love. All our longings for love and ecstasy will be satisfied in Jesus because one day "we shall be like him, for we shall see him as he is" (1 John 2:1). So "we wait for that blessed hope—the glorious appearing of our great God and Savior, Jesus Christ, who gave himself for us to redeem us from all wickedness and to purify for himself a people that are his very own, eager to do what is good" (Titus 2:13–14).

Oddly enough, it is during times of forced stillness that I enjoy a foretaste of what it's like to see my Lord and sense his undying love. When I lie down at night around 7:30, exhausted after a long day, I cannot *do* anything. I can only *be.* As I lie there paralyzed, I choose to be the wise virgin who pours her love into the marriage contract. I sing songs to the Lord for his listening pleasure. I pray, setting my heart and mind on heavenly glories. I "taste and see that the LORD is good" as I ingest favorite Scriptures (Ps. 34:8). Within a short time, I can picture myself kneeling in the throne room where Jesus is seated. And there I enjoy face-to-face intimacy with my betrothed.

HOW TO GET HOME

Where is heaven, and how will we get there? From one standpoint, heaven is far, far away. "To the LORD your God belong the heavens, even the highest heavens" (Deut. 10:14). Our solar system has a diameter of about 700 light-minutes, or eight billion miles. But the galaxy in which our solar system is contained has a diameter of 100,000 light-years. Our galaxy is huge! And even more amazing is that it is only one of billions of other galaxies filled with stars and planets that God created out in the cosmos. The dwelling place of God exists in infinity—yet the dying thief on the cross next to Jesus heard him say, "I tell you the truth, today you will be with me in paradise" (Luke 23:43).

"Today"? How could a dead criminal span billions of light-years in an instant? Jesus gives us a clue in Revelation 1:8 when he laughs at time and distance: "'I am the Alpha and Omega,' says the Lord God, 'who is, and who was, and who is to come, the Almighty.'" Jesus is the Beginning and the End, the One who orchestrated the glorious creation of the world, who laid his glory aside when he came to earth, and who will come again with glory.

When the dying thief on the cross believed in Jesus, he was born again of the Spirit and given the spiritual "genes," so to speak, of God himself—Christ Jesus. So when the thief died, he simply slipped from one dimension to the next, much as the resurrected Jesus could slip through walls from one room to another.

To step into heaven, we, too, must be born again in Christ. Entrance to heaven requires a redeemed body, a body that is rid of the law of sin in its members. We know from 1 Corinthians 15:50 that "flesh and blood cannot inherit the kingdom of God." That's because our bodies are corrupted from sin, and heaven is a high and holy place where only purity dwells (Isa. 57:15). Consequently, our sinful flesh prevents us from seeing God. First Timothy 6:16 says that God "lives in unapproachable light, whom no one has seen or can see." When the prophet Isaiah "saw" the Lord high and exalted on a throne, he caught only a glimpse of the outer edges of the radiance of God. That sight alone caused Isaiah to despair so much over his sin that he cried, "Woe to me! . . . I am ruined! For I am a man of unclean lips" (Isa. 6:5).

We may not realize how heinous sin is until we catch a glimpse of the pure and spotless radiance of God. The closer the apostle Paul got to God, the more he cried, "I am the chief of sinners."

This was not a declaration of false humility; it was the cry of a saint sensitized to sin.

Yet aren't you glad God's love goes deeper than our sin? I echo Paul, who said, "Who will rescue me from this body of death? Thanks be to God—through Jesus Christ our Lord!" (Rom. 7:24–25). Our eternal destiny is secure if we have truly trusted Christ alone—not our own "goodness" or merit—for our salvation.[2] As new creatures in Christ, we can experience peace in our hearts and increasing victory over sin as we submit to his leadership and experience the joy of knowing our Savior even here and now.

DON'T CHOOSE HELL

What about those who reject Jesus as their Messiah? At some future date, the record will be set straight. God will vindicate his holy name and dispense his pure and perfect justice. For a great many people, it will be shocking to behold this Jesus, whom they tried to relegate to a Sunday school room. Terror will strike their hearts as the Lord arrives on the scene, as predicted in Revelation 19:11–16:

> I saw heaven standing open and there before me was a white horse, whose rider is called Faithful and True. With justice he judges and makes war. His eyes are like blazing fire, and on his head are many crowns. He has a name written on him that no one knows but he himself. He is dressed in a robe dipped in blood, and his name is the Word of God. The armies of heaven were following him, riding on white horses and dressed in fine linen, white and clean. Out of his mouth comes a sharp sword with which to strike down the nations. "He will rule them with an iron scepter." He treads the winepress of the fury of the wrath of God Almighty. On his robe and on his thigh he has this name written: KING OF KINGS AND LORD OF LORDS.

This is not a pretty sight. The same mouth that spoke peace and reconciliation will one day use the sharp sword of judgment. The same eyes that glowed with compassion will one day blaze with fire. Finally, impenitent sinners will be judged, and anyone whose name is not found written in the Lamb's Book of Life will be thrown into the lake of fire. Is this my Bridegroom? Yes, this same Jesus is my Lover and Avenger. He is altogether loving in his justice, and just in his love. And because he is perfect, his justice is pure.

How will believers feel on that great and terrible Day of the Lord? We won't cringe during the Judgment, because our sins have been removed as far as the east is from the west. Rather, we will accompany the Judgment with choruses of praise, because we, like God, will love purity and hate the perniciousness of evil. With perfect minds and hearts, we will desire truth and despise lies. We will joyfully agree with all of God's judgments. We are numbered among the angels, the elders, and "the roar of a great multitude in heaven shouting: 'Hallelujah! Salvation and glory and power belong to our God, for true and just are his judgments'" (Rev. 19:1).

Yes, the Day of Christ will be a great and terrible day—great for the righteous and terrible for the unrighteous. C. S. Lewis once said, "There are only two kinds of people in the end: those who say to God, 'Thy will be done,' and those to whom God says, in the end, 'Thy will be done.' All that are in hell, choose it."[3]

But for those who repent and turn their lives over to Jesus the Redeemer, heaven—with its absence of evil and with the presence of God—will be rewarded for all eternity.

CROWNING ACHIEVEMENTS

What will we do in heaven? When I first learned about heaven during the early days of my paralysis, I zeroed in on it because it was the place where I would receive new hands and feet. Heaven was the place I would be freed from the pain, so it became an escape from reality. At times, heaven was so me-centered that I felt as though the whole point of it was to get back all it owed me, all I had lost. Heaven became a death wish for me.

As I studied the Bible and grew in spiritual maturity, it gradually dawned on me that the still-to-come Day of Christ would be the Day of Christ, not the day of Joni. New hands and feet, as well as reunions with loved ones, began to look more like fringe benefits compared with the honor of being able to worship Jesus, the "Lamb, who was slain" (Rev. 5:12), and cast my crowns at his feet.

Crowns? What crowns?

While some people are trying to have a short-lived heaven on earth, we have a chance to "store up treasures in heaven" and to send ahead, so to speak, building materials so that something of eternal worth can be constructed. We will bring to the judgment seat of Christ all that we are and all that we have done. That is why we are warned to be careful and choose as our building materials gold, silver, and costly stones—that is, service rendered out of a pure heart, a right motive, and an eye for giving God the glory. One look from the Lord will scrutinize the quality of what we have built, and anything fashioned from selfish service will be consumed in a fiery flash.

This is sobering. I imagine I will come away a little singed on the edges. Don't misunderstand: I believe I will bask in God's approval for my service on earth, but pride and impure motives have probably sullied a lot of it. Burnt away will be those times I shared the Gospel out of puffed-up pride. Up in flames will go any manipulative behavior or lies that were dressed up like truth.

But even if a lot of people barely survive the judgment seat, keeping only their crown of salvation, that is in itself plenty of cause for rejoicing. Think of those who trusted Christ on their deathbed and had little or no time to build anything for eternity. Yet, if we have been faithful in earthly service, our responsibility in heaven will increase proportionately—or rather, completely *out of proportion.* Consider the formula Jesus gives in his parable of heaven in Luke 19:17: "'Well done, my good servant!' his master replied. 'Because you have been trustworthy in a very small matter, take charge of ten cities.'"

Wow! Ten cities? In exchange for faithfulness in a very small matter? When it comes to blessing us, Jesus thinks exponentially. The more faithful we are in this life, the more responsibility we will be given in the life to come. Keep in mind that success is not the key. *Faithfulness* is. You could have invested thirty years sharing the Gospel in the outback of Zimbabwe with only a handful of converts to show for it, or forty years being faithful in a difficult marriage. But if you were trustworthy to do the work God gave you to do, your service will be greater in eternity. In fact, as sons, daughters, and heirs of God (Rom. 8:17), we get to reign with Jesus forever. "To him who overcomes, I will give the right to sit with me on my throne" (Rev. 3:21).

I want to win as many crowns as possible while on earth. True, greater rewards will enhance my service in heaven, but they will also magnify the glory Jesus will receive. The more crowns, the merrier God's praise. And you and I were chosen to praise him.

I used to think that praising God in heaven would be boring. Won't we run out of Scripture choruses and hymns after a few millennia? I mean, to me, anything changeless has a high boredom factor. Even a great vacation at the beach has a hidden potential to be boring if it goes on too long.

But heaven is more than a place of pleasure and happiness. If that were so, heaven would be boring. What Christ gives us is the joy of heaven—everlasting joy. Like love, joy cannot be contained. It's always moving. It's the real energy of praise. If we are to be praising God for all eternity, as we shall be, then joy will be the dynamic. In heaven, praise will never be boring. In fact, the highlight of heaven won't be what *we* become, receive, and do. Rather, it will be enough simply to be there and to "be for the praise of his glory" (Eph. 1:12).

FINALLY I UNDERSTAND!

For now, our faith allows us only to glimpse at heaven "through a glass, darkly" (KJV), but in heaven we shall "know fully" (1 Cor. 13:12). Not only will we recognize the ones we love, but we will *know* them better than we ever knew them on earth. And we will find out who we truly are. God will give you a new name that's a secret between God and you. Revelation 2:17 says, "To him who overcomes, I will give . . . a white stone with a new name written on it, known only to him who receives it." The fact that no one else has your new name shows how unique you are to God. Another plus: In heaven there will be no room for envy. You will reflect God like the facet of a diamond, and people will say to you, "I love seeing that part of God in you . . . in fact, you seem to show off that trait of his better than anybody up here!"

Also, we will find out how God redeemed our pain and suffering. My sister, Linda, will understand why God took her five-year-old daughter, Kelly, through brain cancer. My friend, Diane, will see how her multiple sclerosis safeguarded her from falling into spiritual indifference. We will lift our hands and glorify God when we see how he used the hundred dollars we sacrificed at a missions conference to reach many hundreds in a Third World country. We will understand how God's plan worked perfectly. Everything fit. Nothing was wasted. "The LORD works out everything for his own ends—even the wicked for a day of disaster" (Prov. 16:4).

Closed doors are no accident. They remind us that this life is not all there is. God wishes to instill within us a deep desire for an inheritance that can never perish, spoil, or fade. And in order to grip our hearts, he will take drastic measures. I was one of those people who needed a broken neck to get my heart focused on heavenly glories instead of the here and now. You may not need a broken neck to start longing for heaven, but perhaps you are a mother who has lost a child, or a boy who has lost his father to cancer. Such sorrows can lead to the contentment of asking less of this life because there is more coming in the next.

Ultimately, one touch of Jesus' scars will provide an answer for the "Why?" questions of our suffering. If he went through so much suffering to secure for us that which we don't deserve, why do we complain when we endure on earth only a tiny fraction of what he went through on our behalf? If, instead, we stifle complaints and rejoice in the privilege of participating in the sufferings of Christ, we will be overjoyed when his glory appears. For "we share in his sufferings in order that we may also share in his glory" (Rom. 8:17).

What matters most is knowing that heaven will feel like home to the believer. All the earthly things we enjoy with our friends here will find a more exalted expression in heaven. We will be co-heirs with Christ. We will rule the world, eat the fruit of the Tree of Life, and be happier in service than we ever dreamed. And best of all, together we will fall on our faces at the foot of the throne and worship our Savior forever.

Notes

Portions of this chapter are adapted from Joni Eareckson Tada, *Heaven: Your Real Home* (Grand Rapids: Zondervan, 1997).

1. See Affirmation and Denial #8. Jesus was the perfect sacrifice for our sins.
2. See Affirmation and Denial #17.
3. See Affirmation and Denial #3.

Study Questions

1. How has the hope of heaven changed your perspective on life?
2. What is even better than having a new body in heaven? Try to name three more things to look forward to in heaven.
3. What is one eternal reason that we should rejoice in suffering?
4. How can we store up treasures in heaven instead of trying to have heaven on earth?
5. Why will we enjoy praising God in heaven?
6. How has your view of heaven changed in reading this chapter?

Salvation is a Trinitarian reality, initiated by the Father, implemented by the Son, and applied by the Holy Spirit. It has a global dimension, for God's plan is to save believers out of every tribe and tongue (Rev. 5:9) to be his church, a new humanity, the people of God, the body and bride of Christ, and the community of the Holy Spirit. All the heirs of final salvation are called here and now to serve their Lord and each other in love, to share in the fellowship of Jesus' sufferings, and to work together to make Christ known to the whole world.

■

We affirm that Jesus Christ is the only way of salvation, the only mediator between God and humanity (John 14:6; 1 Tim. 2:5).

We deny that anyone is saved in any other way than by Jesus Christ and his Gospel. The Bible offers no hope that sincere worshipers of other religions will be saved without personal faith in Jesus Christ.

—*The Gospel of Jesus Christ: An Evangelical Celebration*

9

DOES THE WORLD REALLY NEED TO HEAR THE GOSPEL OF JESUS CHRIST?

I will forever remember one particular exchange I had in 1986 with a person hostile to Christian mission. At the time, I was teaching theology and missiology at the Alliance Theological Seminary in Nyack, New York. I had spent part of the summer speaking at youth camps, conducting seminars, and participating in various ministry assignments in Burkina Faso and Côte d'Ivoire. I was exhausted when I returned home to Nyack.

A few days after my return, I became ill with what I thought was malaria. Seeing that I was not getting well, my wife insisted that I consult a doctor. I hesitated, procrastinated, and, at the urging of my family, finally consented to make an appointment. After a few sentences of casual conversation, the physician realized that I was a foreigner. He inquired about my country of origin, and he stated with obvious delight that he knew a man and his wife who were missionaries in my country. He then asked, "What brings you to this country?" I replied that I was teaching theology and missions at the seminary.

I was startled by the doctor's next statement. Although he formulated it as a question—"So, you are teaching the students how to colonize your country?"—he clearly was not interested in an answer or a presentation that would unsettle his conviction that mission and colonialism are the same thing. He was very convinced that Christian mission is colonial in nature.

I do not recall my response to this physician's allegation that missionaries actually endeavor to subjugate people. I probably muttered something to the effect that I could not be guilty of promoting the colonization of my own country.

After the examination, the doctor concluded that I did not have malaria and that he was unable to ascertain the nature of my ailment. He then sent me home with some general recommendations. While he did not offer me a cure that day, he did provide me with an incentive to keep on examining why Christians should continue to proclaim the Gospel wherever it is not known or accepted.

CONFIDENCE IN THE GOSPEL

For me, this examination begins with the need to recover confidence in the Gospel. Christians must recover confidence in the Gospel because when they lose it, either they will doubt the need to proclaim the Gospel or they will accept the claim that all religions are equally valid.

The recovery of confidence in the Gospel begins with knowing its origin. God is the author of the Gospel Christians are called to proclaim. Like the apostle Paul, Christians acknowledge that the Gospel is "the gospel of God" (Rom. 1:1). So when Christians share the Gospel with others, they do not market their own ideas; they convey a divine message. That is the reason Christians can and should have confidence in the Gospel: It comes from God and belongs to him who is the sole Master of everything (including humans).

This Gospel is neither a plan devised by people nor a program crafted by clever thinkers. It is as dependable as God himself. It is the good news that God, the ruler of the universe, is in the business of extending his saving grace to humans. One can therefore adhere to this Gospel wholeheartedly without fear of disappointment. Indeed "The Gospel is good news, not a good *idea*."[1] It is, as the Statement says, "the best and most important news that any human being ever hears." Humans have an avidity for sharing and hearing news. Thus it is unreasonable to expect Christians to keep silent about the most important news of all. The Gospel can be proclaimed with confidence because it is good news from God.[2]

When Christians have confidence that the Gospel is not the product of a particular culture or the creation of religious specialists and zealots, they are able to withstand all kinds of adversaries. Some of these adversaries oppose the proclamation of the Gospel because, to them, such a proclamation imposes Western religion on non-Western people. But the Gospel of God is not the religious artifact of the West, the East, the North, or the South; it is good news that God addresses to the entire human race. The proclamation of the divine Gospel is not a colonization project from the West; all people, regardless of culture or place of habitation, need to hear God's Good News.

Confidence that the Gospel is from God also enables Christians to distinguish between the real Gospel of God and the many false gospels being peddled today. The Gospel of God must not be identified with such pseudo-gospels as economic success, political ideology, or the eradication of disease and ignorance. All of these may be good, but they are not the Gospel because they are not news about Jesus Christ the Son. The true and real Gospel of God "sets forth Jesus Christ as the living Savior, Master, Life, and Hope of all who put their trust in him." That is why "acts of mercy and charity to our neighbors" cannot constitute "evangelism."[3] True evangelism requires that the Good News of God "regarding his Son" (Rom. 1:3) be proclaimed. The world needs this news more than any other product or commodity.

OPPOSITION TO THE GOSPEL

Why, then, is there so much opposition to the preaching of the Gospel? This is not the place to present a detailed description and analysis of the reasons people oppose the preaching of the Gospel. Such an exercise could be discouraging and distract us from our purpose: Making a case for a renewed commitment to mission and evangelization. We know that opposition to the preaching of the Gospel exists. We can see evidences of it in the reports of protests against Christian missionary thrusts. Whether it is in India or the United States of America, some people seem to be particularly offended when Christians declare their intentions to launch missionary initiatives whereby people are offered the possibility of life in Christ and reconciliation with God. Yet, apparently the same people would not be in favor of curtailing the rights of salespeople, talk show hosts, and others to propagate their ideas or promote their causes. Could it be that opposition to the preaching of the Gospel is owing to the fact that humans prefer error to truth and darkness to light? In any case, opposition alone should not cause Christians to accept the idea that the world no longer needs to hear the Gospel. People everywhere need the Gospel, not because they will accept the Gospel without question or resistance, but because of the Gospel's uniqueness in the way it offers a solution to the human predicament.

None of the problems associated with the human predicament is greater or deeper than our alienation from God, our Maker. Consequently, the greatest human need is reconciliation with God. Only Jesus Christ makes that reconciliation possible. He said: "I am the way and the truth and the life. No one comes to the Father except through me" (John 14:6). Ours is a day "of replacing sin and grace with rich and poor"[4]even in some Christian circles. Poverty and related social ills are considered the most important problems humans face.

It is not surprising, in this context, that some would consider the declaration made by our Lord either irrelevant or an exaggerated claim. It is argued that if one insists on the significance of religion and spirituality, all religions must have validity. Since all religions are equally valid, the argument goes, we should refrain from believing that there can be an exclusive mediation between God and humans. Instead, we are told, we should think that God extends salvation to all. Perhaps Reverend C. Joseph Sprague, a

Methodist bishop from Illinois, offers one of the clearest articulations of this sentiment. Steve Kloehn, the religion writer for the *Chicago Tribune*, reports the following statement made by Sprague: "I'm always fearful when we in the Christian community move beyond the rightful claim that Jesus is decisive for us, to the presupposition that non-Christians . . . are outside of God's plan of salvation. . . . That smacks of a kind of non-Jesus-like arrogance."[5] If Christians agreed with Sprague they would cease all their efforts in mission and evangelism.

Faced with opposition to mission and evangelism even within the ranks of the church, Christians must remember that God is not impressed by one's religion. In fact, the focus on religions as systems to be compared for their merits is an incorrect way of understanding how God relates to humans. God is interested in people and how they relate to him, not in their religious ideas, observances, and systems. Chris Wright accurately summarizes the teaching of the Bible on this when he states that "the Bible is not greatly concerned about religions as systems or structures. It is concerned with human beings before the living God."[6]

God wants to free humans from their alienation. This is what Christians call salvation. No human effort can provide this salvation. Indeed, "Religion does not save anybody—God does."[7] As far as God is concerned, "the hopelessness of the virtuous"[8] is what he sees when he looks at humans and all their religious observances. For God, the religious and the nonreligious, the virtuous and the rascal are all alienated from him and hopeless. And God has chosen to help humans in their hopelessness and save them through Jesus Christ. Since the Gospel tells the story of Jesus Christ, its proclamation to all humans is of utmost importance, because "salvation is found in no one else" (Acts 4:12).

ONLY ONE WAY

The viewpoint advocated here is customarily labeled the "exclusivist" position because it excludes the availability of salvation through other persons or means.[9] "Exclusivists" tend to be branded as intolerant religious bigots and as people whose message produces strife, discord, and violence. In a day when tolerance is perceived as the highest value, especially in religion, this charac-

APOSTLE TO AFRICA

Byang H. Kato descended from a line of fetish priests in the heart of Nigeria and was dedicated by his father to become a fetish priest himself. At age ten he and other boys his age went through the secret initiation rituals of his Jaba tribe. But at age eleven Byang heard the Gospel from an itinerant missionary, and the next year he enrolled in a mission school, where he became a Christian believer.

Gifted with a brilliant mind, Byang pursued higher education in Nigeria, England, and the United States and eventually earned a Th.D. degree with outstanding honors. During that time, he became recognized as an astute leader and a clear-thinking theologian, and at the age of thirty-one he was appointed general secretary of the Evangelical Churches of West Africa (ECWA). A few years later, he was elected general secretary of the Association of Evangelicals of Africa and Madagascar (AEAM) and then in 1974 was appointed secretary of the World Evangelical Fellowship executive council. As such he played a large role in the efforts to preserve evangelical theology in Africa and resist attempts toward a syncretistic "African religion." Although his name was not well-known to laypeople outside Africa, he was having a profound impact on the evangelical church on that continent.

Thus it was a shock for the evangelical world in 1975 when Byang H. Kato, at the age of thirty-nine, drowned one day off the coast of Mombasa, Kenya. Typical was the reaction of Francis Schaeffer, theologian and founder of L'Abri in Switzerland: "I literally wept. The loss for Africa and the Lord's work seemed so great." Yet Kato's vision lives on through other African evangelicals who were inspired and encouraged by his courageous defense of the Gospel of Jesus Christ.

Adapted from "Byang H. Kato: African Prophet"
in *More Than Conquerors,* ed. John D. Woodbridge
(Chicago: Moody Press, 1992), pp. 320–22.

terization of "exclusivists" seals their fate: They must be avoided like the plague; they must be silenced.

One cannot dispute the fact that some "exclusivists" may, indeed, be bigoted and intolerant. One should acknowledge, however, that bigoted and intolerant people are present in many sectors of human society. Moreover, Christians who adopt an "exclusivist" position do so, not because they delight in intolerance, but because they have a passion for Christ and his Gospel. They have come to the conclusion that true allegiance to Jesus Christ requires that they be "Christoexclusivist[s] ... [since] Christ is not only the center—he is the *circumference.* He is the only way to the responsible knowledge of, or participation in, saving truth."[10]

"Exclusivists," like all people, recognize that life is a journey. They agree with Scripture that human beings have veered off course in this journey and are headed in the wrong direction. People "have gone astray, each of us has turned to his own way" (Isa. 53:6); they "have been lost sheep; their shepherds have led them astray" (Jer. 50:6); but God sent his Son, Jesus Christ, "to seek and to save what was lost" (Luke 19:10). Yet multitudes of people continue to follow their own way; some firmly and sincerely believe that they are on the right way. Belief and sincerity are the issues. People can walk into a catastrophic situation by sincerely following their own way if that way is wrong. Such people can avoid catastrophe only by abandoning their way and accepting an alternative one, especially if the alternative way is right. The Gospel is precisely the right way to God. In the Gospel, God says to humans, "This is the way to me, stop following other ways!"

Christians are people who have accepted what God said in the Gospel, have forsaken their wandering ways, and have found *the way* to God through Jesus Christ. They are convinced that the world needs to know about *the way* they found. So when Christians "affirm that Jesus Christ is the only way of salvation, the only mediator between God and humanity" and state that "the Bible offers no hope that sincere worshipers of other religions will be saved without personal faith in Jesus Christ,"[11] they are not motivated by hatred or bigotry. Rather, by these statements Christians seek to clarify to themselves the teachings of Scripture. Furthermore, these statements express the urgency Christians feel about inviting all people to embark on a journey of hope. Indeed, it would be terrible selfishness on the part of Christians if they were to keep the Good News to themselves. Withholding news about the only source of hope of salvation is worse than not sharing information concerning the cure for a dreadful disease. Consequently, proclaiming the Gospel is one of the greatest demonstrations of love toward other human beings because it is the only way of extending God's love to the world (John 3:16).

A PRIVILEGE AND AN OBLIGATION

A Christian realizes that sharing the Gospel of Christ with others is both a wonderful privilege and also a deep obligation. The Statement says precisely this: "To share the joy and hope of this Gospel is a supreme privilege. It is also an abiding obligation." The apostle Paul was convinced of this when he wrote to the Christians in Rome, "I am obligated both to Greeks and non-Greeks, both to the wise and the foolish. That is why I am so eager to preach the gospel also to you who are at Rome" (Rom. 1:14–15). Christians are eager to preach the Gospel, and they do so joyfully because the Gospel is the power of God unto salvation (v. 16). That the power for salvation is found in the Gospel is also the reason why Christians remain under Christ's commission to reach the inhabitants of the whole world.

We must proclaim the Gospel to all people, not only because the church is commanded by God, but also because they have "taste[d] and see[n] that the LORD is good" (Ps. 34:8). The joy of knowing that God is good and encountering him in the person of Jesus Christ, who came to make God known (John 1:18), has motivated countless numbers of Christians in their proclamation of the Gospel. I think of my parents in this respect. They were among the first in their towns to accept the Good News when it was presented there. I recall their anxiety and pain when they would pray for their acquaintances who did not know Christ. I also witnessed their excitement and joy as they shared the Gospel.

They were not coerced into this by powerful, foreign religious zealots. They did it freely because they believed that everybody ought to know the same freedom they found in Christ.

My parents' story is not unique. It is the story of millions of Christians in Africa and elsewhere. For them, proclaiming the Gospel to people near and far is an expression of gratitude to God whose grace they discovered in Jesus Christ.

Christians like my parents are right; they have understood God's plan. They have understood that God commands Christians to keep on forwarding the Gospel to new addresses. In God's plan, people who have received his grace should actively seek to persuade others to accept the divine, free, gracious offer of reconciliation to God in Christ.

SHARING THE GOOD NEWS

Our participation in making the Good News known—or our lack of it—is therefore an indication of our understanding of divine grace. Our activity also expresses the truth that the Gospel must be spoken and heard. The Gospel is not a treasure that must be jealously kept; it is news to be shared. A secret Gospel ceases to be news and loses its goodness. Today the world needs the Good News of Christ because people seem to have lost their optimism concerning unlimited progress and a golden future for all. It is not a time for Christians to retreat into silence. It is time for a renewed commitment to telling the news of Jesus and his love. It is time for telling this story in a new way for varied audiences.

The world needs to hear the Good News of Jesus Christ because only he can liberate people from their propensity to retreat into the isolation of ethnic identities on the one hand and their fear of imperial domination on the other. Many people seek to protect themselves from imperial domination by fighting to maintain or restore their distinct ethnic and religious characteristics. Such people are suspicious of anyone presenting religious propaganda. But the preaching of the Gospel is not mere religious propaganda; it is a call to know God through Jesus Christ. Only the true knowledge of God allows people to see the hideous evils of ethnic isolationism and imperial domination for what they are. Jesus Christ calls people neither to preserve ethnic purity nor to subjugate others, but to worship God "in spirit and in truth" (John 4:24). In Christ, people can worship God that way regardless of ethnicity, social class, gender or economic status. This is wonderful news for people living in a world of increased fragmentation. It is news worth telling again and again.

Christians are entrusted with the preaching of the Gospel to everyone until the end of time. As they do so, they engage in what is important to their Lord. He told his disciples, "This gospel of the kingdom will be preached in the whole world as a testimony to all nations, and then the end will come" (Matt. 24:14). Christians are the agents God has chosen to accomplish this task. They have been preaching this Gospel from the very inception of the church (see Acts 8:12). The church's work of preaching the Gospel to all people continues until the very end. Christians cannot rest as long as the world endures and there are persons in it who do not know God through Christ. May God grant Christians today confidence, faithfulness, and power as they seek to reach all people with the Gospel of God concerning his Son, Jesus Christ.

Notes

1. Chris Wright, "What Difference Does Jesus Make?" *Practicing Truth: Confident Witness in our Pluralistic World*, ed. David W. Shenk and Linford Stutzman (Scottdale, PA: Herald Press, 1999), p. 247. Italics in the original.
2. See Affirmation and Denial #1 in the Statement.
3. See the Preamble and Affirmation and Denial #18.
4. Klaus Bockmühl, "God and Other 'Forgotten Factors' in Theology," *Christianity Today* (February 19, 1982): 48.
5. Steve Kloehn, "Clergy Ask Baptists to Rethink Area Blitz," *Chicago Tribune*, November 28, 1999, sec. 1, p. 17.
6. Wright, "What Difference Does Jesus Make?" p. 246.
7. Ibid., p. 247.
8. Andrew F. Walls, *The Missionary Movement in Christian History: Studies in the Transmission of Faith* (Maryknoll, NY: Orbis Books, 1996), p. 67.

9. *Exclusivism* and *inclusivism* are widely used terms. The first one is "narrow" in that it limits the availability of salvation; the second one is "broad" in that it agrees that all religions are means of salvation. The terms are not necessarily the best or the most accurate portrayals of Christian viewpoints and biblical teaching. I have kept *exclusivism* because this is the label generally attached to the position advocated here."

10. F. Dale Bruner, "Is Jesus Inclusive or Exclusive," *Theology, News and Notes* (October 1999): 4. Italics in the original.

11. Affirmation and Denial #4.

Study Questions

1. What does it mean to you to "have confidence in the Gospel"?
2. How would you respond if someone told you that all religions have validity?
3. What motivates you most to share the Gospel with others?
4. Why is sharing the Gospel with others both an obligation and a privilege?

To share the joy and hope of this Gospel is a supreme privilege. It is also an abiding obligation, for the Great Commission of Jesus Christ still stands: proclaim the Gospel everywhere, he said, teaching, baptizing, and making disciples.

■

We affirm that Jesus Christ commands his followers to proclaim the Gospel to all living persons, evangelizing everyone everywhere, and discipling believers within the fellowship of the church. A full and faithful witness to Christ includes the witness of personal testimony, godly living, and acts of mercy and charity to our neighbor, without which the preaching of the Gospel appears barren.

We deny that the witness of personal testimony, godly living, and acts of mercy and charity to our neighbors constitutes evangelism apart from the proclamation of the Gospel.

—The Gospel of Jesus Christ: An Evangelical Celebration

10

HOW CAN I SHARE MY FAITH WITH OTHERS?

Lee Strobel

It was a hectic and harried day at the newspaper where I worked as an editor. Several major stories erupted shortly before deadline. Reporters scurried around as they frantically tried to squeeze information out of uncooperative sources. With their emotions frayed, just about everyone lost their tempers.

On many days the stress of daily journalism had caused me to lose my composure, too. But as a fairly new Christian, I chose on this day to fervently pray for God's help. Thanks to him, I was like an island of calm amidst the chaos of the day.

After the last story was edited, I slumped back in my chair, weary but grateful. I knew that without God's intervention I could never have remained composed on my own.

Looking up, I saw my boss standing over my desk. "Strobel, how did you get through the day without blowing your top?" he asked. Then, apparently suspecting a connection with my faith, he added: "What's this Christianity thing to you?"

Nobody had ever asked me that before. For a moment I froze. I didn't know what to say or how to say it. I was afraid I would utter the wrong words. I was fearful of embarrassing myself or having him make fun of me. But I made the split-second choice to take a spiritual risk and tell him about my faith in Jesus.

We ended up talking for forty-five minutes. I fumbled around quite a bit and wasn't as clear or concise as I should have been, but I managed to explain how I had met Jesus Christ and how he had changed my life and eternity. And an amazing thing happened.

When I emerged, I was thoroughly invigorated. There were no words to adequately describe the fulfillment and thrill I felt in having been used by God to communicate his message of forgiveness and hope to someone who was far from him. The closest analogy would be to say that my entire life up to that point had been like a movie shot in very grainy black-and-white film with scratchy sound—but that forty-five minutes was in vivid technicolor with rich Dolby stereo!

Have you ever taken the opportunity to share your faith with someone who does not know Jesus personally? If not, you are missing one of the most humbling experiences and exciting adventures of Christianity: communicating the only message in the world that can rewrite a person's eternal destination.

Jesus was crystal clear about his mission: "For the Son of Man came to seek and to save what was lost" (Luke 19:10). He wants you to join in that mission. He told his followers: "As the Father has sent me, I am sending you" (John 20:21). As the Statement points out, we have both "a supreme privilege" and "an abiding obligation" as followers of Jesus to be his ambassadors to a world that is in desperate need of his saving grace.

It is comforting to know that the power of the Gospel doesn't ultimately rest on our eloquence, techniques, or persuasion. God is, after all, the supreme evangelist; it is the Holy Spirit who is responsible for convicting people of sin and drawing them into

God's kingdom. Yet God has chosen to use ordinary people like you and me to be his servants in this extraordinary drama of human redemption. As the Statement affirms, we should be ready at all times to actively participate in the global effort to "proclaim the Gospel to all living persons, evangelizing everyone everywhere."

Perhaps you have shied away from sharing your faith because, like me in the newsroom, you have felt ill-prepared. I have found that we are much more apt to get involved in talking about Jesus if we are equipped to do so. And there are eight steps we can take to be ready when God opens up opportunities for us to experience the life-changing adventure of personal evangelism.

We will never fully embody each of these steps, but as we grow in these areas we will find ourselves more and more willing to reach out to people who are not yet part of God's family. The result: fresh purpose for life, new growth in our spiritual development, a unique sense of fulfillment—and more people hearing about God's plan of salvation.

STEP 1: ASK GOD TO INCREASE YOUR LOVE FOR LOST PEOPLE

Jesus demonstrated deep compassion for people who were alienated from God. He wept over Jerusalem because he envisioned all the sheep without a shepherd. In Luke 15 he told three rapid-fire parables about a lost coin, a wayward sheep, and a prodigal son to make it abundantly clear that lost people matter to God.

Each day, countless people pass through our lives, but we will not be motivated to reach out to them with the Gospel until we see them through heaven's eyes—as sinners by both birth and choice, yet people who are nevertheless engraved with the image of God and valued by him.

Unlike Jesus, our hearts tend to develop calluses toward "outsiders." Sometimes we slip into an "us versus them" mentality, as if they're the enemy. But they weren't viewed that way by Jesus. His primary emotion toward them was love—even to the point of dying for them on the cross. As Romans 5:8 says, "But God demonstrates his own love for us in this: While we were still sinners, Christ died for us."

Pause for a moment and ask yourself: Is your heart compassionate toward spiritually lost people? Do you care about their eternal destination? If not, there are two things you can do to help reverse the heart disease that may be afflicting you.

First, spend time reading about Jesus' attitude toward people outside God's family. Linger over John 4, where he purposefully breached Jewish custom by interacting with a reviled Samaritan woman, or the trilogy of parables in Luke 15, or the Beatitudes in Matthew 5, where he offered hope and tenderness to the brokenhearted and downtrodden of his day. Peruse the Gospels and take special note of how Jesus behaved toward lost people.

Second, ask God to instill in your heart a renewed passion for the spiritual cynics, skeptics, and seekers of your world. Tell him you want to have the same kind of concern, empathy, and sacrificial love that he expressed toward the people he met. After all, what prayer could be more squarely within the will of God than that?

STEP 2: PRAY CONSISTENTLY FOR THE SPIRITUALLY LOST

As British pastor John Stott has pointed out, Jesus' prayers for the lost continued right up until his last moments on the cross. "Jesus seems to have prayed for his tormentors actually while the iron spikes were being driven through his hands and feet; indeed, the imperfect tense (of the original Greek) suggests that he kept praying, kept repeating his entreaty, 'Father, forgive them; for they know not what they do.'"[1]

So consider this question: Are you praying *consistently*, *specifically*, and *fervently* for lost people in your life? Are you praying that God would pull them toward himself; open their eyes to the emptiness of life without him; help them see their need for forgiveness; remove the confusion they have about him and the life he offers; help them grasp the meaning and importance of the cross of Christ; and open their heart to his love and truth? Are you praying that God would open up opportunities for you to share your faith with them?

You can begin by writing down the names of three people in your sphere of influence who are far from God and then committing yourself to praying regularly for them.

One time as I was about to baptize a woman in front of a large crowd at church, I turned to her husband, who was standing with her. "Have you given your life to Jesus?" I asked him.

This tough construction worker stunned me when he burst out crying. "No," he sobbed, "but I want to right now." So I prayed with him to receive Christ as his forgiver and leader, and then I baptized the two of them together.

As the service ended, a woman ran up to me, threw her arms around me, and kept saying through her tears, "Nine years! Nine years! Nine years!"

She was the man's sister. She and her sister-in-law had been praying for him for nine long years, seeing no glimmer of spiritual interest on his part. But they persevered and kept praying. "And look what God did today!" she exclaimed.

You may have been praying for a spouse, a parent, a child, or a friend for a lot longer than nine years. Maybe you have lost heart. But if you were to ask those two women, they would tell you never to give up hope and never stop praying!

STEP 3: REACH OUT IN A WAY THAT FITS WHO YOU ARE

My friend, Mark Mittelberg, lost his enthusiasm for evangelism when he spent the summer serving in a church whose main outreach strategy was to knock on doors of strangers and try to talk to them about Jesus. Some Christians thrive in this approach. But although Mark desperately wanted to help people come to faith in Christ, he found this strategy extremely difficult and uncomfortable for him.

Today, however, he is a leading writer, speaker, and trainer on evangelism. What happened to change his attitude? He discovered that there are different styles of sharing the faith. When he learned that he could reach out to others in a way that is consistent with the personality and temperament God has given him, he became an influential evangelist who has led many people to Christ.

Six styles are identified in a book Mark coauthored with Bill Hybels. It is important to understand that all Christians should be able to testify to God's work in their lives, answer questions about the faith, and point people toward God by serving them. However, some people are especially effective in certain areas because of their personalities. Consider which of these approaches resonates with you:

- **The Confrontational Style**, exemplified by Peter in Acts 2, where he boldly accuses a crowd of murdering the Messiah. People with this style tend to be confident, assertive, and direct.
- **The Intellectual Style**, illustrated by Paul in Acts 17, where he reasons with philosophers in Athens. Those with this style are inquisitive, analytical, and logical.
- **The Testimonial Style**, shown in John 9 by the blind man who was healed by Jesus and then declared, "One thing I do know. I was blind but now I see!" (v. 25). People with this style are particularly adept at being clear communicators, effective storytellers, and good listeners.
- **The Interpersonal Style**, lived out by the disciple Matthew, who threw a party where his sinful tax-collecting friends could rub shoulders with Jesus and his followers (Luke 5:29). People with this style are warm, conversational, and friendship oriented.
- **The Invitation Style**, illustrated by the woman at the well in John 4, who runs into town to invite people to come meet Jesus. People with this style are good at bringing non-Christians to places where they can hear the Gospel. They tend to be hospitable, relational, and persuasive.
- **The Serving Style**, exemplified by Dorcas in Acts 9, who made clothing for the widows of her community. Those with this style are particularly able to evangelize through the way they provide practical assistance to people. They are generally others-centered, humble, and patient.[2]

When my friend Mark discovered he has the intellectual style, he immediately felt motivated and liberated to further develop that approach so he could reach out to people who have questions or objections concerning Christianity. Perhaps you, too, will find freedom in knowing that you can be yourself while sharing your faith in a way that is natural to you.

STEP 4: BUILD BRIDGES OF FRIENDSHIP WITH LOST PEOPLE

Some non-Christians are reached through impersonal styles of evangelism, such as billboards, mass mailings, and door-to-door efforts. Today many people seem impervious to these strategies, yet they remain receptive to hearing about Jesus from friends with whom they have a trust-filled relationship.

Jesus was a friend of sinners who spent time with lost people. When the tax collector Zacchaeus called out to him, Jesus invited himself over for a meal (Luke 19:1–9). While the disciples went into town to get food, Jesus lingered at Jacob's Well to get to know a Samaritan woman who was leading an immoral life (John 4). As we develop authentic relationships with spiritually lost people, we can build trust with them, listen to their questions and concerns, and get into spiritual conversations through which we can share the Gospel.

Think about the three people for whom you are praying regularly. Are there ways you can purposefully deepen your friendship with them so that God might open up opportunities for you to share your faith in an environment of love and trust? Here are a few tips to keep in mind:

- *Have a no-strings-attached attitude.* Enter into these relationships with the approach that you are going to be their friend regardless of whether they ever make a decision to follow Jesus. Otherwise, they will feel like an evangelistic project instead of someone you authentically care about.
- *Drop hints early that you are a Christian.* You will be surprised at how often they will bring up spiritual topics if they are aware that you take your faith seriously. For instance, merely mentioning that you regularly attend church can set the groundwork for a future discussion about God.

- *Spend time together.* Include your friends in activities you are already planning to do, such as going to sporting events or dining out. Look for interests that you have in common and build on those in strengthening your relationship.
- *Cultivate the art of listening.* Put the other people first in your relationship by caring about their attitudes, issues, and questions. As you listen to their concerns, you will better understand how to get into a conversation about Christianity. For example, if they have been talking about certain fears about life, you can easily segue into talking about how God has helped you deal with anxieties.

We need to be careful to always be the dominant spiritual influence in the relationship and not get pulled into activities that would violate God's teachings. But as we take relational risks and cultivate honest and heartfelt friendships with spiritually lost people, we will often find that they are open and willing to hear about our faith.[3]

STEP 5: DON'T JUST SHARE YOUR FAITH—SHOW IT

We show our faith in at least two ways. First, we can live a humble, honest, authentic, surrendered Christian life. Nonbelievers are constantly scanning Christians with their "hypocrisy radar," looking for excuses to reject them, their church, and the Gospel. Our words carry much more weight when they are backed up by a lifestyle that reflects the love and teachings of Jesus.

As one non-Christian put it: "I'm not looking for perfect, but I am looking for real. Integrity is the word that comes to mind. I need to hear real people talk about real life, and I need to know if God is—or can be—a part of real life." This young woman, who had been poisoned against God by inauthentic Christians, eventually gave her life to Christ after encountering Christians whose lives of grace were consistent with Christ's message of grace.

Second, we can show our faith by serving neighbors and strangers in practical ways. Jesus said, "For even the Son of Man did not come to be served, but to serve, and to give his life as a ransom for many" (Mark 10:45). He served the blind by granting them sight, he served lepers by restoring their health, he served the disciples by calming the sea, he served thousands of people on a hillside by multiplying the fish and bread, and in the ultimate act of servanthood, he gave his life to pay for the sins of the world.

Jesus tells us in Matthew 5:16: "Let your light shine before men, that they may see your good deeds and praise your Father in heaven." By "good deeds" he meant acts of servanthood that are winsome and that prompt people to turn their eyes heavenward in search of the One who motivates such countercultural compassion and kindness.

So look at the spiritually lost people around you and ask, *What specific need can I help meet in that person's life?* As the Statement reminds us, a full and faithful witness to Christ includes "godly living, and acts of mercy and charity to our neighbor, without which the preaching of the Gospel appears barren."

STEP 6: BE READY TO TELL OTHERS HOW YOU MET GOD

Once I was listening as a newspaper reporter interviewed a pastor for a story he was writing about our church. Suddenly the journalist turned to me and asked, "So, Lee, what's your story?"

Freeze that scene for a moment. If someone were to unexpectedly ask you to recount how you became a Christian, could you tell him clearly and concisely? I was glad someone had earlier challenged me to be ready to tell the story of my spiritual journey in a simple but compelling way. So I was ready. The reporter responded by printing it in the newspaper for thousands to see.

Several times in addressing nonbelievers, Paul told the story of how he first encountered Jesus and how his life had been changed forever. While our testimony might not be as dramatic as Paul's, each of us has a story about how we became followers of Christ. When we have a trusting relationship with a lost person, he or she is usually very interested in hearing about it—especially if we can tell it succinctly and relate it to our listener's personal situation.

So take time to think through your story of coming to Christ. Try the three-point outline that Paul used when speaking to King Agrippa in Acts 26:

- **Point 1: What your life was like before Christ.** What was your spiritual attitude prior to the time you became a Christian? What issues did you struggle with? What prompted you to consider Christianity?
- **Point 2: How you became a Christian.** Specifically, how did you pray to receive Jesus as your forgiver and leader?
- **Point 3: How your life is different now.** How has your life begun to change? In what way has God helped you with the issues you struggled with before you became a Christian?

You can unify your story by emphasizing a theme that began before you encountered God, and which he resolved or is helping resolve, now that you're in a relationship with him. For example, perhaps before you were a Christian you struggled with rejection, but now you are able to relax in God's unconditional love. Maybe you once felt hopeless regret over the sins you had committed, but now God has flowed a sense of forgiveness and peace into your life. It could be that you wrestled with anxiety over the brevity of life, but now you are resting confidently in God's promise of eternity in heaven. Be careful not to exaggerate by saying God instantly solved all your emotional struggles. Instead, talk with honest and authenticity about how God has been helping you.

If you became a Christian as a youngster, you won't have much to say about what your life was like before you encountered Christ. However, you can talk about what your life might have been like if you had never become a Christian. You know the areas where you are easily tempted; these provide clues to the direction your life would have headed if you had never become a follower of Jesus.

Most of all, be yourself. Don't preach or slip into stilted Christian language or clichés. You might want to write out your story and let a friend read it and give you suggestions about how you can be more concrete and concise. See if you can hone it down so you can tell it in three or four minutes.

Once you feel confident in relating your spiritual journey to others, your apprehension over sharing your faith will probably diminish. That is especially true when you spend some time mastering the next step as well.

STEP 7: BE PREPARED TO EXPLAIN GOD'S MESSAGE

I could take you to the very spot where someone explained to me for the first time how a person becomes a Christian. With clarity and simplicity, Bill Hybels spelled out precisely how I could commit my life to Christ. It took him only a few minutes to cut through twenty-eight years of ambiguity, misinformation, and confusion. While I wasn't at the point yet of wanting to receive Christ, at least I knew what step to take when I was ready.

As Christians we need to be prepared to explain the Gospel at a moment's notice. I remember the time I was showing some fellow journalists the slides of a trip I had taken to India. The photos included baptisms in the Krishna River, and I explained that these people had just become Christians.

At the end, one reporter asked, "What do you mean they 'became Christians'? How does a person become a Christian?"

Glancing at the clock, I saw that I only had a few minutes to explain the Gospel before we had to return to work. I was thankful someone had previously trained me to articulate God's plan of salvation in an easy-to-understand way.

Numerous illustrations are popularly used to communicate the essentials of the Gospel. While none is able to fully explain all the theological nuances of conversion, they can be useful in summarizing how nonbelievers can commit their lives to Jesus if they are ready to do so.

One easy-to-master explanation is called the Roman Road, because it uses three verses from Romans. You can mark these verses in your Bible and commit them to memory. Here is what you might say:

- Romans 3:23: *For all have sinned and fall short of the glory of God.* "The Bible tells us that *all* have fallen short. I've certainly sinned. Would you agree that you have, too?"

- Romans 6:23: *For the wages of sin is death, but the gift of God is eternal life in Christ Jesus our Lord.* "We both just admitted we have sinned and fallen short. This verse shows we're in a real predicament, because *the wages of sin is death*, or eternal separation from God. In other words, this is what we have earned as a result of falling short. On our own, we're totally without hope."
- "The good news comes in the second half of the verse. We don't have to suffer this spiritual death on account of our sins, because *the gift of God is eternal life in Christ Jesus our Lord.* He lived a perfect life and died on the cross as our substitute to pay the penalty for all our wrongdoing. He graciously offers us forgiveness and heaven as a gift—one that we could never earn or obtain on our own. But it is not enough just to know this; we have to act on it."
- Romans 10:13: *Everyone who calls on the name of the Lord will be saved.* "This verse shows that if we are willing to humbly receive Jesus as our forgiver and leader, then we will be saved. Are you ready to take this step?"

A second illustration is called "Do Versus Done." You pique the person's curiosity by saying that there's a big difference between "religion" and "Christianity." You might say:

> Religion is spelled D-O—people *do* good deeds, like praying, being nice to others, or giving money to the poor, in order to try to earn their way to heaven. The problem is, they never know how many good deeds they need to do. Even worse, the Bible says they can never do enough to merit eternal life.
>
> But Christianity is spelled D-O-N-E. Jesus has *done* for us what we could never do for ourselves. He lived the perfect life and died as our substitute to pay for all of our wrongdoing. But merely knowing is not enough. We must receive Jesus as our forgiver and leader. Are you ready to take that step?

Notice that at the end of each illustration, the person is given an opportunity to act on what you have just explained. If she responds affirmatively, you can lead her in a prayer in which she confesses and repents of her sins, receives God's forgiveness and cleansing, and commits herself to following Jesus as Lord.

Often, however, the other person's spiritual progress is being blocked by questions. For instance, she may wonder why you believe the Bible is true or why there's so much suffering in the world if God is loving and powerful. First Peter 3:15 says, "Always be prepared to give an answer to everyone who asks you to give the reason for the hope that you have."

While we need to be ready with answers to their questions, sometimes people will raise an issue you are not familiar with. If so, don't panic. Sometimes the best response is simply to say, "That's a great question, and frankly, I don't have a great explanation for you right now. But if you're willing to keep an open mind, I'll help you get an answer." Then explore with the person some good Christian books that offer replies to the most common inquiries concerning the faith.[4]

These seven steps can equip you and put you in a position to be able to share your faith in Christ. Yet there remains one crucial step that will help you turn good intentions into real action.

STEP 8: TAKE RISKS TO REACH PEOPLE WITH THE GOSPEL

Jesus was willing to take risks to reach out to people who were outside the family of God. Interacting with the Samaritan woman in John 4 was a tremendous social risk, since Jews didn't talk to Samaritan women, especially ones who had led such immoral lives. And Jesus risked his reputation by inviting himself to Zacchaeus's house. Luke 19:7 says, "All the people saw this and began to mutter, 'He has gone to be the guest of a "sinner."'"

We need to be willing to take risks as well. In fact, don't wait until you are faced with a split-second opportunity to share your faith and then try to decide whether you will take a spiritual risk. Usually, that's too late. You will hesitate, and the window of opportunity will close before you act.

Instead, decide right now. Resolve today that when you are faced with a choice either to play it safe or to take a risk by going down the spiritual road, you will choose the spiritual path.

I will never forget the elderly man who approached me during the third week of an evangelism course I was teaching at church. He told me he had visited a woman from his trailer park who had been in the hospital.

TO THE ENDS OF THE EARTH

Billy Graham's name keeps appearing on lists of the most admired people in the world. The lad born on a dairy farm in North Carolina became an evangelist, and it is commonly held that he has preached the Gospel in person to more people than anyone else ever. He is a friend of presidents and royalty, has preached on every continent but Antarctica, and has proclaimed the Gospel to hundreds of millions of others on radio and television.

Many stories can be (and have been) told that illustrate the kind of impact William Franklin Graham has had in the cause of spreading the Gospel of Jesus Christ. One venture in India is typical. Billy's first trip to Asia, in 1956, included a crusade in Kottayam in southern India. Girls, with only baskets to remove the dirt, had carved out a giant amphitheater on the side of a hill—three tiers. Kottayam had only about 50,000 people, yet 25,000 showed up at a preliminary service that had gotten almost no publicity. At the first scheduled meeting the next night, 75,000 came. The people who attended the meetings were all dressed in white. They brought palm leaves to sit on. Many who came a long distance brought their own food.

Billy and several of his staff stayed in the home of Bishop Jacob, the highly respected leader of the Church of South India. While they liked the idea of

"She wasn't a Christian, and while I was talking with her, I could have easily brought up spiritual matters," he said. "I mean, the door was open several times. But I played it safe. When I got home, I was so angry with myself that I decided to go back in a couple of days and take the risk. But then I got a phone call; it turned out that she had died."

He looked at me with great pain on his face and said: "Keep telling people, when those split-second decisions come—take a deep breath, trust God, and take the spiritual road!"

When someone at work asks what you did over the weekend, you are faced with a split-second opportunity. You can either play it safe by saying, "I washed the car, watched football on TV, and went out to dinner," or you can take a spiritual risk by saying, "I

staying in a private residence, they had second thoughts when the bishop informed them some snake charmers had captured twenty-six cobras in his yard the week before! But the bishop assured them that the cobras seldom came into the house. On their first night in the home, Billy and the others were awakened about four in the morning by amplified music blaring outside. As Billy describes it, "I had been dreaming I was on an airplane, and when this booming started, I thought the plane had crashed. When I looked out of my window, I realized that the music was coming from the roughly 5,000 people who had already gathered for a prayer service."

The numbers grew with each evangelistic service, and on the last night the total reached 100,000. Within just a few days, a third of a million people had heard the Gospel. The truth fell on open ears and hearts. In Billy's words, "Any doubts I might have had about the relevancy of the Cross in a cultural setting so different from everything I had known were instantly dispelled." The Gospel of Christ knows no barrier, cultural, linguistic, or otherwise.

—Adapted from Billy Graham, *Just As I Am: The Autobiography of Billy Graham* (New York and Grand Rapids: Harper Collins and Zondervan, 1997), pp. 268–70.

washed the car, watched football on TV, went out to dinner, and I heard a terrific sermon at church about the purpose of life. Do you ever think about stuff like that?"

A friend once told me, "What's the worst possible thing that could happen? They might say, 'Thanks, but I'm not interested.' Is that really going to shatter your life? Christians in the first century were dipped in tar, set ablaze, and hung on posts to light garden parties at night because they shared their faith. It isn't the end of the world if someone says to you, 'No thanks, I don't want to hear about Jesus.'"

The unparalleled adventure of evangelism begins when you are equipped to share your faith and then take risks to do it. Ask God to give you the attitude of the apostle Paul, who wrote, "Telling the Good News is my duty—something I must do" (1 Cor. 9:16 NCV). It's a responsibility—and an incredible privilege—that each Christian shares. Once you begin to live out the evangelistic mission God has given you, you will never want to go back to being a mere armchair spectator in the most important enterprise on the planet.

Notes

1. John Stott, *The Message of the Sermon on the Mount* (Downers Grove, IL: InterVarsity Press, 1985), p. 119.

2. Bill Hybels and Mark Mittelberg, *Becoming a Contagious Christian* (Grand Rapids: Zondervan, 1994), pp. 119–32. For a diagnostic tool and further teaching, see the *Becoming a Contagious Christian Training Course* (Grand Rapids: Zondervan, 1995).

3. A belief in pluralism as an obstacle to the Gospel is mentioned elsewhere in this book. Perhaps one benefit of pluralism when Christians want to share their faith is that it can give people an openness to hearing the Gospel of Jesus Christ.

4. For example, see Paul Little, *Know Why You Believe* (Downers Grove, IL: InterVarsity Press, 1988); Cliffe Knechtle, *Give Me an Answer* (Downers Grove, IL: InterVarsity Press, 1986); Lee Strobel, *The Case for Christ* (Grand Rapids: Zondervan, 1998) and *The Case for Faith* (Grand Rapids: Zondervan, 2000); Norman Geisler and Ronald Brooks, *When Skeptics Ask: A Handbook on Christian Evidences* (Wheaton, IL: Victor Books, 1990); and R. C. Sproul, *Reason to Believe* (Grand Rapids: Zondervan, 1982).

Study Questions

1. Like a fuel gauge on a car, imagine a meter that measures the condition of your heart toward non-Christians: 0 means a granite-hard heart, 10 a compassionate heart like Jesus'. What would your gauge register? What are some concrete steps you can take to develop an attitude more like Jesus'?
2. Which of the six evangelism styles seems to fit you the best? Can you think of three ways you could further develop this style in your own life?
3. Using the outline suggested in this chapter, write out the story of how you became a Christian. Ask a Christian friend to give you feedback and then make the appropriate revisions. Then pray for and look for an opportunity to tell your story to a non-Christian friend this week.
4. Identify three non-Christians in your sphere of relationships. In addition to praying consistently for them, what actions can you take to deepen your friendship with them, as suggested in steps 4 and 5?
5. Practice both the Roman Road and the Do Versus Done illustrations verbally with a Christian friend. Ask for suggestions on how to improve the way you relate them.
6. Can you identify times when you could easily have taken a risk and gotten into a spiritual conversation with someone? How might you handle the situation differently today?

All Christians are called to unity in love and unity in truth. As evangelicals who derive our very name from the Gospel, we celebrate this great good news of God's saving work in Jesus Christ as the true bond of Christian unity, whether among organized churches and denominations or in the many transdenominational cooperative enterprises of Christians together.

The Bible declares that all who truly trust in Christ and his Gospel are sons and daughters of God through grace, and hence are our brothers and sisters in Christ.

■

We affirm that the doctrine of the imputation (reckoning or counting) both of our sins to Christ and his righteousness to us, whereby our sins are fully forgiven and we are fully accepted, is essential to the biblical Gospel (2 Cor. 5:19–21).

We deny that we are justified by the righteousness of Christ infused into us or by any righteousness that is thought to inhere within us.

—*The Gospel of Jesus Christ:*
An Evangelical Celebration

11

THE EVANGELICAL FAMILY

ITS BLESSINGS AND BOUNDARIES

When our children were small, Thanksgiving celebrations were held at my sister's home in the country. The wonderful smells of the turkey in the oven and pies and baked goods made a perfect backdrop to the happy noise of the children's playing and the adults' newsy chatter. It was one of the highlights of the year for all of us. On one occasion, my four-year-old niece, beaming with delight, said, "Aren't we having a good time of familyship?"

There is something wonderful about getting along. Families, congregations, and friendships that are free of conflict nourish and refresh the soul. And it is not just the absence of conflict. It is the joy of commonality, of sharing common experiences, common interests, common passions, and mutual commitments that connect us at the deepest levels and provide an ongoing flow of the joy and satisfaction of true companionship.

The psalmist had it right when he wrote,

> How good and pleasant it is
> when brothers live together in unity!
> It is like precious oil poured on the head,
> running down on the beard,
> running down on Aaron's beard,
> down upon the collar of his robes.
> It is as if the dew of Hermon
> were falling on Mount Zion.
> For there the LORD bestows his blessing,
> even life forevermore (Psalm 133:1–3).

The imagery of this text is profound. In the ancient world, people celebrated guests of honor by anointing them with oil. The more highly honored the guest, the more expensive the oil. Expensive oils were filled with exotic aromatic herbs. And these anointings were not sparse ceremonial sprinklings. The richly fragrant oils would be generously poured on the head of the guest, running down onto his robes. For days and even weeks later the robes of the anointed one would carry the fragrance of the honor, thereby blessing others who found themselves in their company.

The psalmist refers to the anointing of Aaron, which was an Old Testament symbol of the highest level of the priesthood. It was the clearest statement yet of God's presence among his people in terms of a human mediator. To the psalmist, oneness among God's people is like the fragrance of expensive oils anointing the presence of God in our midst and thereby blessing all who come near.

The second metaphor is equally instructive. In the psalmist's day, Mount Hermon was covered with snow most of the year. As the day dawned, the warmth of the sun melted the snow and the wind would spread condensing moisture in a plentiful dew that watered the barrenness of the surrounding land. This is a picture of the bountiful blessing that unity brings to dry and undernourished hearts. We must remind ourselves that throughout the history of the church, barren and broken lives have found refreshment in the community of belief. The church at its best is a place where we bind one another's wounds and share the salve of unifying love with barren, hurting souls.

The psalmist clearly knew what most of us already know, that harmony in relationships is one of life's greatest rewards.

UNITY: ITS BEARING ON DISCIPLESHIP AND WITNESS

But oneness is not important just because it is fulfilling and satisfying to us. It is important because of what it means to God. It should give us pause to read that "there are six things the Lord hates, seven that are detestable to him" (Prov. 6:16). The last item on the list is "a man who stirs up dissension among brothers" (v. 19). The sobering thing about the statement is that it's not just the division that deeply offends God but also the person who perpetrates this behavior. It is as though God says, "If you are so proud and self-absorbed that you would drive a brother or sister from you and from one another, then I will separate myself from you as well."

Other passages that underscore God's love for unity abound. In John 13:34–35 Jesus transitions the old command that we should "love the Lord your God and your neighbor as yourself" to a deeper, more intimate application. He tells us that we are to love one another as he has loved us. This implies that Christ's love for us and our love for one another are inseparably linked.

But then Christ ups the ante by adding that when we show this Christlike, unifying love to one another, it will be the proof of the authenticity of our claim that we are followers of Christ. We have unfortunately come to believe that a watching world will know that we are Christians by the worldly things we avoid or by the churchy things we do. Christ has a different perspective. Our identity with him is marked by the oneness that comes from our mutual love for each other.

Not only is our unity important to God as a witness to a watching world, but it also provides tangible evidence that Jesus Christ is indeed the One sent by him (John 17:21). In addition, Paul argues that unity across normally impenetrable lines is one of the fundamental outcomes of our being in Christ. He writes that having "clothed yourselves with Christ. There is neither Jew nor Greek, slave nor free, male nor female, for you are all one in Christ Jesus" (Gal. 3:27–28). Later in the book Paul adds, "For in Christ Jesus neither circumcision nor uncircumcision has any value. The only thing that counts is faith expressing itself through love" (Gal. 5:6).

The scandalous divisions at the church in Corinth occupy a major portion of Paul's remedial instructions in 1 Corinthians. He caps the call for oneness in chapter 13 with a poetic treatise on the useless emptiness of loveless lives and the beauty and attractive qualities of a life that is committed to love. He concludes by saying that these three ultimate principles prevail; faith, hope, and love. But, he says, the greatest of these is love.

If our hearts do not strive for unity with brothers and sisters in Christ we have stepped out of the mainstream of unifying love that flows from the heart of God.

HINDRANCES TO UNITY

Setting our hearts on unity, however, is not always an easy thing. Preferences, personalities, traditions, temperaments, offenses, pride, desire for power and platform, and a host of other worldly pests lurk in the bushes of life waiting to ambush our togetherness. Even the most committed among the followers of Christ are not exempt from the seduction of divisive impulses. One of the most telling moments for the disciples—who had given up everything to follow Christ—was the event recorded in Matthew 20. The mother of James and John came to Jesus and asked that her sons be allowed to occupy the positions of power and prestige in the coming kingdom. The reaction among the other ten disciples was less than admirable; when they heard the request, they were moved with indignation. It may be that they, too, wanted to have the power and platform, but James and John had beaten them to the punch. In fact, these brothers had leveraged the situation way out of bounds by having their mother make the request. The same kind of divisive capacity of the desire for power and recognition has left the landscape of the church littered with stories of personal jealousies and broken fellowship.

Nor is our propensity toward prejudice a friend of unity. For Christ to talk to the woman at the well (John 4) was a bold and tradition-shattering statement about the worth and dignity of everyone across gender, racial, and moral lines. Returning from a trip into town to get food, the disciples were mortified that Christ would be speaking to a woman of Samaria. Their consternation would have deepened had they known about her promiscuous lifestyle. They were not the last persons among Christ's followers to find themselves far from the heart of Christ by living inside the divisive walls of prejudice.

Other potentially divisive influences are exclusivist attitudes of denominations and a variety of theological systems. It is not hard to see why oneness seems to be such an illusive dream—one that always gives way to the nightmare of broken fellowship, which in turn offends Christ.

UNITY AND TRUTH

Nonetheless, it must be noted that there is a refreshing wind blowing today. In the five decades of my walk with Christ, I don't know when I have ever heard more talk among God's people about unity. But as refreshing as this wind may be, we must sound a cautionary note. A wind that blows too hard can inflict serious damage. As I measure the velocity of the wind, it seems as though we are beginning to incur some damage.

As important as unity is, it is not our most important value. Jesus Christ taught that truth transcends unity as a priority. It is critical to recall that in Christ's high priestly prayer, before he prayed that we would be one, he prayed that we would be set apart in the truth (John 17:17). From God's point of view, truth is not only more important than unity but is in fact the basis for unity. The Bible does not know a unity that is just for unity's sake. Authentic Christian unity is a unity forged in a common cause, a common conviction, a common interest. Biblical unity is forged in our mutual bondedness to the truth in Christ, "the way and the truth and the life" (John 14:6). When we embrace the truth, we are free to embrace one another in the truth.

Admittedly, this is not always an easy course. Many factors work against the biblical prerequisite of truth as the ground for authentic unity. For instance, living in a culture that is philosophically dominated by postmodernity creates for us a huge challenge. Relativism long ago took away any notion of absolutes. Pluralism has taught our culture to believe that there is no ultimate truth, or as Francis Schaeffer would say, no "true truth." The gospel according to pluralism says that everyone is entitled to his or her own truth claims. If you can validate a particular thought in your own worldview, then that thought can weigh in as truth for you. Postmodernity has followed this relativism and pluralism by

A SHINING LIGHT

In Peru, the guerilla group known as The Shining Path was greatly agitated by the advance of the Gospel among Indian tribes. One night an assassin from the Shining Path knocked on the door of a pastor's home and asked if the pastor were in the house. Rómulo Sauñe (1953–1992), who was in the house, responded through the closed door that the minister was not at home.

The next morning the assassin returned and knocked on the door again. When Rómulo opened the door, the assassin told him that he had actually come the night before to kill him. But earlier, in attempting to ingratiate himself with the Christians in Rómulo's church, the assassin had attended services and even memorized Scripture. Now he confessed to Rómulo what the effect of the Word of God had been on his soul: "Last night I was tortured by those Bible verses that I had learned. They were like a hammer pounding inside my head. Finally I couldn't stand it anymore. So this morning I decided to come and talk with you about your faith, about your God. I don't want to kill you anymore."

The assassin became a Christian. Rómulo declared, "God's Word says that the angels rejoice when someone enters the kingdom of God."

Why was Rómulo targeted by the guerilla group? He was known as a heartfelt evangelist and as a leader in the distribution of the Bible and other deconstructing reason and logic and revising history to be interpreted according to one's politically correct agenda.

Presenting the precept that truth is the grounds for unity makes little sense in the mindset of a non-truth, subjective, self-

Christian literature to the Ayacucho, his people. On June 23, 1992, the World Evangelical Fellowship awarded Rómulo the Religious Liberty Award in Manila, the Philippines. But back home, just a few weeks later, on September 5, Rómulo was slain by the guerillas. One killer commented, "We finally got him." Yes, they "got him," but not in the ultimate sense. The killer did not understand that the Christian who dies for Christ and His Gospel is never defeated. The apostle Paul wrote, "For to me, to live is Christ and to die is gain" (Phil. 1:21).

Rómulo Sauñe knew very well that following Jesus Christ could cost him his life, yet he joyfully assumed that risk. He fearlessly ministered to his people, preaching the Gospel and giving out God's Word. Nor is he alone. The most typical evangelical Christian does not live in Europe or the United States but somewhere else. And it is more than likely that he or she is facing poverty and confronting persecution. Throughout the world, millions of evangelical Christians experience a situation much like the one Rómulo encountered. They face persecution daily, some just for the simple fact of being a Christian. Despite the risks, many continue to proclaim the Gospel of Christ to their friends and neighbors.

Adapted from "Rómulo Sauñe: Slain by the Shining Path"
in *Ambassadors for Christ,* ed. John D. Woodbridge
(Chicago: Moody Press, 1994), pp. 137–40.

absorbed culture. As a result of the loss of "true truth," the defining value of our culture has become tolerance. If there is no truth, then everything should be tolerated. It is difficult enough for most people to stomach the notion that there really is truth, let alone pronounce that truth ought to be a standard for authentic fellowship. Unfortunately, the church has not remained insulated from the impact of this cultural worldview.

Embracing truth as the standard for unity is also difficult given the fact that our culture is so fragmented. This is particularly a problem for younger generations. Sadly, we have handed them a broken world. Government is broken, education is broken, the environment is broken; their families are broken, and as a result they have deep, innate longings for togetherness. Anything that smacks of division or exclusion runs against the longing of their hearts. Even the thought that faith and truth authenticate legitimate divisions is difficult for them to embrace.

Truth as the standard struggles to make its point in the face of competing notions. For instance, many people who do not embrace the truth of the Gospel are far more likable, seemingly more spiritual and kind, than some of us who do embrace that truth. It is easy to assume that a good and likable person—particularly if that goodness is wrapped in spiritual rhetoric with a tip of the hat to Christ—is one with us in Christ.

Another common but misplaced assumption about unity is that we will know we are one with someone or a group if we hear them say that Jesus is Lord. While Romans 10 seems to indicate this, we must remember Jesus' response to some who had called him Lord: "I never knew you. Away from me!" (Matt. 7:23). It may very well be that Paul's use of the verbal affirmation of Jesus as Lord as a mark of authenticity was related to the early Christians' unwillingness to say that Caesar was lord. To confess Christ as Lord, and not Caesar, when this bold act could cost your life would clearly be a work of the Spirit.

TRUTH AND UNITY

To keep truth as the standard or basis for unity has been an ongoing struggle for the church. Charles H. Spurgeon, in the face of similar pressures, wrote,

> To remain divided is sinful! Did not our Lord pray, 'that they may be one, even as we are one'? (John 17:22). A chorus of ecumenical voices keep harping the unity tune. What they are saying is, 'Christians of all doctrinal shades and beliefs must come

> together in one visible organization, regardless. . . . Unite, unite!'
>
> Such teaching is false, reckless and dangerous. Truth alone must determine our alignments. Truth comes before unity. Unity without truth is hazardous. Our Lord's prayer in John 17 must be read in its full context. . . . 'Sanctify them through thy truth: thy word is truth.' Only those sanctified through the Word can be one in Christ. To teach otherwise is to betray the gospel."[1]

Spurgeon's counsel is wise and should be taken seriously. But it prompts an obvious follow-up question, "What is the truth that forges our unity in Christ?" What kind of truth was Jesus talking about in John 17? Since Jesus states that we are set apart by the Word of God and that the Word is truth, it is clear that unity demands a mutual affirmation that God's Word is truth to us. But given that, what are the additional truths of his Word that mark the grounds for unity? Jesus does not define the specific truths that dictate legitimate unity, but the apostles do. While the early church fathers marked the doctrine of the Trinity as a core truth of orthodoxy, the New Testament especially elevates two other fundamental doctrines as standards for unity. They are the doctrine of salvation and the doctrine of Jesus Christ.

One never hears the apostles pleading for unity among the different factions that threatened these two fundamentals. Quite the opposite. The constant struggle of the early church was to defend the Gospel against the legalistic influences of the Judaizers. These were false teachers who added works to the grace of God as a means of achieving redemption. In the face of this, Paul in no uncertain terms designates the doctrine of salvation as a point of demarcation. In Galatians 1:8 he writes, "But even if we or an angel from heaven should preach a gospel other than the one we preached to you, let him be eternally condemned!"

The second truth used to define New Testament oneness is the doctrine of Jesus Christ. Second John 7–11 makes this clear. The Gnostic sects had infiltrated the early church with teachings that undermined the biblical claims regarding Christ. Jesus' virgin birth, his deity, his bodily resurrection, and his bodily return were all contradicted by the teachings of the Gnostics.

Sometime ago, a friend was telling me about her Mormon neighbor. She rejoiced in their friendship and said how much she appreciated the times they prayed together. She asked me, "Have you ever prayed with a Mormon?" The inference was that she and her friend were wonderfully one in prayer. While one could cultivate a friendship with Mormons, praying with them would be quite another issue. Because they deny the doctrine that Christ is God, spiritual oneness with them is not only wrong but impossible, according to the Bible. Historically the church has persistently held to the fundamental realities of truth about Christ as a test of faith: his virgin birth, divinity, resurrection, and return.

In our day, not only is the doctrine of Christ under attack but the doctrine of salvation as well. What could be more important than knowing how a person becomes right with God? Eternal destinies hang in the balance of this truth. Paul devoted much of Romans, Galatians, and Ephesians to clarifying what salvation is. For salvation to be properly actualized in our lives and for repentance to be complete, we must know that it is all of Christ and not of ourselves. The Bible teaches that it is always and only by grace alone through faith alone in the finished work of Christ—apart from works or merits—that we are made right with him (see, for example, Ephesians 2:8–10).

A proper understanding of the grace-only orientation to salvation is significant not only for redemption but also for a transformed view of all of life. The power of the Gospel to transform a life is beautifully illustrated in the career of Michelangelo. As we all know, Michelangelo produced masterpieces heralded today as among the best artistic works of all time. His sculpture of David and his paintings in the Sistine chapel are especially familiar. Nearly all of his subject matter was religious in nature, and he often worked at the bidding of the pope. A deeply religious man, he no doubt could justifiably take appropriate pride in what he was doing for God.

Toward the end of his life, under the influence of his dear friend Vittoria Colonna, Michelangelo became intrigued with what the Reformers were teaching about justification through faith by grace alone apart from any works of his own. Accepting the reality that all of his good works were of no avail to settle the question of his sin, he embraced Christ as his forgiving Savior. It changed everything for him. He now realized that what he had supposedly done for God had actually become his god—a controlling idol in his life.

In a sonnet penned in his later years, he confessed,

> ... Whence the loving fancy that made of art
> my idol and my king,
> I know now well that it was full of wrong....
> Painting and sculpture shall no longer calm
> the soul turned to that love divine
> that spread its arms on the cross to take us in.

Rejoicing in the finished work of his Savior, he wrote,

> O flesh, O blood, O wood, O extreme sorrow,
> only by you my sin is done....
> Thou alone art good.

Although an accurate understanding of the truth about salvation changed his entire perspective on life, Michelangelo never stopped expressing himself through art. He was busy until the day he died. But now he engaged in art for another reason—not for merit, but for love. As one observer notes, "Michelangelo worked down to the end.... Nonetheless, the change was a radical one: art, which had become the primary interest, the 'idol and king' of his life, now becomes a means to serve God humbly."[2] Without a proper orientation to the truth that salvation is by grace through faith alone, his art would have remained his idol and king and his good works would have been of no avail to him in the end. But now his life was an expression of love and gratitude to a costly redemption.

Because proclaiming and defending salvation as described in the Bible impacts our lives and ministries in the present and our eternal destiny in the future, we dare not compromise the Gospel in any way, no matter how much we may desire unity.

THREATS TO A PURE GOSPEL

The quest to keep the truth of salvation intact is being challenged on more than one front. Neo-universalism, liberation theology, and process theology all hold the threat of dismantling this central tenet of our faith. Moreover, the well-intentioned desire among evangelicals to bridge differences through dialogue with representatives of other Christian traditions can also have unexpected negative consequences. We must underscore that if a person from another Christian tradition embraces "justification by faith alone through Christ alone," he or she may very well be a brother or sister in Christ. The challenge is not so much about our relations with other individuals who belong to Christ. Rather, the danger is that we will not maintain clarity about what the Gospel essentially is by striking alliances with doctrinal and churchly systems that clearly are not friends of salvation through grace alone and faith alone. We need to discern carefully the theology that lies behind the words of any dialogue. The same words used in one theological context can have other connotations in another theological framework. Once again, it must be reiterated, authentic unity can only be built upon truth.

As evangelical Christians we believe that we are justified by faith alone. This doctrine gives all glory to Christ for our salvation. As Scott Hafemann has expounded earlier in this book, this is what the Bible teaches. Only through Christ's substitutionary death on the cross in payment for our sins are we saved, without mediation by others or by merits of our own or by engaging in rituals. Our salvation is simply due to Jesus' amazing grace. Paul wrote; "For it is by grace you have been saved, through faith—and this not from yourselves, it is the gift of God—not by works, so that no one can boast" (Eph. 2:8–9).

The Statement underscores these same points: "We affirm that the doctrine of the imputation (reckoning or counting) both of our sins to Christ and of his righteousness to us, whereby our sins are fully forgiven and we are fully accepted, is essential to the biblical Gospel (2 Cor. 5:19–21). We deny that we are justified by the righteousness of Christ infused into us or by any righteousness that is thought to inhere within us."

While some would wish that evangelicals and other Christians were not so unbending about these matters, it is simply the case that there can be no true unity without a clear articulation of the truth regarding salvation. If we strive for unity apart from a pure Gospel, we will have done the Gospel a tragic disservice and will have confused many about their own eternal destiny.

UNITED IN THE GOSPEL AND IN THE SPIRIT

As evangelicals, then, we are one with each other in the truth of the Gospel of Jesus Christ. It is this Gospel that evangelicals believe is truly "good news" for the world. The Statement begins, "The Gospel of Jesus Christ is news, good news: the best and most important news that any human being ever hears. This Gospel declares the only way to know God in peace, love, and joy is through the reconciling death of Jesus Christ the risen Lord."

In all of this, we should keep in mind what is not included in the "truth" standards for unity. The Bible does not indicate that modes of baptism, the timing or details of our Lord's return, church polity, ministry roles, and such matters are points that should necessitate divisions. It is not that some of these things are unimportant. But differing viewpoints about them should not cause evangelical divisions.

Westminster Seminary, for example, is unapologetically Calvinistic in its theology and Reformed in its hermeneutic. As such, I doubt that the school would invite John Wesley (if he were alive today) to teach on its faculty. His theology would be inconsistent with a number of the seminary's theological perspectives. But I am quite certain that Westminster Seminary would fully embrace John Wesley as a brother in Christ. While these particular and diverse distinctions are important in their own context, we should be careful that we do not see the particular doctrinal emphases of our schools and churches as setting the exclusive parameters for defining the body of Christ. Rather, our unity is grounded in the Gospel of Jesus Christ and supported in other historic, foundational truths that reflect the Bible's teachings.

As we seek for unity in the truth of the Gospel of Jesus Christ, we must remember that the way we treat other Christians is highly significant. In Ephesians 4:1–15, the apostle Paul encouraged Christians to endeavor to "keep the unity of the Spirit through the bond of peace" (v. 3). He also encouraged them to be "completely humble and gentle; be patient, bearing with one another in love" (v. 2). He urged "speaking the truth in love" (v. 15). Paul's counsel should direct the way we interact respectfully and lovingly with other Christians. Our concern for the purity of the Gospel will appear quite barren to the watching world and to each other if we do not "keep the unity of the Spirit" through peace and love and the other fruit of the Spirit (Gal. 5:22–23). For that matter, it will appear quite barren if we do not love those who have not yet become grace-born followers of Christ.

THE EVANGELICAL FAMILY

Evangelicals, then, are a family united in the Gospel of Jesus Christ. We come from many nations, races, economic circumstances, denominations, and churches. The geographical boundaries for the family are as large as the world itself. But the doctrinal boundaries are circumscribed by a commitment to the Gospel of Jesus Christ, and in particular and to the historic tenets of orthodox Christian truth in general, as described in Holy Scripture.

Evangelicals will experience the blessings of oneness as we love the Lord our God with all our hearts, souls, and minds and our neighbors as ourselves. Moreover, in loving, caring, and praying for other members of the household of faith, the body of Christ, we will demonstrate to a watching world that indeed we are Christ's disciples.

The Statement summarizes well many of these points regarding family life in Christ: "As evangelicals united in the Gospel, we promise to watch over and care for one another, to pray for and forgive one another, and to reach out in love and truth to God's people everywhere, for we are one family, one in the Holy Spirit, and one in Christ. Centuries ago it was truly said that in things necessary there must be unity, in things less than necessary there must be liberty, and in all things there must be charity. We see all these Gospel truths as necessary."

Notes

1. Charles H. Spurgeon, "The Essence of Separation," sermon.
2. Enzo Noe Girardi, in *The Complete Work Of Michelangelo* (New York: Reynal and Co., 1966), pp. 552, 554.

Study Questions

1. What aspects of "familyship" do you value most in your church experience?
2. What hindrances to unity do you deal with most in your life? What steps can you take to overcome them?
3. Explain why truth is not only more important than unity but also the basis for unity.
4. Why is it important that different points of view not cause divisions among evangelicals?

This Gospel of Jesus Christ which God sets forth in the infallible Scriptures combines Jesus' own declaration of the present reality of the kingdom of God with the apostles' account of the person, place, and work of Christ, and how sinful humans benefit from it. The Patristic Rule of Faith, the historic creeds, the Reformation confessions, and the doctrinal bases of later evangelical bodies all witness to the substance of this biblical message.

The heart of the Gospel is that our holy, loving Creator, confronted with human hostility and rebellion, has chosen in his own freedom and faithfulness to become our holy, loving Redeemer and Restorer.

■

We affirm that the church is commanded by God and is therefore under divine obligation to preach the Gospel to every living person (Luke 24:47; Matt. 28:18–19).

We deny that any particular class or group of persons, whatever their ethnic or cultural identity, may be ignored or passed over in the preaching of the Gospel (1 Cor. 9:19–22). God purposes a global church made up from people of every tribe, language, and nation (Rev. 7:9).

—*The Gospel of Jesus Christ: An Evangelical Celebration*

12

THE BIG PICTURE

DOES GOD HAVE A PLAN FOR THE WORLD?

Timothy George

In her book *Mystery on the Desert*, Maria Reiche describes a series of strange lines on the Nazca Plain in Peru, some of them covering many square miles. For years people assumed that these lines were the remnants of ancient irrigation ditches. Then in 1939, Dr. Paul Kosok of Long Island University discovered that their true meaning could only be seen from high in the air. When viewed from an airplane, these seemingly random lines form enormous drawings of birds, insects, and animals.

In a similar way, people often think of the Bible as a series of individual, unconnected stories. But if we survey the Scriptures as a whole, we discover that they form one Great Story of redemption—from the opening scenes of Genesis to the final chapter of Revelation.

In this concluding chapter I plan to place the Gospel of Jesus Christ into the larger context of biblical history. We will view the overarching story of what

God has been up to in the rescue and restoration of fallen human beings from the first nanosecond of creation through the final cry of victory at the end of time. Why is it important to get an overall grasp of the whole story? Let me suggest three reasons.

First, the Christian faith has a purpose and a goal and is going somewhere. Unlike many religions and popular philosophies today, Christians do not see the world as a great wheel swirling endlessly around and around in cyclical repetitions that go on forever. No, Christians believe that the world, and everyone in it, has a special destiny, a rendezvous with eternity for which our life on earth is but a preparation. The Christian view of history is linear but centered, with everything and everyone related to Jesus Christ, whose coming to earth is still acknowledged every time someone speaks of our living in the *third* millennium.

Second, the Bible is an interrelated, coherent unity that makes sense ultimately only when we read it as a connected story rather than as a series of proof texts or theological axioms. True enough, the Bible is also a book of incredible diversity. It was written over a millennium of time in scores of documents by dozens of human authors from various cultural backgrounds, using a wide variety of styles and literary genres. This is what the author of Hebrews means when he says that God spoke "at many times and in various ways" (1:1 NIV). But the Bible does not present itself as a mere object to be studied and admired as one religious book among many. The narrative structure of the Bible itself, from creation to the world's forthcoming end, makes the imperious claim to be the one true story in the light of which all other stories—and, indeed, the reality of the universe itself—must be understood.

Some people try to study the Bible the way a geologist might study a piece of petrified wood in a lab—interesting perhaps, but cold, inert, dead. To them the Bible's story line is a "myth," a fanciful, made-up history. But if you read the Bible without such blinders, you may discover something quite different. The Bible is a living book. You cannot read it and put it down the way you might the sports page or a Stephen King novel. It addresses you, provokes you, questions you, commands you, calls out to you. It has your number. Slowly you come to see, as Christians have through the centuries, that what the world calls "myth" is really a true and trustworthy account of your life and of life itself. At the same time, you realize that what the world calls reality and history is the real myth! You come to see that what the Bible claims to be so really is so, and not just so "for me," but so for everybody everywhere.

Finally, Christian worship makes sense only in light of God's plan for the ages. Believing that the Bible is true and that God is real, Christians worship their Creator and Redeemer, celebrating his marvelous deeds in praise and prayer. In worship, Christians respond to who God is and to what he has done in ages past and in their own lives, too. Christians worship on Sunday to celebrate Jesus' resurrection. For them the new year begins, not on January 1, but on the first Sunday of Advent, as they recall the messianic prophecies of the Old Testament and their fulfillment in the Incarnation. Both baptism and the Lord's Supper recall not only what happened in Palestine two thousand years ago but also the presence of Christ here and now as well as what will take place in the future when Jesus comes again. In worship, Christians give expression to "the mighty acts of God" from creation to the end of time. In doing so, they worship and glorify God Almighty, the One who says, "I'm A to Z. I'm THE GOD WHO IS, THE GOD WHO WAS, AND THE GOD ABOUT TO ARRIVE. I'm the Sovereign-Strong" (Rev. 1:18 THE MESSAGE).

ACCORDING TO PLAN

"For God so loved the world . . ."

Christians love to quote John 3:16. It is a beautiful summary of the entire Gospel in less than thirty words. If the whole Bible had been destroyed or lost except for John 3:16, that would still be enough for any person to come to know God and receive eternal life. But in fact, John 3:16 presupposes some very important things about God and the world he created and loved so much.

The Christian account of history does not begin with the birth of Jesus, nor with the calling of Abraham in the Old Testament, but with God's creation of the world "out of nothing" *(ex nihilo)*. This understanding of the origin of the universe is unique in the history of ideas. Pantheism equates God and the creation, blurring all distinction. Dualism posits two primal principles, God and matter, or God and some other reality, locked in an eternal cosmic battle. The Bible teaches that the world is utterly distinct from God while totally dependent upon him. In the beginning, God said, "Let there be," and there was. God spoke, and his word (*dabar* in Hebrew) was so powerful that it shattered the silence of eternity, spangling the sky with stars and causing the sun to burst forth with radiance and the earth to vibrate with teeming animal and plant life—dolphins, elephants, caterpillars, glowworms, ospreys, the whole menagerie. When all this was in place, God created human beings, males and females, making them in his own image, endowed with special dignity and intended for intimate fellowship with their Creator.

But who is God, and why did he make the world in the first place? Some people teach that the reason God made the world is that, way back in the vast stretches of eternity past, he had grown lonely. He created the world, so this theory goes, in order to have something to love. But this is an utterly pagan notion of God. It supposes that in his innermost being, God is utterly alone, a monad, superior and transcendent to be sure, but isolated and aloof in his omnipotence. This is the God of Arius, a false teacher of the fourth century A.D., who wrote, "We know there is one God, alone unbegotten, alone eternal, alone without beginning, alone true, alone immortal...."

The Bible gives us a very different picture of God. Here we learn that within the being of God himself there is a mysterious living love, a dynamic reciprocity of surrender and affirmation, of giving and receiving, among the Father, the Son, and the Holy Spirit. The Maker of heaven and earth is at once the Triune God of holiness and love.

God's ultimate reality is not expressed in terms of brute power and force alone. This is not the most decisive mark of God's divinity. What makes God God is the relationship of total and mutual self-giving by which the Father gives everything to the Son, and the Son offers back all that he has to glorify the Father, the love of each being established and sealed by the Holy Spirit, who proceeds from both.

If all this is true, then why on earth did God make the world? Not because he had to, but because he chose to. God is the Lord of creation, not its midwife. God did not need to create something outside of himself as an object for his love, for God is Love (1 John 4:8). There is nothing missing or lacking in God. He is the fountain of being. In him dwells all holiness, glory, light, power, happiness, joy.

Yet—this is the amazing thing!—out of the richness and utter sufficiency of his own being, God creates the world and human beings within it, granting them a creaturely reality and freedom and inviting them to share in the out-splashing of his divine love for all eternity. Indeed, the Bible speaks of God as "jealous" for his own glory and honor: He will brook no rivals. But he is not a grudging, stingy God like a Silas Marner counting his gold coins for fear that one of them might have gotten away. No, at the heart of God there is a freedom, an unthreatenedness, a generosity that is a reflection of his own character. This is the basis of all human reality and freedom. This is also the source of wonder and awe, the kind of wonder that prompted Martin Luther to find sermons in peach stones and to adore the living God who made heaven and earth (and me too, Luther says), "of his sheer fatherly kindness and compassion, apart from any merit or worthiness of mine: For all of which I am bound to thank and praise Him, to serve Him and to be obedient, which is assuredly true."

Some people accept the idea of God's creation of the world, but they cannot imagine that he has much to do with its continuing operation, much less with our human lives. The British poet and novelist Thomas Hardy once wrote in disparaging terms about God as "the dreaming, dark, dumb Thing that turns the handle of this idle Show." This is the God of deism: He created the world, and still cranks it along from time to time, but wouldn't think of getting his hands dirty in the daily muck and mess of it all. He is an absentee landlord God who neither knows nor cares very much about the tenants who occupy his property. This God is an idol of the modern imagination—he has crippled feet and withered hands, eyes that see not, and ears that hear not.

No wonder so many people find it hard, even useless, to believe in such a God! How different is the God of the Bible, who is everywhere active, alive, and involved. Jesus said that no act is too insignificant for the Father's care. He knows every time a sparrow is caught in a hailstorm and falls to the ground. In his great and boundless wisdom, God knows even how to use evil instruments to do good—including the devil himself, as Paul makes clear in 2 Corinthians 12:7, where he describes his "thorn in my flesh" as something "given" by God through the agency of Satan. Through God's providential care, even painful episodes such as this can become occasions for grace.

In his great mercy, God did not leave the world to its own devices, nor turn it over to the stratagems of Satan. Even before Creation, God devised a plan to rescue fallen human beings from their foreseen sin and misery. God was not caught off guard by Adam's sin, nor surprised by the subsequent apostasy of his chosen people, Israel. Thus, the last book in the Bible describes Jesus as "the Lamb that was slain from the creation of the world" (Rev. 13:8).

The biblical word for God's sovereign freedom in salvation is election. God chose, or elected, Israel as the special bearers of revelation, not because it had the biggest army or the most thriving economy of any nation in the ancient world. Quite the contrary: "The LORD did not set his affection on you and choose you because you were more numerous than other peoples, for you were the fewest of all peoples. But it was because the LORD loved you ..." (Deut. 7:7–8). Throughout the Bible, God's election is always absolutely unconditional.

Throughout the Old Testament, God is described as ever faithful in all his undertakings. The pattern of redemption is unfolded century after century through the Exodus and the desert, the conquest of Canaan and the exile to Babylon. Again and again God reaches out to his people and communicates his love to them through the patriarchs, the poets, and the prophets, coming finally to a dénouement in the final book of the Old Testament, which announces the "burden" (*nasa* in Hebrew) of the Lord to Israel through Malachi. "'I have loved you,' says the LORD" (Mal. 1:2). It is the burden of love, the burden of God's covenant love that comes finally to rest on a baby in a manger and a man on a tree.

THE CRUX OF HISTORY

"*. . . That he gave his one and only Son . . .*"

In 1980 Samuel Levine published a book with the title *You Take Jesus, I'll Take God: How to Refute Christian Missionaries*. It was an attempt to prove that Christians misunderstand the Old Testament when they apply passages such as Psalm 22 and Isaiah 53 to Jesus.

The true identity of Jesus Christ is one of the most controversial issues in the history of religion. Just look at the different views people had of Jesus in his own day. Some saw him as a healer, a teacher, a prophet, maybe even Elijah come back from the dead. Others saw him as a demon-possessed man, a political troublemaker, or simply Joseph the carpenter's kid. At one point Jesus asked his disciples outright, "Who do you say I am?"—to which Peter answered, "You are the Christ [the Messiah], the Son of the living God" (Matt. 16:15–16).

The British philosopher Norman Kemp Smith spoke for many of his contemporaries when he remarked, "I have no difficulty with the idea of God, but I do with that of Christ: One time, one place. Very difficult." His comment points to the fact that when we say the words *Jesus Christ*, we are not talking about an idea or a symbol or a principle. No, we are dealing with a specific historical figure, a particular person whose time on earth was bracketed by the political power structures of the day. He was born in the reign of Caesar Augustus, and he died when Pontius Pilate was governor of Judea. There is an inescapable "then and thereness" about Jesus Christ that we cannot spiritualize away.

In recent years, New Testament scholars have emphasized the Jewishness of Jesus, placing him in the context of the history and culture of the people of Israel. After all, the word "Jesus" is the English translation of the Hebrew name "Joshua," which means literally "Yahweh helps" or "God is our salvation." It was a familiar name in Jesus' day, as it still is in ours in some cultures. The Gospel writers portray the life and ministry of Jesus in terms of the fulfillment of God's covenant with his people Israel.

MORE THAN MIND

Biblical Christianity is more than a matter of the mind. This is what one brilliant young Oxford University undergraduate discovered during the 1940s. James Innell Packer early on became fond of reading and developed a passion for writing. This was in part due to a near-fatal accident at the age of seven that left a one-inch hole in his head and prevented him from ever fulfilling another passion—riding a bicycle. It is not surprising, then, that the young man ended up at Oxford.

At Oxford, Packer believed mentally in Christ and had once defended the Trinity in an argument with a friend. But one day some classmates invited him to a meeting of the Christian Union (a branch of InterVarsity Christian Fellowship), where he heard the Gospel of Jesus Christ presented in a way he had not known before. He later described what it was like observing Christians who were enjoying their faith so much:

"I saw myself standing outside a house looking in on a tremendous party with laughter and joy. The Lord tracked me down and found me. I was surprised

Indeed, this is how Jesus explained his own mission to those befuddled disciples on the road to Emmaus:

> "How foolish you are, and how slow of heart to believe all that the prophets have spoken! Did not the Christ have to suffer these things and then enter his glory?" And beginning with Moses and all the Prophets, he explained to them what was said in all the Scriptures concerning himself (Luke 24:25–27).

Jesus is the last Adam, the seed of Abraham, the son of David, and the true Prophet. He is the Servant King whose greatness exceeds that of Solomon (Luke 11:31). He cleanses the house of God, identifying himself as the true temple (John 2:13–22). When he is taken to Egypt as a baby, he reenacts the Egyptian bondage experienced centuries before by the people of Israel. His going up to Jerusalem to suffer and die is the new Exodus. He is the paschal lamb whose poured-out blood brings rescue and redemption.

by grace. I became an avid Bible reader and my initial doubts soon evaporated in the atmosphere of solid Bible exposition at the Christian Union."

That was the beginning of a career devoted to writing, teaching, expounding on theology, and ironically, reestablishing the place of the mind in the Christian life. While Christianity is more than a matter of the mind, at its best it nevertheless does include the mind. Soon after his conversion experience at Oxford, J. I. Packer became acquainted with the great Puritan writers and thinkers of an earlier era. As a result of his fascination with them, he has done much to revive the wisdom and the teachings of the Puritans in the church of the late twentieth century. He contends that by standing on their shoulders he can see today's world better. And in so doing, he has helped the evangelical church understand the world better and to know how to confront it effectively with the Gospel.

Adapted from "J. I. Packer: Surprised by Grace"
in *More Than Conquerors,* ed. John D. Woodbridge
(Chicago: Moody Press, 1992), pp. 317–19.

With the coming of Jesus, God's reign has arrived. God's kingdom, Jesus announced, is now "among you" (Luke 17:21). Satan has been routed, as Jesus' work as an exorcist shows (Matt. 12:28). All that God has promised in the Old Testament Jesus fulfills. As the apostle Paul puts it, "Whatever God has promised gets stamped with the Yes of Jesus. In him, this is what we preach and pray, the great Amen, God's Yes and our Yes together, gloriously evident" (2 Cor. 1:20 THE MESSAGE).

Christians believe that in the unique person of Jesus Christ, God himself came and lived our human life with all its difficulties, temptations, and hurts. The verse in the Bible that explains this best is John 1:14: "The Word became flesh and blood, and moved into the neighborhood" (THE MESSAGE). In the Incarnation, God the Son became *sarx*, flesh and blood, that part of the human person that is most vulnerable, most susceptible to suffering, decay, and death. Thus Jesus was no phantom, ghostlike figure, but truly human, of the same reality as we are as to his humanness.

But in Jesus Christ we also have to do with one who is perfectly divine, actually deity, of the same reality as God from all eternity. This is what the early Christians meant when they confessed that Jesus Christ was "the only-begotten Son of God, begotten of his Father before all worlds, God of God, Light of Light, Very God of Very God, begotten not made, being of one substance with the Father, by whom all things were made: Who for us and for our salvation came down from heaven" (Nicene Creed).

When John 3:16 says that "God so loved the world that he gave his one and only Son," this "giving" refers not only to Jesus' birth, life, teachings, and miracles but also to his sacrificial death on the cross. The death of Jesus was not an accident, nor—although he was crucified by evil men—was he an unwilling victim. His death was part of God's eternal design for the salvation of sinners. *It is important to say emphatically that God does not love us because Jesus died for us; rather, Jesus died for us because God loves us.* Through his work on the cross, Jesus turned aside the wrath of God, absorbing the punishment due to sinners, securing forgiveness and a right standing before God for all who trust in him. The Bible describes Christ's finished work on the cross, not only as a settling of accounts in heaven, but also as a triumphant victory over all the powers of darkness.

These themes are reflected in two classic prayers of the Christian church. The first is the prayer of consecration from the sixteenth-century *Book of Common Prayer:* "Almighty God, our heavenly Father, who of Thy tender mercy didst give Thine only Son Jesus Christ to die upon the cross for our salvation, who made there, by his one oblation of himself once offered, a full, perfect and sufficient sacrifice, and satisfaction for the sins of the whole world. . . ." The second is a simple affirmation from an ancient Syrian liturgy: "The Lord hath reigned from the tree."

In the fourth century, Athanasius, who defended the true deity and equality of the Son with the Father, declared, "The power of the cross of Christ has filled the world." But the meaning of the cross, and its power, too, were released by Jesus' resurrection from the dead. Paul does not hesitate to put everything on the line here: If Jesus has not been raised, it's all useless, smoke and mirrors. "And if Christ wasn't raised, then all you're doing is wandering about in the dark, as lost as ever" (1 Cor. 15:14–21 THE MESSAGE). But Paul goes on to say that the truth is that Christ *has* been raised up, a fact attested by the first eyewitnesses and by millions of believers since then who have known and worshiped the risen Christ.

When Christians of any era looked back on Jesus—on his life, death, and resurrection—they saw him as the Turning Point of History, the One in whom the hopes of Israel had been fulfilled and God's plan of salvation for humanity itself accomplished. In the light of Jesus Christ, we see history not, as Henry Ford described it, "the succession of one damned thing after another," but rather as a sequence of events pregnant with purpose, laden with eternal meaning. The Lord still reigns from the tree, and one day his rule will be acknowledged by every living creature in the universe.

THE PROGRESS OF THE GOSPEL

"*... That whoever believes in him shall not perish ...*"

The book of Acts opens with two great events of salvation-historical importance: The going up of Jesus from earth into heaven (the Ascension), and the coming down of the Holy Spirit upon the disciples (Pentecost). Jesus' resurrection from the dead inaugurated God's new beginning, which the New Testament calls "the last days." In Jesus Christ, the future has invaded the present, and Christians are those "on whom the fulfillment of the ages has come" (1 Cor. 10:11). When Jesus returned to heaven, this did not mean that he was absent from his followers, but rather that he would now be present in another form.

Before Jesus died, he said to his disciples, "I will not leave you as orphans; I will come to you" (John 14:18). From Pentecost on, the Spirit of God, who is also called the Spirit of Jesus and the Spirit of

Christ, would come to live within every person who repented of one's sins and believed in Jesus. This is what Christians mean when they describe their new relationship with God as having Jesus in their heart. "You can tell for sure that you are now fully adopted as his own children because God sent the Spirit of his Son into our lives crying out, 'Papa! Father!'" (Gal. 4:6 THE MESSAGE). To truly know God in this way is the greatest thing that can happen in anyone's life. The Bible says it is like being born again, or raised from the dead, or coming out of the deepest darkness into the light of day. But none of this would be possible without the witness and work of the Holy Spirit, who not only makes us aware of our need for God and puts us into a right relationship with the Father through the Son but also fills us and empowers us to walk with Christ every day and to grow in our love for him and for one another.

It is important to say that what we are talking about here is not a matter of self-improvement, of turning over a new leaf. Nor is it a question of our having some ecstatic, mystical experience. The saving knowledge of God is unattainable by human effort. This is why justification—our being declared right before God—is by faith alone, apart from any good works or personal merit we can claim. Christians sometimes sing this song to Jesus, "In my hand no price I bring, simply to thy cross I cling." Salvation is based solely on what God has once and for all done for us in the life, death, and resurrection of Jesus Christ. What Christ has done for us, though, must be appropriated personally through our turning away from sin (repentance) and our turning in reliant trust to the Savior himself (faith). John Calvin, a great teacher of the church, put it this way: "As long as Christ remains outside of me, and we are separated from Him, all that He has suffered and done for the salvation of the human race remains useless and of no value to us" (*Institutes* 3.1.1.).

Imbued with the "glad tidings" of new life in Jesus Christ, the early Christians fanned out from Jerusalem and Judea to carry this Gospel into all the world. They went everywhere—into the arena, the academies of learning, and the marketplace, to faraway lands such as India and Ethiopia, into every nook and cranny of the

Roman Empire. When, in the early fourth century, Eusebius of Caesarea set out to chronicle the course of Christian history from the days of the apostles up to his own time, he described the activity of those heralds of faith through whom the spread of the Gospel was first carried out:

> Leaving their homes, they set out to fulfill the work of an evangelist, making it their ambition to preach the word of the faith to those who as yet had heard nothing of it, and to commit to them the books of the divine gospels. They were content simply to lay the foundations of the faith among these foreign peoples: They then appointed other pastors, and committed to them the responsibility for building up those whom they had merely brought to the faith. Then they passed on to other countries and nations with the grace and help of God.

The last word in the Greek text of Acts is "unhindered" *(akölutös)*, an adverb used to describe the unstoppable progress of the Gospel from Jerusalem to Rome. This does not mean, of course, that the early Christians faced no opposition. Indeed, they often came into dramatic and violent conflict with the ruling authorities. It is not coincidental that the word "martyr" derives from the Greek *marturia*, meaning "witness."

In the twentieth century, Dietrich Bonhoeffer claimed that when Christ calls one to follow him, he bids him to take up his cross and die. This was literally true for many Christians for whom there was only one *Dominus et Deus*, "Lord and God," an imperial title the Christians refused to ascribe to anyone but Christ. The martyrs were revered, and the dates of the executions remembered as their "birthdays." In seeking to stamp out Christianity, the Roman authorities provided it with an effective means of evangelism! The blood of the martyrs became the seed of the church. Still today, many thousands of Christians are put to death every year because of their faith in Jesus Christ.

The course of Christian history is not marked by smooth and inevitable progress. There have been many setbacks. With the establishment and toleration of the Christian religion came a new freedom to go out into the world. But at the same time, in a new and dangerous way, the world entered into the church. There have been periods of decline, apostasy, and unbelief. And there have also been great moments of reformation, revival, and renewed faith.

Several years ago I had the experience of being in a worship service and receiving communion from the Bishop of Durham, a high official in the Church of England who had become notorious for denying some of the most basic truths of the Christian faith such as the virginal conception of Jesus and his bodily resurrection from the dead. His sermon was really bad, and I was quite depressed. After the service, I stayed in the cathedral to think and pray. As I walked through this massive Romanesque structure, I became aware of many evidences of the Gospel all around me. There was the Lord's Prayer and the Apostles' Creed engraved on a wall. Here was a prayer book and a Bible used by faithful Christians for generations. There were the stained-glass windows portraying the saints and martyrs of ages past. The building itself was in the shape of a cross. I suddenly realized that while bishops may come and go, and heretics rise and fall, the Word of the Lord abides forever. God has never left himself without a witness, even when that witness is silent and unobserved and contradicted by foolish thoughts and wayward words. The stones cry out and the Gospel goes forth!

HOMEWARD BOUND

". . . But have eternal life."

One of the great metaphors of the Christian life is that of a journey. We think of Abraham and Sarah setting out for a land where they had never been, of the children of Israel trekking through the desert toward the Promised Land, of St. Augustine's pilgrimage toward what he called his *Patria*, his true homeland, of Dante's journey toward the beatific vision. John Bunyan gave us one of the greatest interpretations of this theme in *The Pilgrim's Progress* with Christian's long journey from this world to the next. This is a journey from which no one is exempt. By God's grace, heaven is a destination no one who trusts in Jesus can miss.

It has been some two thousand years now since Jesus was born, lived, died, and rose again. Before he ascended to heaven, Jesus promised that he would come again, and Christians live in the earnest expectation of his return. Baptism is a picture of our future resurrection, just as the Lord's Supper is a foretaste of that heavenly banquet we shall one day share with Christ and all the blessed departed. One of the earliest refrains in Christian worship points to this hope: "Christ has died, Christ has risen, Christ will come again."

At some definite point in the future—and only God knows when that will be—Jesus will return to consummate the drama of redemption. Satan will be conquered, and Jesus will reign on earth in a world filled with justice and peace. At the resurrection, we shall receive new transformed bodies, comparable to the body Jesus himself had after he came back from the dead (1 John 3:2). There will be a final solemn separation when the wicked are forever banished from the presence of God in hell.

There is much about the future we do not know. Will there be time in heaven? What kind of food will we eat there? Will babies who die in infancy be raised as adults? It is useless to speculate about such matters, for God has not chosen to reveal these details to us. But one thing we can know for sure: Life with God in heaven will be an utterly transformed existence. Eternal life is not simply endless life; life everlasting is not merely life that lasts forever. Some people mistakenly think of heaven as "an everlasting church service with highbrow music in insipid surroundings," as Peter Jensen puts it.[1] No, heaven will be a place of unutterable beauty and over-splashing joy. There we shall know even as also we are known. There we shall see Jesus face-to-face. There we shall be reunited in loving fellowship with our godly loved ones who have gone on before, and indeed with all the saints of the ages. There we shall worship and adore the one triune God of love and glory, sharing forever in his never-wearing-down life and never-growing-tired love.

When C. S. Lewis came to the conclusion of the Chronicles of Narnia, he noted that for himself and his readers, "this is the end of all the stories." But for the Narnia characters, he said, "it was only the beginning of the real story. . . . now at last they were beginning Chapter One of the Great Story, which no one on earth has read: which goes on forever: in which every chapter is better than the one before."[2]

In the meantime, the journey continues, for the God who created the world out of nothing, who sustains it by his daily care, and who has redeemed it once and for all in his Son Jesus, will not forsake it to its own wicked devices. Every moment, every event in history is filled with divine meaning even though that meaning is often not evident to us. Christians are called not to abandon the world but to love it, even as Jesus loved it and died for it. But we can do this fully only when we realize that God's eternal plan does not terminate on the world as it is now, with its racism, cancer, and death, but on the new heaven and the new earth where, with the multitude of the heavenly hosts, unseen but eternal, we shall join the choir and sing a new song, gathered around the throne of God and of the Lamb.

And what will it be like to enter this eternal world? The late Edward John Carnell perhaps said it best: "We are alone when we enter the world, but when we leave it we shall feel the abiding presence of the Lord. As death draws near and we dread the dark journey ahead, the Lord will assure us that our lives are precious in the sight of God. He will gently say, 'Child, come home.' Jesus has given his word that he will never leave us or forsake us, and his word is as firm as his character."

Notes

1. Peter Jensen, *At the Heart of the Universe* (Wheaton, IL: Crossway Books, 1997).

2. C. S. Lewis, *The Last Battle*, Book 7 in the Chronicles of Narnia (New York: Macmillan/Collier Books, 1970), p. 184.

Study Questions

1. Why is it important to see clearly the "big picture" portrayed in biblical history?
2. Why did God make the world and create mankind?
3. Why is it important to believe in a "personal" God? What would you tell a friend who says that God created the world and then left it on its own?
4. Why is it easier for some people to believe in God than to believe in Jesus as the Son of God?
5. How would you describe your journey in the Christian life? What have been the best parts? Which parts would you rather had never occurred?

APPENDIX ONE

THE GOSPEL OF JESUS CHRIST: AN EVANGELICAL CELEBRATION

> For God so loved the world that he gave his one and only Son, that whoever believes in him shall not perish but have eternal life.
>
> —John 3:16

> Sing to the Lord, for he has done glorious things; let this be known to all the world.
>
> —Isaiah 12:5

PREAMBLE

The Gospel of Jesus Christ is news, good news: the best and most important news that any human being ever hears.

This Gospel declares the only way to know God in peace, love, and joy is through the reconciling death of Jesus Christ the risen Lord.

This Gospel is the central message of the Holy Scriptures, and is the true key to understanding them.

This Gospel identifies Jesus Christ, the Messiah of Israel, as the Son of God and God the Son, the second Person of the Holy Trinity, whose incarnation, ministry, death, resurrection, and ascension fulfilled the Father's saving will. His death for sins and his resurrection from the dead were promised beforehand by the prophets and attested by eyewitnesses. In God's own time and in God's own way, Jesus Christ shall return as glorious Lord and Judge of all (1 Thess. 4:13–18; Matt. 25:31–32). He is now giving the Holy Spirit from the Father to all those who are truly his. The three Persons of the Trinity thus combine in the work of saving sinners.

This Gospel sets forth Jesus Christ as the living Savior, Master, Life, and Hope of all who put their trust in him. It tells us that the eternal destiny of all people depends on whether they are savingly related to Jesus Christ.

This Gospel is the only Gospel: there is no other; and to change its substance is to pervert and indeed destroy it. This Gospel is so simple that small children can understand it, and it is so profound that studies by the wisest theologians will never exhaust its riches.

All Christians are called to unity in love and unity in truth. As evangelicals who derive our very name from the Gospel, we celebrate this great good news of God's saving work in Jesus Christ as the true bond of Christian unity, whether among organized churches and denominations or in the many transdenominational cooperative enterprises of Christians together.

The Bible declares that all who truly trust in Christ and his Gospel are sons and daughters of God through grace, and hence are our brothers and sisters in Christ.

All who are justified experience reconciliation with the Father, full remission of sins, transition from the kingdom of darkness to the kingdom of light, the reality of being a new creature in Christ, and the fellowship of the Holy Spirit. They enjoy access to the Father with all the peace and joy that this brings.

The Gospel requires of all believers worship, which means constant praise and giving of thanks to God, submission to all that he has revealed in his written word, prayerful dependence on him, and vigilance lest his truth be even inadvertently compromised or obscured.

To share the joy and hope of this Gospel is a supreme privilege. It is also an abiding obligation, for the Great Commission of Jesus Christ still stands: proclaim the Gospel everywhere, he said, teaching, baptizing, and making disciples.

By embracing the following declaration we affirm our commitment to this task, and with it our allegiance to Christ himself, to the Gospel itself, and to each other as fellow evangelical believers.

THE GOSPEL

This Gospel of Jesus Christ which God sets forth in the infallible Scriptures combines Jesus' own declaration of the present reality of the kingdom of God with the apostles' account of the person, place, and work of Christ, and how sinful humans benefit from it. The Patristic Rule of Faith, the historic creeds, the Reformation confessions, and the doctrinal bases of later evangelical bodies all witness to the substance of this biblical message.

The heart of the Gospel is that our holy, loving Creator, confronted with human hostility and rebellion, has chosen in his own freedom and faithfulness to become our holy, loving Redeemer and Restorer. The Father has sent the Son to be the Savior of the world (1 John 4:14): it is through his one and only Son that God's one and only plan of salvation is implemented. So Peter announced: "Salvation is found in no one else, for there is no other name under heaven given to men by which we must be saved" (Acts 4:12). And Christ himself taught: "I am the way, the truth and the life. No one comes to the Father except through me" (John 14:6).

Through the Gospel we learn that we human beings, who were made for fellowship with God, are by nature—that is, "in Adam" (1 Cor. 15:22)—dead in sin, unresponsive to and separated from our Maker. We are constantly twisting his truth, breaking his law, belittling his goals and standards, and offending his holiness by our unholiness, so that we truly are "without hope and without God in the world" (Rom. 1:18–32; 3:9–20; Eph. 2:1–3, 12). Yet God in grace took the initiative to reconcile us to himself through the sinless life and vicarious death of his beloved Son (Eph. 2:4–10; Rom. 3:21–24).

The Father sent the Son to free us from the dominion of sin and Satan, and to make us God's children and friends. Jesus paid our penalty in our place on his cross, satisfying the retributive demands of divine justice by shedding his blood in sacrifice and so making possible justification for all who trust in him (Rom. 3:25–26). The Bible describes this mighty substitutionary transaction as the achieving of ransom, reconciliation, redemption, propitiation, and conquest of evil powers (Matt. 20:28; 2 Cor. 5:18–21; Rom. 3:23–25; John 12:31; Col. 2:15). It secures for us a restored relationship with God that brings pardon and peace, acceptance and access, and adoption into God's family (Col. 1:20; 2:13–14; Rom. 5:1–2; Gal. 4:4–7; 1 Peter 3:18). The faith in God and in Christ to which the Gospel calls us is a trustful outgoing of our hearts to lay hold of these promised and proffered benefits.

This Gospel further proclaims the bodily resurrection, ascension, and enthronement of Jesus as evidence of the efficacy of his once-for-all sacrifice for us, of the reality of his present personal ministry to us, and of the certainty of his future return to glorify us (1 Cor. 15; Heb. 1:1–4; 2:1–18; 4:14–16; 7:1–10:25). In the life of faith as the Gospel presents it, believers are united with their risen Lord, communing with him, and looking to him in repentance and hope for empowering through the Holy Spirit, so that henceforth they may not sin but serve him truly.

God's justification of those who trust him, according to the Gospel, is a decisive transition, here and now, from a state of condemnation and wrath because of their sins to one of acceptance and favor by virtue of Jesus' flawless obedience culminating in his voluntary sin-bearing death. God "justifies the wicked" (ungodly: Rom. 4:5) by imputing (reckoning, crediting, counting, accounting) righteousness to them and ceasing to count their sins against them (Rom. 4:1–8). Sinners receive through faith in Christ alone "the gift of righteousness" (Rom. 1:17; 5:17; Phil. 3:9) and thus become "the righteousness of God" in him who was "made sin" for them (2 Cor. 5:21).

As our sins were reckoned to Christ, so Christ's righteousness is reckoned to us. This is justification by the imputation of Christ's righteousness. All we bring to the transaction is our need of it. Our faith in the God who bestows it, the Father, the Son, and the Holy Spirit, is itself the fruit of God's grace. Faith links us savingly to Jesus, but inasmuch as it involves an acknowledgment that we have no merit of our own, it is confessedly not a meritorious work.

The Gospel assures us that all who have entrusted their lives to Jesus Christ are born-again children of God (John 1:12), indwelt, empowered, and assured of their status and hope by the Holy Spirit (Rom. 7:6; 8:9–17). The moment we truly believe in Christ, the Father declares us righteous in him and begins conforming us to his likeness. Genuine faith acknowledges and depends upon Jesus as Lord and shows itself in growing obedience to the divine commands, though this contributes nothing to the ground of our justification (James 2:14–26; Heb. 6:1–12).

By his sanctifying grace, Christ works within us through faith, renewing our fallen nature and leading us to real maturity, that measure of development which is meant by "the fullness of Christ" (Eph. 4:13). The Gospel calls us to live as obedient servants of Christ and as his emissaries in the world, doing justice, loving mercy, and helping all in need, thus seeking to bear witness to the kingdom of Christ. At death, Christ takes the believer to himself (Phil. 1:21) for unimaginable joy in the ceaseless worship of God (Rev. 22:1–5).

Salvation in its full sense is from the guilt of sin in the past, the power of sin in the present, and the presence of sin in the future. Thus, while in foretaste believers enjoy salvation now, they still await its fullness (Mark 14:61–62; Heb. 9:28). Salvation is a Trinitarian reality, initiated by the Father, implemented by the Son, and applied by the Holy Spirit. It has a global dimension, for God's plan is to save believers out of every tribe and tongue (Rev. 5:9) to be his church, a new humanity, the people of God, the body and bride of Christ, and the community of the Holy Spirit. All the heirs of final salvation are called here and now to serve their Lord and each other in love, to share in the fellowship of Jesus' sufferings, and to work together to make Christ known to the whole world.

We learn from the Gospel that, as all have sinned, so all who do not receive Christ will be judged according to their just deserts as measured by God's holy law, and face eternal retributive punishment.

UNITY IN THE GOSPEL

Christians are commanded to love each other despite differences of race, gender, privilege, and social, political, and economic background (John 13:34–35; Gal. 3:28–29), and to be of one mind wherever possible (John 17:20–21; Phil. 2:2; Rom. 14:1–15:13). We know that divisions among Christians hinder our witness in the world, and we desire greater mutual understanding and truth-speaking in love. We know too that as trustees of God's revealed truth we cannot embrace any form of doctrinal indifferentism, or relativism, or pluralism by which God's truth is sacrificed for a false peace.

Doctrinal disagreements call for debate. Dialogue for mutual understanding and, if possible, narrowing of the differences is valuable, doubly so when the avowed goal is unity in primary things, with liberty in secondary things, and charity in all things.

In the foregoing paragraphs, an attempt has been made to state what is primary and essential in the Gospel as evangelicals understand it. Useful dialogue, however, requires not only charity in our attitudes, but also clarity in our utterances. Our extended analysis of justification by faith alone through Christ alone reflects our belief that Gospel truth is of crucial importance and is not always well understood and correctly affirmed. For added clarity, out of love for God's truth and Christ's church, we now cast the key points of what has been said into specific affirmations and denials regarding the Gospel and our unity in it and in Christ.

AFFIRMATIONS AND DENIALS:

1. We affirm that the Gospel entrusted to the church is, in the first instance, God's Gospel (Mark 1:14; Rom. 1:1). God is its author, and he reveals it to us in and by his Word. Its authority and truth rest on him alone.

We deny that the truth or authority of the Gospel derives from any human insight or invention (Gal. 1:1–11). We also deny that the truth or authority of the Gospel rests on the authority of any particular church or human institution.

2. We affirm that the Gospel is the saving power of God in that the Gospel effects salvation to everyone who believes, without distinction (Rom. 1:16). This efficacy of the Gospel is by the power of God himself (1 Cor. 1:18).

We deny that the power of the Gospel rests in the eloquence of the preacher, the technique of the evangelist, or the persuasion of rational argument (1 Cor. 1:21; 2:1–5).

3. We affirm that the Gospel diagnoses the universal human condition as one of sinful rebellion against God, which, if unchanged, will lead each person to eternal loss under God's condemnation.

We deny any rejection of the fallenness of human nature or any assertion of the natural goodness, or divinity, of the human race.

4. We affirm that Jesus Christ is the only way of salvation, the only mediator between God and humanity (John 14:6; 1 Tim. 2:5).

We deny that anyone is saved in any other way than by Jesus Christ and his Gospel. The Bible offers no hope that sincere worshipers of other religions will be saved without personal faith in Jesus Christ.

5. We affirm that the church is commanded by God and is therefore under divine obligation to preach the Gospel to every living person (Luke 24:47; Matt. 28:18–19).

We deny that any particular class or group of persons, whatever their ethnic or cultural identity, may be ignored or passed over in the preaching of the Gospel (1 Cor. 9:19–22). God purposes a global church made up from people of every tribe, language, and nation (Rev. 7:9).

6. We affirm that faith in Jesus Christ as the divine Word (or Logos, John 1:1), the second Person of the Trinity, co-eternal and co-essential with the Father and the Holy Spirit (Heb. 1:3), is foundational to faith in the Gospel.

We deny that any view of Jesus Christ which reduces or rejects his full deity is Gospel faith or will avail to salvation.

7. We affirm that Jesus Christ is God incarnate (John 1:14). The virgin-born descendant of David (Rom. 1:3), he had a true human nature, was subject to the Law of God (Gal. 4:5), and was like us at all points, except without sin (Heb. 2:17; 7:26–28). We affirm that faith in the true humanity of Christ is essential to faith in the Gospel.

We deny that anyone who rejects the humanity of Christ, his incarnation, or his sinlessness, or who maintains that these truths are not essential to the Gospel, will be saved (1 John 4:2–3).

8. We affirm that the atonement of Christ by which, in his obedience, he offered a perfect sacrifice, propitiating the Father by paying for our sins and satisfying divine justice on our behalf according to God's eternal plan, is an essential element of the Gospel.

We deny that any view of the Atonement that rejects the substitutionary satisfaction of divine justice, accomplished vicariously for believers, is compatible with the teaching of the Gospel.

9. We affirm that Christ's saving work included both his life and his death on our behalf (Gal. 3:13). We declare that faith in the perfect obedience of Christ by which he fulfilled all the demands of the Law of God on our behalf is essential to the Gospel.

We deny that our salvation was achieved merely or exclusively by the death of Christ without reference to his life of perfect righteousness.

10. We affirm that the bodily resurrection of Christ from the dead is essential to the biblical Gospel (1 Cor. 15:14).

We deny the validity of any so-called gospel that denies the historical reality of the bodily resurrection of Christ.

11. We affirm that the biblical doctrine of justification by faith alone in Christ alone is essential to the Gospel (Rom. 3:28; 4:5; Gal. 2:16).

We deny that any person can believe the biblical Gospel and at the same time reject the apostolic teaching of justification by faith alone in Christ alone. We also deny that there is more than one true Gospel (Gal. 1:6–9).

12. We affirm that the doctrine of the imputation (reckoning or counting) both of our sins to Christ and of his righteousness to us, whereby our sins are fully forgiven and we are fully accepted, is essential to the biblical Gospel (2 Cor. 5:19–21).

We deny that we are justified by the righteousness of Christ infused into us or by any righteousness that is thought to inhere within us.

13. We affirm that the righteousness of Christ by which we are justified is properly his own, which he achieved apart from us, in and by his perfect obedience. This righteousness is counted, reck-

oned, or imputed to us by the forensic (that is, legal) declaration of God, as the sole ground of our justification.

We deny that any works we perform at any stage of our existence add to the merit of Christ or earn for us any merit that contributes in any way to the ground of our justification (Gal. 2:16; Eph. 2:8–9; Titus 3:5).

14. We affirm that, while all believers are indwelt by the Holy Spirit and are in the process of being made holy and conformed to the image of Christ, those consequences of justification are not its ground. God declares us just, remits our sins, and adopts us as his children, by his grace alone, and through faith alone, because of Christ alone, while we are still sinners (Rom. 4:5).

We deny that believers must be inherently righteous by virtue of their cooperation with God's life-transforming grace before God will declare them justified in Christ. We are justified while we are still sinners.

15. We affirm that saving faith results in sanctification, the transformation of life in growing conformity to Christ through the power of the Holy Spirit. Sanctification means ongoing repentance, a life of turning from sin to serve Jesus Christ in grateful reliance on him as one's Lord and Master (Gal. 5:22–25; Rom. 8:4, 13–14).

We reject any view of justification which divorces it from our sanctifying union with Christ and our increasing conformity to his image through prayer, repentance, cross-bearing, and life in the Spirit.

16. We affirm that saving faith includes mental assent to the content of the Gospel, acknowledgment of our own sin and need, and personal trust and reliance upon Christ and his work.

We deny that saving faith includes only mental acceptance of the Gospel, and that justification is secured by a mere outward profession of faith. We further deny that any element of saving faith is a meritorious work or earns salvation for us.

17. We affirm that, although true doctrine is vital for spiritual health and well-being, we are not saved by doctrine. Doctrine is necessary to inform us how we may be saved by Christ, but it is Christ who saves.

We deny that the doctrines of the Gospel can be rejected without harm. Denial of the Gospel brings spiritual ruin and exposes us to God's judgment.

18. We affirm that Jesus Christ commands his followers to proclaim the Gospel to all living persons, evangelizing everyone everywhere, and discipling believers within the fellowship of the church. A full and faithful witness to Christ includes the witness of personal testimony, godly living, and acts of mercy and charity to our neighbor, without which the preaching of the Gospel appears barren.

We deny that the witness of personal testimony, godly living, and acts of mercy and charity to our neighbors constitutes evangelism apart from the proclamation of the Gospel.

OUR COMMITMENT

As evangelicals united in the Gospel, we promise to watch over and care for one another, to pray for and forgive one another, and to reach out in love and truth to God's people everywhere, for we are one family, one in the Holy Spirit, and one in Christ.

Centuries ago it was truly said that in things necessary there must be unity, in things less than necessary there must be liberty, and in all things there must be charity. We see all these Gospel truths as necessary.

Now to God, the Author of the truth and grace of this Gospel, through Jesus Christ, its subject and our Lord, be praise and glory forever and ever. Amen.

APPENDIX TWO

SIGNATORIES TO "THE GOSPEL OF JESUS CHRIST: AN EVANGELICAL CELEBRATION"

THE DRAFTING COMMITTEE

John N. Akers
John Ankerberg
John H. Armstrong
D. A. Carson
Keith Davy
Maxie Dunnam
Timothy George
Scott Hafemann
Erwin Lutzer
Harold Myra
David Neff
Thomas C. Oden
J. I. Packer
R. C. Sproul
John D. Woodbridge

OTHER SIGNATORIES

A partial list of those who have already endorsed the statement includes the following:

Danny Akin
Eric Alexander
C. Fitzsimmons Allison
Gregg Allison
Bill Anderson
Darrell Anderson
J. Kerby Anderson
Don Argue
Hudson T. Armerding
Kay Arthur
Myron S. Augsburger
Theodore Baehr
B. Clayton Bell Sr.
Joel Belz
Bryan Beyer
Henri Blocher
Donald G. Bloesch
Kenneth Boa
Scott Bolinder
John Bolt
William Bouknight
Todd Brady
Gerald Bray
Gerry E. Breshears
Bill Bright
Harold O. J. Brown

Stephen Brown
George Brushaber
David Cerullo
Peter Cha
Daniel R. Chamberlain
Bryan Chapell
Ian M. Chapman
David K. Clark
Brian Clarke
Sam Clarke
Arthur M. Climenhaga
Edmund Clowney
Robert Coleman
Chuck Colson
Clyde Cook
David Cook
W. Robert Cook
Mike Cordle
John R. Corts
Michael Cromartie
Roger Cross
Jimmy Davis
Alan Day
Lane T. Dennis
David S. Dockery
David Dryer
Michael Duduit
Paul Engle
Ted Engstrom
Stuart Epperson
James Erickson
Tony Evans
Jerry Falwell
Sinclair Ferguson
R. Scott Foresman
Michael Friend
John Galbraith
Kenneth L. Gentry
Dwight Gibson
James A. Gibson
Billy Graham
Brad Green
Wayne Grudem
Stan N. Gundry
David Gushee
Brandt Gustavson
George Guthrie
Corkie Haan
Ronald Habermas
Mimi Haddad
Ben Haden
Kevin G. Harney
B. Sam Hart
Bob Hawkins Jr.
Wendell Hawley
Jack W. Hayford
Stephen A. Hayner
Jim Henry
Hutz H. Hertzberg
Roberta Hestenes
Paul Hiebert
Ed Hindson
Oswald C. J. Hoffman
Woo Jun Hong
James M. Houston
Jeanette Hsieh
R. Kent Hughes
Bill Hybels
Paul Jackson
Frank James
Kay Coles James
David Jeremiah

Ronald Johnson
Arthur P. Johnston
Howard Jones
Walter C. Kaiser Jr.
Kenneth Kantzer
D. James Kennedy
Jay Kesler
Craig Klamer
In Ho Koh
Woodrow Kroll
Beverly LaHaye
Tim LaHaye
Timothy Lam
Lewis C. Lampley
Richard D. Land
Richard G. Lee
James Leggett
Don Lester
Arthur Lewis
David H. Linden
Duane Litfin
Crawford Loritts
Max Lucado
John MacArthur
Stephen A. Macchia
Marlin Maddoux
C. J. Mahaney
Ronald F. Marshall
Ray M. Mathsen
Victor Matthews
Richard McBride
Bill McCartney
Jerry McComber
David Melvin
Ron Merryman
Mike Messerli
Jesse Miranda
Beth Moore
Peter C. Moore
T. M. Moore
Richard J. Mouw
Kenneth Mulholland
Toby Nelson
Thomas J. Nettles
Roger Nicole
William Nix
Phil Olsen
John Orne
Luis Palau
Earl F. Palmer
Hee Min Park
James Patterson
Cary M. Perdue
Zolton J. Phillips
Hal Poe
Phillip Porter
Paul Pressler
Ray Pritchard
Richard W. Reiter
Kurt Anders Richardson III
Robert Ricker
Pat Robertson
John Rodgers
Adrian Rogers
Tom Rosebrough
Doug Ross
Hugh Ross
Joseph F. Ryan
Ken Sande
H. David Schuringa
John Scott
Paul Scroggins

Frank Severn
Warren Shelton
David Short
Ronald J. Sider
Stephen Smallman
John T. Sneed
Russell Spittler
James J. Stamoolis
Charles F. Stanley
Brad Stetson
C. Bruce Stewart
Brian Stiller
John Stott
Joseph Stowell
Stephen Strang
Lee Strobel
Douglas Sweeney
Charles Swindoll
Joni Eareckson Tada
Paul Tambrino
Peter W. Teague
Greg Thornbury
Kimberly Thornbury
Thomas E. Trask
Augustin B. Vencer Jr.
Marion Von Rentzell
Billy Walker
Paul L. Walker
John F. Walvoord
Raleigh Washington
Greg Waybright
Jim Weaver
Timothy Weber
Collins D. Weeber
David F. Wells
Luder Whitlock
Bruce H. Wilkinson
David K. Winter
Charles J. Wisdom
Mike Womack
Richard F. Woodcock
Ravi Zacharias
Anne Zaka

APPENDIX THREE

A PERSONAL AFFIRMATION

I have read the declaration, "The Gospel of Jesus of Christ: An Evangelical Celebration."

Because, as it states,

- "The Gospel of Jesus Christ is news, good news: the best and most important news that any human being ever hears,"
- "This Gospel is the only Gospel: there is no other,"
- "All Christians are called to unity in love and unity in truth," and
- "To share the joy and hope of this Gospel is a supreme privilege,"

I embrace this declaration and affirm my commitment to the task of proclaiming this Gospel, and with it my allegiance to Christ himself, to the Gospel itself, and to my fellow cosigners as evangelical believers.

Name:______________________________

Date:______________________________

news: The best and

news that any hea

hears. ... This Go

message of the

and is the true k

ding them. ... This

the only Gospel

and to change it

is to pervert and in

Preaching and Worship Resources

■

written by Kevin G. Harney

ABOUT THE WRITER

Kevin G. Harney (B.A., Azusa Pacific University; M.Div., Fuller Seminary; D.Min., Western Theological Seminary) is the preaching pastor of Corinth Reformed Church, Grand Rapids, Michigan. His current church has grown from 350 worshipers to over 1,000 in the past six years. During his ministry he has served congregations from 200 to 10,000 members. For the past fifteen years he has done extensive speaking to groups of youth, men, and couples, has written or cowritten more than forty small-group study guides, and has published over 200 articles. He has written with, or edited for, authors, pastors, and scholars such as Charles Swindoll, Bill Hybels, John Ortberg, Alister McGrath, Walter Kaiser, and Mark Mittelberg. Although preaching is his vocation and calling, Kevin says that writing is one of his favorite hobbies. Kevin has been married to his wife, Sherry, for over fifteen years, and they have three boys —Zach, Josh, and Nate. Although he had said they would never have a dog, he has discovered that sons can be very persuasive, and the family now has a very friendly pup named Buddy.

USING THESE RESOURCES

KEVIN G. HARNEY

A WORD ABOUT THE TASK OF PREACHING

When I received the invitation to write twelve sermons (and related worship resources) to accompany the book *This We Believe*, I was both thrilled and humbled. Thrilled because I love preaching and the creative, Spirit-anointed process of preparing a sermon. Humbled because every time a preacher opens the Word of God and proclaims the life-changing truth of the Gospel, there is a profound sense of inadequacy for the task at hand. With this in mind, please know, as one preacher to another, that I have come to the throne of grace as I have prepared these preaching and worship resources. I have asked for the leading of the Spirit and the power of Jesus, and I have prayed that all the glory would go to our heavenly Father.

I live with the joyous responsibility of preaching three times every Sunday. This preaching includes two different sermons (one preached twice in the morning and the other preached in the evening). I love to learn from others and receive insights from scholars, preachers, family, and friends who love Jesus. As I read *This We Believe*, I discovered a wonderful resource for preaching and teaching. Each of the authors has communicated the truth of the Gospel with clarity and conviction.

In this preaching guide, I have sought to draw from the wealth of biblical truth in each chapter as well as from the great reservoir of illustrative material in this book. I have tried to present these resources in a way that is:

- Thoroughly biblical
- Theologically sound
- Deeply practical

I have also tried to keep in mind my many friends who are preachers of God's Word. Each of us approaches this great task of preaching from a slightly different angle. Some are more expository, others find a three-point approach very helpful, while others seek to find a way to lock key points into the memory banks of God's people by using words that rhyme or start with the same letter. I would not begin to pretend I have discovered the best of all possible ways to preach. In my mind, when preaching is true to the Word of God, theologically sound, Spirit led, and deeply practical, then God is pleased and the people of God are edified—no matter what stylistic approach is used.

I have sought to provide basic outlines any preacher can use and easily modify for a particular context and congregation. My prayer is that these sermon outlines will help you find a way you can faithfully and powerfully communicate these core beliefs to the body of believers God has called you to lead.

If you get a little nervous about the prospect of preaching a series of sermons that focuses on doctrinal orthodoxy, remember these clarifying words of G. K. Chesterton: "People have fallen into a foolish habit of speaking of orthodoxy as something heavy, humdrum and safe. There never was anything so perilous or so exciting as orthodoxy" (*Orthodoxy*).

God's Word is truth. It gives life. Preach it with conviction and the power of the Holy Spirit!

A WORD ABOUT THE INVITATION TO WORSHIP

Someone once asked me, "What is God looking for?" I balked, having no idea what to say. Years later I know how to answer that question. God is looking for worshipers. The heart of God longs for those who will worship him in Spirit and truth (John 4:23). He searches this vast universe looking for faithful worshipers.

As a preacher and pastor, you certainly know the challenge of planning a weekly worship service that is authentic, relevant, joy filled, faithful to Scripture, and God honoring. This is no small task. We live in a day when worship styles range from high liturgy to an unplanned, free-flowing format. Some churches use drama, dance, praise bands, and powerful media visuals. Others use traditional liturgies, hymns, and organ music. Many churches attempt to blend varied worship styles.

Yet churches all over the world, from every possible stylistic vantage point, faithfully lead God's people into the most holy place. The curtain has been torn in two from top to bottom. Access to the Father has been won through the death and resurrection of Jesus Christ. We are invited—called—to worship. Style is not our primary concern, but the glory of the Living God is the passion of our hearts.

In an effort to help in the worship planning process, I have reflected not only on the sermon, but also on other aspects of the worship service. If you choose to spend a number of weeks (we have provided resources for a twelve-week sermon series) preaching on the themes from this book, you will find ideas for each worship service that will help you develop a holistic worship experience around the central theme of each chapter. I have provided resources, such as hymn and praise chorus suggestions, responsive readings, prayers, drama ideas, and more. I offer these knowing that some of the suggestions may fit naturally into your worship service and style, and others may not. These are simply ideas to get your creative juices flowing as you plan worship services that bring honor and glory to the King of kings.

A WORD ABOUT THE NEED FOR CLEAR DOCTRINAL STATEMENTS

Fuzzy at best.

That is how we would have to describe the doctrinal position of many people. We live in a day when crystal-clear declarations are few and far between and often evoke scoffing rather than praise. Many in the church today will express great concern over a change in the worship order, inclusion of a new instrument, or some stylistic idiosyncratic concern. They won't notice or express concern, however, when teaching is no longer biblical. Many in the church are not tuned in to the deep and abiding need for clear biblical doctrine.

There are also those who get upset when a preacher declares the truth and seeks to stand on the unchanging foundation of God's Word. In our relativistic age, some get upset when anyone, even a preacher, declares this is what we believe and this is what we do not believe. They say things like, "Who are you to claim you know the truth?" "That might be your truth, but I have my own truth!" "You are free to believe whatever you want, but don't try to make any declaration that is going to be normative or binding on anyone else." Sadly, even church leaders make such statements. Relativism rules supreme. Subjectivity is on the throne. Clear doctrinal statements are offensive to many and are becoming a vestigial remnant of a day gone by.

This should not be so! One of the greatest gifts we can give to the church and to a lost world is a clarion call to the truth. The statement being examined in this book, "The Gospel of Jesus Christ: An Evangelical Celebration," is no new prophecy for this generation. It is an impassioned affirmation of what the church has believed since its birth.

Are statements like this helpful? In our day, they are essential!

A WORD ABOUT THIS MOMENT IN TIME

There are critical moments in history that cry out for a fresh word, a clear statement, a decisive declaration. As we enter the opening years of this new millennium, I believe we are in such a time.

The document "The Gospel of Jesus Christ: An Evangelical Celebration" is a call to evangelical unity that grows out of a passionate desire to celebrate the power, joy, and clarity of the Gospel. It is bold and unapologetic. It is just what we need in this moment of time!

In our relativistic day, many want to remake the Gospel to fit the ever-lowering standards of a world whose heart has wandered far from God. This temptation has existed from the very beginning, and God has spoken plainly about the seriousness of the call to keep the purity of the Gospel. Hear the apostle Paul's warning:

> I am astonished that you are so quickly deserting the one who called you by the grace of Christ and are turning to a different gospel—which is really no gospel at all. Evidently some people are throwing you into confusion and are trying to pervert the gospel of Christ. But even if we or an angel from heaven should preach a gospel other than the one we preached to you, let him be eternally condemned! As we have already said, so now I say again: If anybody is preaching to you a gospel other than what you accepted, let him be eternally condemned! (Gal. 1:6–9)

With the proliferation of false "gospels" and the compromise of the true Gospel in many places, it is time for the church to stand with a united voice and declare what it believes. This series of sermons and the related worship tools are designed to help as you call the people of God to hold firmly to the Gospel.

If you choose to take a season in the life of your congregation to preach a series of sermons on these topics, know you will be in good company, for other preachers and worship leaders all over the world will be bringing a similar word to the people of God in their churches. Let us lift our voices in unison with the saints of God who have gone before us and declare without compromise, *This We Believe!*

A WORD ABOUT USING THESE RESOURCES

I do not presume that any preacher would present these sermons just as they are. Preaching is far too dynamic for that. Each of us needs to allow time for prayer, reflection, additional study, and grappling with the text of Scripture. Each person who uses the materials from the book *This We Believe* and these worship resources will need to leave room for a unique work of the Spirit as he or she prepares and proclaims the truth of the Gospel.

With this in mind, please review these materials carefully and prayerfully. Glean what you can use and what fits your ministry context. I trust there will be a wealth of scriptural passages, ideas, illustrations, and tools that will help you in your sermon preparation. My prayer is that these resources will move you into a deep place of preparation and passion for the topics on which you will preach.

Chapter 1

DOES MY LIFE HAVE ANY MEANING?

SERMON TITLE:
DISCOVER THE MEANING OF LIFE

The drama of this sermon unfolds in three acts. We begin with a familiar and common scene—the reality of meaninglessness. The goal here is not to convince people that life is meaningless without God; it is simply to acknowledge the common feeling experienced by human beings. All of us come to a point where we ask, "Why am I here? Isn't there more to life? Why does my heart feel so vacant?" As the curtain goes up on this sermon, speak to the reality of how so many people in our world live with a daily sense of deep meaninglessness.

1. The Despair of Meaninglessness

- Tell the story of Sisyphus. It can be read from the book, but it would be better if you put it in your own words (pp. 25–26).
- Read Ecclesiastes 2:10–11. Acknowledge the universal place that all people come to at some point along the journey of life, the profound sense that life has a feeling of emptiness and lack of meaning.
- Speak to the reality of so many who live day by day in a state of utter emptiness.
- Pray for God to reveal the source of hope and lasting meaning in an empty world.

As the curtain goes up for the second scene of this tragedy, we begin to discover the "why" of meaninglessness. We open our eyes to some of the pursuits and attitudes that leave our hearts empty and our spirits dry.

2. Empty Wells and Broken Cisterns

- Reflect on the human desire to drink deeply of life and find ultimate meaning.
- Look at the three examples of meaninglessness (draw from pp. 26–29):

  — materialism's despair
  — pleasure's concession
  — naturalism's vanity

- Read Jeremiah 2:12–13. Reflect on the heartbreak of God over his children who have fountains of living water provided by his grace but choose to dig their own wells and make their own cisterns, only to discover that this leads to greater emptiness and meaninglessness.
- Reflect on the utter despair that comes when we try to fill ourselves, dig our own wells, and drink from our own cisterns.

If you have ever been in the Middle East, you know that water is life. If a person is dehydrated and comes to a well hoping to find the life-giving water he desperately needs, he ends up disappointed, discouraged, and depressed if he finds the well dry. When a family dug a cistern and filled it with water, they often would expect this water supply to get them through months of arid weather. If the cistern cracked and the water soaked into the ground, they could end up in dire straits.

Jeremiah moves us from this earthy illustration of dry wells and broken cisterns to the spiritual condition of people who seek to find refreshment in wells of their own making—without God.

- Our lives are spiritually parched, and we thirst for a filling of living water that will satisfy our hearts and bring lasting meaning to our lives.

As we take an intermission between the second and third acts of this tragic drama, we become quite sober. We find ourselves mouthing the words of Ecclesiastes:

When I surveyed all that my hands had done
and what I had toiled to achieve,
everything was meaningless, a chasing after the wind;
nothing was gained under the sun (2:11).

Yet, as the curtain goes up on the third act, we discover something amazing. This is not a tragedy that gets worse and worse with each scene. This is no Romeo and Juliet, *no Shakespearian story with only tears at the end. This story ends with joy. The final scene reveals a source of living water for our thirsty souls. In the final act we see Jesus and discover that he is ready and able to fill us with himself. He brings meaning to the whole of life.*

3. The Fountain of Life's Meaning: The Person of Jesus

- Explain the four stages of life and how Jesus is the one who satisfies and fills us in each new chapter of life. He is our source of meaning amid the vanity of life. Ravi Zacharias does a wonderful job of describing and illustrating this in chapter 1 of this book (pp. 30–40).

  — the childlike sense of wonder
  — the quest for truth in adolescence (John 14:6)
  — the passion for love in young adulthood (1 John 4:7–8)
  — the essential need for security (John 11:25)

- Testimony: You may want to have a church member stand up and give a brief testimony to how Jesus Christ has brought meaning in this season of life. If you know a person who can develop a video and are able to show it during the service, you might have four people (one in each stage of life) give a very brief testimony as to how Jesus is bringing meaning to life. This could be shown before the sermon or at this point in the sermon before the conclusion.
- All of these components of meaning are found in Jesus—fully and completely! Address this reality and challenge people to commit themselves to look only to him for their meaning, not to the empty wells that fail to satisfy.
- Extend an invitation to come and drink deeply of the fountain and discover the meaning of life fully revealed and experienced in Jesus Christ.

Closing Prayer

OTHER IDEAS FOR THIS WORSHIP SERVICE

Hymn Suggestions

"Because He Lives" (William J. and Gloria Gaither)
"Blessed Assurance" (Fanny J. Crosby/Phoebe P. Knapp)
"Jesus Is King" (Wendy Churchill/arranged by Tom Fettke)

Praise Chorus Suggestions

"Better Is One Day" (1995, Kingsway's Thankyou Music)
"Breathe" (1995, Mercy/Vineyard)
"I Exalt Thee" (1977, Pete Sanchez Jr.)
"I Will Not Forget You" (1999, Blue Renaissance Music)
"Knowing You" (1993, Make Way Music)
"Let Everything That Has Breath" (1997, Kingsway's Thankyou Music)

Prayer Suggestion

This following prayer is from *Prayers of the Martyrs*, ed. Duane W. H. Arnold (Grand Rapids: Zondervan, 1990).

Now at last I am beginning
 to be a disciple.
No earthly pleasure can
 bring me any good,
 no kingdom of this world.
It is better for me to perish
 and obtain Jesus Christ
 than to rule over
 the ends of the earth.
Let me win through to the light;
 that done, I shall be complete.
Let me suffer as my Lord suffered.

—*Ignatius of Antioch, A.D. 107, after his capture in the Syrian persecution and just before being martyred by being thrown to wild beasts in Rome*

Additional Scripture Texts

John 10:7–18 (key verse: John 10:10)
Ecclesiastes 1:1–11

Drama Suggestion

"Livin' in Adverse City," from *Sunday Morning Live*, vol. 9 (Grand Rapids: Zondervan, 1998).

Responsive Reading

Leader: How have we come to know the Gospel of Jesus Christ?

Congregation: We affirm that the Gospel entrusted to the church is, in the first instance, God's Gospel. God is its author, and he reveals it to us in and by his Word. Its authority and truth rest on him alone.

Leader: If God alone is the author of the Gospel, then what must the church deny?

Congregation: We deny that the truth or authority of the Gospel derives from any human insight or invention. We also deny that the truth or authority of the Gospel rests on the authority of any particular church or human institution.

—From "The Gospel of Jesus Christ: An Evangelical Celebration"

Reflection

You may want to print this brief reflection on the Gospel on the cover of your church bulletin or project it for reflection at the beginning of your worship service:

> This Gospel sets forth Jesus Christ as the living Savior, Master, Life, and Hope of all who put their trust in him. It tells us that

the eternal destiny of all people depends on whether they are savingly related to Jesus Christ.

This Gospel is the only Gospel: there is no other; and to change its substance is to pervert and indeed destroy it. This Gospel is so simple that small children can understand it, and it is so profound that studies by the wisest theologians will never exhaust its riches.

SMALL-GROUP DISCUSSION RESOURCES

At the end of each chapter, the author has offered some questions for discussion and reflection. If you wish to use this book or these sermons as a springboard for small-group discussion, here are a few more questions that may help in the process:

Biblical Understanding

1. Read Ecclesiastes 2:1–11. How does this passage express the seeking and longing of every person in every generation?
2. Read Revelation 3:14–18. What is God saying to the church in Laodicea? How does this word speak to the church today?

Theological Reflection

1. Respond to this statement: We can have all of the world's goods, all of the world's praise, and all of the world's wisdom, but if we are not in a living relationship with God, life will always be meaningless.
2. How has the truth of God's Gospel brought meaning to your life?

Practical Application

1. What is one meaningless pursuit you have invested in that needs to be forsaken so you can walk more closely with Jesus Christ, the giver of all meaning?

2. Identify one person you care about deeply who has not yet discovered the true meaning of life in Jesus Christ. How can others pray for you and encourage you as you seek to share the true meaning of life with this person?

Chapter 2

DOING IT MY WAY: ARE WE BORN REBELS?

SERMON TITLE:
ARE WE BORN REBELS?

It is a new millennium, but some things never change. In a hospital a baby is born. A precious little girl—beautiful, precious, perfect! Perfect? Perfection is such a fragile thing. As the doctors do their testing and look more closely, they discover something is wrong. She is physically flawless, but something in the very DNA of her soul is corrupt—something passed down from both of her parents and from their parents before them. From the very beginning this little girl has a sickness in her soul called sin. *With time the symptoms will surface and everyone will see them—this little one is born a rebel. There is no denying it; sin has infected this little life.*

1. The Diagnosis

- Tell the story of St. Michael's Cathedral (pp. 43–44). Read it from the book or tell it in your own words. The key theme is captured in these words by J. I. Packer: "*The remnants of great dignity are still apparent, but the ruins are useless for their intended purpose until they undergo a rebuilding more radical than anyone contemplating the scene can imagine.*" Linger on the sad and painful reality of the human condition due to sin. What is true of this great cathedral is far more true and tragic when we see this reality in the life of a person loved by God yet devastated by sin.

- Read Romans 1:18–32. It is time to call sin what it is! No glossing, no avoiding, and no pretending here. Imagine a doctor receiving a report on a patient and discovering that she has cancer. If dealt with immediately, this cancer is very treatable, but if ignored, it will spread and take the life of this person. What would you think of this doctor if he decided not to tell the patient about the condition and the treatment that is available? What if the doctor said, "I want to spare this person the pain of hearing bad news. I don't want her to feel sad. I will protect her by withholding the results of her test." No one would stand for this. We would be outraged. How much more should we be outraged when people withhold the truth that all people are sinful and heading for death but that there is a remedy for their soul and treatment for their condition in Jesus Christ?
- Make an honest assessment. Our sinful condition is no deep dark secret—it is plain to see.

  —G. K. Chesterton's insights are helpful here (p. 47).
  —J. I. Packer has a powerful and poignant insight on this point:

> It is ironic that while the modern West has been lurching wholesale into a new barbarism beyond our wildest nightmares (genocide, massacre, torture, systematic rape and cruelty, organized crime, and so on), psychologists, educationists, social theorists, and opinion-makers have been laboring to assure us that original sin was only a neurotic myth and that it would be very bad for us all to revert to it. To pump out such oracles in face of the above facts is perhaps the greatest example of cognitive dissonance that ever was! (p. 48)

Packer's insights (pp. 47–56) will be very helpful as you develop this section.

The natural response of every person who gets news of an illness is to ask some basic questions. How did this happen? Where did it come from? And most of all, what do I have to do to get rid of this? Can I change my diet? Should I exercise more? Maybe if I stop a few bad habits. Yet the sickness the Bible calls sin is so deep, so woven into the fabric of our being, there is no easy fix. We can't work it off, drive it out, or heal it up on our own. We lack the strength, abilities, or even the will to deal with this sickness of the soul.

2. Our Inability to Heal Ourselves

- Tell the story of the patient who thought he was dead but was really alive (page 49). We, on the other hand, think we are alive when we are really dead due to sin.
- Use the great exposition on this reality by Packer. Continue to expound on the powerful picture of Romans 1. We are in a downward spiral of sin, going farther and farther from God. We are dying, and we don't know it! Not only do we continue sinning, but we approve and applaud when others enter in (Rom. 1:32).

  — We don't know ourselves (p. 50).
  — We lack standards for moral and spiritual self-assessment (pp. 50–51).
  — We do not think self-centeredness is a moral flaw (p. 51).

We have an illness, and we can do nothing to remedy our condition. Things look hopeless until we realize there is a Great Physician who can do for us what we could never do for ourselves. Through Jesus Christ, God has extended healing to all who believe in his name. Jesus is our one hope for healing.

3. Our One Hope for Healing

Packer offers helpful and insightful commentary on the opening chapters of Romans that will be very valuable as you develop this section (pp. 54–56).

- The universal human need for righteousness (Rom. 1:18–3:20)
- The gift of righteousness (Rom. 3:21–5:21)

Point to the coming week's sermon and let people know you will be digging much more deeply into our source of healing—Jesus Christ.

Closing Prayer

OTHER IDEAS FOR THIS WORSHIP SERVICE

Hymn Suggestions

"At the Cross" (Isaac Watts/Ralph E. Hudson)

"Grace Greater Than Our Sin" (Julia J. Johnson/Daniel B. Towner)
"One Day" (J. Wilbur Chapman/Charles H. Marsh)

Praise Chorus Suggestions

"Coming Back" (1994, Curious? Music)
"Create in Me a Clean Heart" (1979, Singspiration)
"In the Light" (1991, Sparrow Song/Andi Beat Goes On)
"Light the Fire Again" (1994, Mercy/Vineyard)
"Sweet Mercies" (1995, Mercy/Vineyard)
"Wonderful, Merciful Savior" (1990, Word Music)

Prayer Suggestion

The following has been adapted to contemporary language.

Heavenly Father, merciful and everlasting God, we acknowledge and confess before Your divine Majesty that we are poor miserable sinners, conceived and brought forth in sin and corruption. We are prone to all evil. We cannot, without You, do anything that is good. And we daily, and in many ways, transgress Your holy commandments. Therefore we provoke Your anger against us, and draw down upon ourselves, by Your just judgments, death and destruction.

But Lord, we repent and are sorry from our hearts that we have so displeased You. We condemn ourselves and our misdoings, and pray that Your grace may bring help to our distress and misery.

The Reformation Confession of Sins, 1525

Additional Scripture Texts

Jeremiah 17:9
Romans 8:9–11
Ephesians 2:1–10

Drama Suggestion

"A Nice Guy," from *Sunday Morning Live*, vol. 2 (Grand Rapids: Zondervan, 1993).

Responsive Reading

Leader:	What can we affirm about the condition of the human heart outside of Christ?
Congregation:	We affirm that the Gospel diagnoses the universal human condition as one of sinful rebellion against God, which, if unchanged, will lead each person to eternal loss under God's condemnation.
Leader:	If this is true, then what must we deny?
Congregation:	We deny any rejection of the fallenness of human nature or any assertion of the natural goodness, or divinity, of the human race.

—The Gospel of Jesus Christ:
An Evangelical Celebration

SMALL-GROUP DISCUSSION RESOURCES

At the end of each chapter, the author has offered some questions for discussion and reflection. If you wish to use this book or these sermons as a springboard for small-group discussion, here are a few more questions that may help in the process:

Biblical Understanding

1. Read Romans 1:18–32. Describe the downward spiral of sin that the apostle Paul portrays in this passage. How does sin lead to more sin?
2. Read Ephesians 2:1–10. The apostle Paul paints a picture of those who are "dead" and those who are "alive." According to this pas-

sage, what does a spiritually dead person look like? What does a spiritually alive person look like?

Theological Reflection

1. What do you think the apostle Paul means when he says, "[God] gave them over" (Rom. 1:24, 26, 28) to their sins? Why would God do this?
2. How does moving from death to life (Eph. 2:1–10) happen all at once? How does it happen over time?

Practical Application

1. We live in a cultural climate of unexamined tolerance and mindless political correctness. How do the apostle Paul's words in Romans 1:32 express the spirit of our day? "Although they know God's righteous decree that those who do such things deserve death, they not only continue to do these very things but also approve of those who practice them." What examples do you see around you?
2. How can Christians offer a voice filled with grace and truth as we call sin what it is yet extend the message of the Gospel?

Chapter 3

JESUS CHRIST: WHO DO WE SAY THAT HE IS?

SERMON TITLE:

JESUS CHRIST: WHO DO WE SAY THAT HE IS?

Imagine a defense attorney standing up in court with every intention of defending his client. The judge gives the familiar instructions: "Please call your first witness." The attorney responds, "Your Honor, I have no witnesses." Silence falls over the courtroom. There is an awkward pause. Everyone present knows that this young attorney has all but lost the case. "No witnesses" is not what a defense attorney wants to say.

Same scene, different attorney. The question comes again: "Please call your first witness." The attorney brings out a list of witnesses that is not only pages long, it is volumes long! The witnesses line up in the aisle of the courtroom, out the back door, down the hall, and into the street in front of the courthouse, streaming as far as the eye can see. Character witnesses, expert witnesses, eyewitnesses—one by one they take the stand, take the oath, and speak clearly and boldly about the defendant. This attorney has a solid case.

When it comes to Jesus, we find a list of witnesses as long as history. From Moses to the prophets, from the Gospel writers to John in exile, the witnesses line up. From the first century to this very moment in history, countless witnesses take their place on the witness stand and declare that they have come to know that Jesus Christ is the holy one of God, the Savior of the world. Jesus Christ is Lord.

Introduction

- Read excerpt from "One Solitary Life" (p. 61).

1. Who Do People Say Jesus Is?

- Read Matthew 16:13–16. Jesus asked, "Who do people say the Son of Man is?" Look at some of the opinions that have existed through history and that continue today.
- Pray for God to open the eyes of every person gathered for worship to see the real Jesus.
- Share Gallup's findings (p. 62). Discuss the word on the street about who Jesus is.
- Does each generation create a new Jesus to accommodate their tastes (pp. 62–63)?

In some court cases, the last thing the defense attorney wants is his or her client on the stand. The attorney tells the client to invoke the Fifth Amendment and to remain silent. Not so in Jesus' case. The most convincing, powerful, and poignant testimony comes from the very lips of Jesus. His life gives witness to who he is. So Jesus takes the stand.

2. Please Call Your First Witness!

- Discuss Jesus' testimony (draw from pp. 64–66 as you develop this section).

  — the "I am" sayings of Jesus
  — the "Son of Man"
  — the parables as they point to Jesus' identity

- Discuss some confirmations of Jesus' identity.

  — voice of God at Jesus' baptism (Matt. 3:17)
  — Jesus' power to do miracles (Luke 11:20)
  — victory of the resurrection (Acts 2:32)

Jesus gives testimony to who he is. Yet the jury members may wonder if self-testimony alone can be trusted. Are there corroborating witnesses? Do others give testimony that what Jesus said of himself is true?

Now the judge asks, "Do you have any other witnesses?" The defending attorney hands the list over to the judge. Page after page after page. Volume after volume of names. There seems to be an endless list of witnesses ready to take the stand and testify to who Jesus is and what he has done. They span every cultural, economic, and age group. Some witnesses have traveled from the other side of the earth, and some give testimony in writing that was penned thousands of years earlier. How long will it take to hear all of the witnesses? Well, how long do you have?

3. Do You Have Any Other Witnesses?

- Discuss the witness of the Gospel writers (pp. 66–69). Here we find eyewitness accounts and the testimony of those who have carefully researched the life and teaching of Christ. Remember, these are not academicians who are sitting down two thousand years after the fact and trying to decide what Jesus did and said. These are Jesus' contemporaries, those who researched his life. Some are firsthand witnesses and participants in much of what Jesus did.

  —Mark testifies: Jesus is the Son of God!
  —John testifies: Jesus is the Word!
  —Matthew testifies: Jesus is the Christ!
  —Luke testifies: Jesus is the Servant of the Lord!

- Examine Paul's testimony: Jesus is Lord!

  —Read Philippians 2:5–11 and Colossians 1:15–20. Take time to reflect on these powerful and clear statements of the apostle Paul.
  —Paul uses "in Christ" two hundred times. Discuss the rich meaning of this term (p. 69).

- Discuss the witness of the church. Throughout the history of the church, prayerful efforts have been made to bear witness to what Christians believe about Jesus Christ. These statements have grown out of a desire to crystallize the core teaching of Scripture. Two of these testimonies are:

  —The Council of Nicea: Jesus is the same substance as the Father. (You may want to develop the images used on pages 73–74: parent and child versus carpenter and table.)

—The Council of Chalcedon: Jesus is one person with two natures.

One by one, the voices from history have spoken. From Moses, the prophets, the Gospels, the early church, the councils—all have stood and given testimony. The judge asks, "Are there any more witnesses?" Silence. Eyes are looking around the room, and suddenly you realize they have fallen on you! It is now your turn to take the stand. Are you ready to add your voice to the countless cloud of witnesses who have gone before you?

4. The Power of Your Witness to Christ

- Are you prepared to give an account for the hope that is in you (1 Peter 3:15)?
- Take time for testimonies. You may want to have someone ready to stand up and tell how Jesus Christ has revealed himself as Lord and Savior in his or her life. If your worship service style and time constraints allow, you may wish to have an open microphone(s) and allow people to line up and give their testimonies as a response to the message. Let them take the witness stand!
- Your story is Jesus' story! How has God impacted your life through Jesus Christ? Extend an invitation for each believer present to commit in a new and fresh way to bearing witness to the life-changing reality of Jesus Christ.

Closing Prayer

OTHER IDEAS FOR THIS WORSHIP SERVICE

Hymn Suggestions

"I Would Be Like Jesus" (James Rowe/Bentley D. Ackley)
"Lord, I Want to Be a Christian" (Traditional spiritual)
"Open My Eyes, That I May See" (Clara H. Scott)

Praise Chorus Suggestions

"All Hail King Jesus" (1981, Glory Alleluia Music)

"Ancient of Days" (1985, Mercy)
"Meekness and Majesty" (1986, Integrity's Hosanna! Music)
"We Bow Down" (1982, Singspiration)
"We Will Worship the Lamb" (1989, Shepherd's Heart Music)
"Your Name Is Holy" (1999, Vineyard)

Prayer Suggestion

The following prayer is from *Prayers of the Martyrs*, ed. Duane W. H. Arnold (Grand Rapids: Zondervan, 1990).

I bless you, Jesus,
  to you belong all blessings.
I bless you, Jesus,
  you are the only begotten of the Father.
I bless you, Jesus,
  you are the true vine,
  the crown upon the throne of the Father.
I bless you, Jesus,
  you walked upon the water,
  and your feet remained dry.
I bless you, Jesus,
  you made the bitter waters sweet.
I bless you, Jesus,
  you are the staff held by the Father.
I bless you, Jesus,
  you are the unmovable rock.
I bless you, Jesus,
  you command the angels.
I bless you, Jesus,
  and your good Father, in whose hands
  is our breath, and who gives us life.
For yours is the power and the glory forever, Amen.

—*Shenoufe the Copt, said to have been arrested during the Diocletianic persecution along with eleven family members who all died under torture*

Additional Scripture Texts

John 14:6 and Acts 4:12
Exodus 3:14 and John 8:58
Matthew 1:23

Drama Suggestion

"Security Check," from *Sunday Morning Live*, vol. 4 (Grand Rapids: Zondervan, 1993).

Reflection

You may want to print this brief reflection on the Gospel on the cover of your church bulletin or project it for reflection at the beginning of your worship service:

> The Gospel of Jesus Christ is news, good news: the best and most important news that any human being ever hears. This Gospel identifies Jesus Christ, the Messiah of Israel, as the Son of God and God the Son, the second person of the Holy Trinity, whose incarnation, ministry, death, resurrection, and ascension fulfilled the Father's saving will. His death for sins and his resurrection from the dead were promised beforehand by the prophets and attested by eyewitnesses.

SMALL-GROUP DISCUSSION RESOURCES

At the end of each chapter, the author has offered some questions for discussion and reflection. If you wish to use this book or these sermons as a springboard for small-group discussion, here are a few more questions that may help in the process:

Biblical Understanding

1. Read Philippians 2:5–11 and Colossians 1:15–20. If you were to meet the apostle Paul and ask him, "Who is Jesus Christ?" and

"What has Jesus done for us?" what do you think he would say in light of these passages?

2. Read Matthew 16:13–16. What was the word on the street about who Jesus was? What did all three of the people the disciples mentioned have in common? What implications does this have on how the people viewed Jesus?

Theological Reflection

1. Someone says to you, "I don't believe Jesus was God, and I don't believe he is really the savior for anyone. What I believe is that Jesus was a good person and a wonderful moral teacher." In light of what Paul writes in Philippians 2:5–11 and Colossians 1:15–20, how would you respond?
2. One of the clearest and most powerful affirmations made by Jesus is: "I am the way and the truth and the life. No one comes to the Father except through me. If you really knew me, you would know my Father as well. From now on, you do know him and have seen him" (John 14:6–7). What is Jesus claiming in this passage? What implications does this have on those who claim to be sincere in their own religious devotion but do not believe in Jesus Christ as Savior?

Practical Application

1. If Jesus is who he says he is, how should this impact the way we worship him? What is one thing you can you do to more surrender your life to Jesus as Lord in the coming days?
2. Since Jesus is "the way and the truth and the life," what can you do to help fortify and expand the evangelism/mission ministry of your local church? How can you enter into prayer, service, and giving that will strengthen the outreach of your congregation?

Chapter 4

AM I NOT GOOD ENOUGH? WHY JESUS HAD TO DIE FOR MY SINS

SERMON TITLE:

WHY DID JESUS HAVE TO DIE?

Opening Illustration

Tell the story of Luther's conversion (pp. 79–80). Focus on Luther's struggle to reconcile the twin realities of God's wrath and love. This same struggle takes place in the hearts of many people today. Yet as we look at Luther, we discover what he came to see so clearly: the same Christ who is judge (Rom. 3:9–18) is also our loving Savior (1 Tim. 1:15).

Radically distorted reality. Unclear, blurred, and obscured. We can't begin to see things from God's perspective, for all we have is our own distorted point of view. When it comes to our understanding of ourselves and God, everything is clouded.

Infected by sin, our vision and perspective have been damaged. We actually believe that, if there is a God, he exists to serve us. We see God as our lucky genie in a bottle. We keep him under our control confined on a shelf. But when we need him, we take down the bottle, rub it a little, and in a puff of smoke, God appears and greets us with a cheerful, "Your wish is my command!" When we say jump, God is supposed to cry out, "How high?" He exists to serve us, make us happy, and meet our needs.

If he fails in this calling, we are disappointed and may even become angry with God. Talk about a distorted view of reality—outside of Christ we see ourselves on the throne and God as our servant!

1. The Reason for God's Judgment

- Read Romans 3:9–18. Expound on Paul's teaching about the condition of the human heart. He does not paint a pretty picture. He holds up a mirror and lets us see the true condition of our hearts and lives outside of Christ. Attractive? No! The truth? Yes!
- Talk about our selfish hearts and pursuits (pp. 81–82). We are in love with the world and hate God! We tend to seek first our desires and wants, not the things of the kingdom (Matt. 6:33).

  — A wonderfully powerful set of images can be found on page 82: "Like a fish in water, we are unaware of the very thing to which we owe our every breath, namely God himself. And like an addict in denial, we gorge ourselves on the very things that destroy us, namely the false gods that we have made out of ourselves and the other created things in the world."

- Reflect on the idolatry of our age and our sinful hearts (pp. 83–84). We worship ourselves and the creation rather than the Creator (Exod. 20:3, 17; Rom. 1:25).
- Judgment is the real and certain fruit of our sinful and idolatrous ways (Jer. 2:20–37).

Like a fun-house mirror, sin distorts what we see. But this is no cheap amusement; this is life! Our ability to see reality as God sees it is so limited that we will never get a clear picture without God's help. Sin clouds our vision so that everything is blurred. Only as we see things through God's eyes can our vision be restored. He reveals the true condition of our heart, the absolute glory and splendor of the Father, and our abounding need of healing, redemption, and a new beginning. The problem is, when God shows us reality, we may not like what we see.

2. Our Need for Mercy

- Read Psalm 51. David was confronted with the reality of his own heart, actions, and sinful condition. He had allowed himself to stay blinded to the truth. He thought that if he covered his tracks, no one would ever know about his sin. It took God's intervention to get David to open his eyes and finally repent. This is also true for us. God, in his grace, helps us see our need for his great mercy (exposition on pp. 84–86).

- Our *eyes* must be opened. Before we are ready to cry out for God's mercy, we must see ourselves as we are. (Tell the story of William Carey, pp. 84–85.)
- Our *heart* must be changed. Like David, when we see our sinful hearts and lives through the lens of the Holy Spirit, our heart can be broken.
- Our *lips* must confess. When we see ourselves as we are, we can cry out for God's mercy (Rom. 10:9–10). Important reminder: Even our strength to cry out for help comes from the very grace of God.

And now we see! When we finally realize our great need and the even greater love God extends to us in Christ, our vision is restored. When by faith we receive Christ, our eyes are opened to the spiritual realities that were always there but we never saw. This is one of the most amazing things about God's grace. When we first receive it, we think we comprehend and see its fullness. But only after we receive Christ and have our eyes opened do we begin to really understand how wide and deep God's grace is! Through the eyes of faith, the fog melts away, the picture clears, and we finally see life through God's eyes.

3. The Heart of the Gospel

- Tell the story of the daughter and the judge (p. 87). This is the heart of God for his children.
- The heart of the Gospel is the life, death, and resurrection of Jesus Christ (Mark 10:45; see Hafemann's exposition on pp. 88–89).
- Read 1 Peter 3:18 and 2 Corinthians 5:17–21. Read the story from *A Tale of Two Cities* on pages 89–90. Though an imperfect example, because Carton was not a perfect sacrifice, it certainly brings alive the reality of a costly exchange to save a life. Christ did this perfectly on the cross.
- Close by giving the basic message of salvation in Christ alone (pp. 91–97).

- We do not trust God so that Christ might die and be raised from the dead for us. We trust God because Christ has *already* died and been raised from the dead (Rom. 4:24–25). When we trust God *alone* because of what he *alone* has already done for us in Christ, God *alone* gets the glory. The giver gets the glory.

Closing Prayer

OTHER IDEAS FOR THIS WORSHIP SERVICE

Hymn Suggestions

"Behold the Lamb" (Dottie Rambo)
"For God So Loved the World" (Frances Townsend/Alfred B. Smith)
"O How He Loves You and Me" (Kurt Kaiser)

Praise Chorus Suggestions

"At the Cross" (1993, Mercy/Vineyard)
"I Will Offer Up My Life" (1996, Kingsway's Thankyou Music)
"Message of the Cross" (1993, Curious? Music)
"O the Blood of Jesus" (1992, Word Music)
"Once Again" (1995, Kingsway's Thankyou Music)

Additional Scripture Texts

Romans 3
Ephesians 2:8–9

Drama Suggestion

"These Parts," from *Sunday Morning Live*, vol. 2 (Grand Rapids: Zondervan, 1993).

Responsive Reading

Use a responsive reading from the Heidelberg Catechism, Q & A 34 and 45.

Leader: Why do we call Jesus "our Lord"?

Congregation: Because—not with gold or silver, but with his precious blood—he has set us free from sin and from the tyranny of the devil, and has bought us, body and soul, to be his very own.

Leader: How does Christ's resurrection benefit us?

Congregation: First, by his resurrection he has overcome death, so that he might make us share in the righteousness
He won for us by his death. Second, by his power we too
Are already now resurrected to a new life.
Third, Christ's resurrection
Is a guarantee of our glorious resurrection.

SMALL-GROUP DISCUSSION RESOURCES

At the end of each chapter, the author has offered some questions for discussion and reflection. If you wish to use this book or these sermons as a springboard for small-group discussion, here are a few more questions that may help in the process:

Biblical Understanding

1. Read Romans 3:9–18. Paul says Jews and non-Jews are all alike. He then gives a brief look at the anatomy of sinful people. Record what Paul teaches about our

   Mind
   Heart
   Mouth
   Feet

2. Read Psalm 51. In this powerful prayer of confession, record what David

   Admits to God
   Asks from God
   Promises to God

Theological Reflection

1. In light of what Paul writes in Romans 3:9–18, respond to this statement: "I admit that people have some flaws, but Paul is *overstating* how bad we are."
2. As you read Psalm 51, what do you learn about David's understanding of God's character?

Practical Application

1. How have you seen the damage and devastation that can come from harsh words spoken by sinful lips?
2. James 5:16 tells us to "confess your sins to each other and pray for each other so that you may be healed." What are ways we can enter into confession and prayer with other Christians? Why do we find this difficult?

Chapter 5

DID JESUS CHRIST REALLY RISE FROM THE DEAD?

SERMON TITLE:

DID JESUS ACTUALLY ARISE FROM THE DEAD?

Opening Illustration

Every pastor has had the painful experience of walking with a family through the valley of the shadow. Tell a story from your own experience of standing at a graveside with a family of nonbelievers, and reflect on the reality of remorse and hopelessness. Then tell a story of standing at the graveside of someone who died with the certain hope of resurrection in Jesus Christ. Discuss the differences between these two scenes. Why is it that Christians do not grieve as those who have no hope?

Skeptics have been around from the beginning. Ever since the religious leaders of Jesus' day fabricated their lie about what happened to Jesus' body, the trend has continued. People launch attacks on the resurrection of Jesus Christ, attempting to build a case against the reality that Jesus actually died and rose again on the third day. Just as such voices cried out two thousand years ago, they still cry out today.

How should we respond? The best way is to invite questions and skepticism with no fear or resistance. We need to listen and then ask clear and probing questions. Are the skeptics' assertions reasonable? Do their theories make sense? As we ask these questions in light of the history of the Christian church, we will often discover that even the toughest skeptic can see things a new way. When skeptics stop and look closely at the history of the early church, the teaching of the Bible, and the impact Christ is still having on lives today, they are struck by the reality that their skepticism is not nearly as well founded as they once thought. Some even come to a point of changing their minds and opening their hearts to Christ.

1. The Voices of the Skeptics

- Read 1 Corinthians 15:1–19. The apostle Paul clearly believed in the bodily resurrection of Jesus Christ. Yet people in his day, as in ours, resisted affirming this reality. What are some of the theories skeptics pose, and how do these measure up in light of reason? This will be the focus of the sermon.
- Read Matthew 28:11–15. Deceptions began from the time Jesus' body was discovered missing. Investigate and respond to some of the theories that persist in our day. Present each of the following theories—one at a time—as clearly and convincingly as you can. Then show why each does not make sense in light of the beliefs, actions, and history of the first-century church.

  —Christ did not really die (swoon theory, p. 104).
  —Someone stole the body (theft theory, pp. 104–5).
  —The disciples made up the story (projection theory, pp. 105–8).

Skeptics two thousand years after Jesus' resurrection look back and come up with the same theories that have circulated for two millennia. Yet as loud as they speak, the voices of the first-century believers are louder! Their faith, their sacrifice, and their confidence in the resurrection of Jesus Christ help us realize that this was no mass hysteria or hoax. They were transformed through their encounter with a risen Lord. The church today needs to listen closely to the voices of these witnesses.

2. The Voice of the First-Century Church

- The lives of Christ's followers were radically transformed. Something happened that made them new people, gave them new power, and birthed a commitment in their hearts so deep that they were willing to suffer and die for the name of Jesus (pp. 108–9). Read Matthew 26:69–75 and Acts 2:14–15, 40–41. What happened to transform Peter from a terrified denier into a bold proclaimer? He met the risen Christ!

- The resurrection narratives were recorded during the lifetime of many who had been firsthand witnesses to Jesus' life and death. Investigate the narratives themselves and how they are our primary source of what happened after Jesus' crucifixion and death (pp. 109–110).
- Investigate the meaning of the resurrection for early Christians (pp. 110–17).

— Thomas Oden offers a compelling and clear exposition of how the early church saw the resurrection of Jesus as the hinge point in human history.

> We today must learn to think historically in the Hebraic sense if we are to grasp the full meaning of this central proclamation of Christianity. Seen in this frame of reference, Christ's resurrection is so decisive that all other events pale in comparison. It discloses nothing less than the final revelation of the will of God in history (p. 113).

— Teaching of Justin Martyr (p. 110).

We hear the voices of the first witnesses of Jesus Christ, the risen Lord. Yet each new generation of believers needs to add their voices to this chorus and proclaim the truth of the resurrection in a way that their contemporaries will understand. The core message is always the same, but each generation of Christ's followers must speak in a new and fresh voice. What is the meaning of the resurrection in the lives of Christ's followers today, and in turn, how can this resurrected Christ impact the lives of others?

3. The Voice of Christians in All Generations

Even if people will admit that Jesus rose from the dead, this generation will always ask the big question: So what? What difference does his resurrection make? We need to be ready to help people understand the deliverance, power, and purpose that come into our lives when we enter a living relationship with the resurrected Christ. Oden offers great commentary on this (pp. 114–17).

- The resurrection *delivers us from the power of sin and death* (Rom. 8:2).
- The resurrection *is the seal of God's work on the cross* (Phil. 3:10).
- The resurrection *gives us a new understanding of Sabbath.*
- The resurrection *makes sense of history* (past, present, and future) (1 Cor. 15:20).
- The resurrection *ratifies all that Jesus taught and did* (Mark 8:31).

Closing Prayer

OTHER IDEAS FOR THIS WORSHIP SERVICE

Hymn Suggestions

"Because He Lives" (Gloria and William Gaither)
"Christ the Lord Is Risen Today" (Charles Wesley/*Lyra Davidica*)
"Crown Him with Many Crowns" (Matthew Bridges/George J. Elvey)
"He Lives" (Alfred H. Ackley)

Praise Chorus Suggestions

"Celebrate Jesus, Celebrate" (1988, Integrity's Hosanna! Music)
"I Believe in Jesus" (1987, Mercy/Vineyard)
"I Will Call Upon the Lord" (1981, Sound III Music)
"Our God Reigns" (1978, Leonard E. Smith Jr./New Jerusalem Music)
"That's Where I Am" (Rich Mullins, *The Jesus Record*)

Prayer Suggestion

Let the estates I own be ravaged,
or given to others;
Let me lose my life, and
let my body be destroyed;

Rather than that I should speak one word
against you, O Lord, who made me.
If they take from me a small portion
of this earth and its wealth,
I shall exchange it for heaven.

—*Julitta of Caesarea, a wealthy Christian widow arrested under the edicts of Diocletian and condemned to death by fire in A.D. 303*

This prayer could be read to the congregation as you address the power and confidence that comes when we know Jesus in his resurrection glory. It could also be printed in your church bulletin or projected on a screen prior to the service as people enter the sanctuary.

Additional Scripture Texts

John 20, 21
Romans 6:1–14
1 Corinthians 15

Study Idea and Witnessing Tool

You might want to purchase a copy of *An Anchor for the Soul* by Ray Pritchard (Chicago: Moody Press, 2000) to review as you preach, teach, and call the congregation to be witnesses to the resurrection of Jesus. Because, like *This We Believe*, it is based on "The Gospel of Jesus Christ: An Evangelical Celebration," the book is also a great resource to give to people who are investigating the Christian faith.

SMALL-GROUP DISCUSSION RESOURCES

At the end of each chapter, the author has offered some questions for discussion and reflection. If you wish to use this book or these sermons as a springboard for small-group discussion, here are a few more questions that may help in the process:

Biblical Understanding

1. Read 1 Corinthians 15:1–19. According to the apostle Paul, what is the core of the Gospel?
2. Describe how the apostle Paul would respond to this statement: "Even if Jesus did not rise from the dead, living as a Christian is still the best way to live."

Theological Reflection

1. What is the relationship of the resurrection of Jesus Christ and our hope of resurrection?
2. Some people claim that the "concept" of Jesus rising from the dead is really only a word picture to bring us hope and encouragement in the difficult journey of this life. They would say that it does not really matter if Jesus rose bodily. What would you say to a person who has this understanding of the resurrection?

Practical Application

1. Read 1 Corinthians 15:50–57. How does the hope of the resurrection influence the way you see this life and your death?
2. Describe a time you genuinely sensed the resurrection power of Christ filling your life and giving you power to live in a way that was pleasing to God.

Chapter 6

BEING A CHRISTIAN: WHAT DIFFERENCE DOES IT MAKE?

SERMON TITLE:

BEING A CHRISTIAN: WHAT DIFFERENCE DOES IT MAKE?

Can a leopard change its spots? Can an old dog learn new tricks? Can a sinner become a saint? Some people would give a resounding "No!" to each of these questions. But Jesus is in the life-changing business. He brings healing and harmony to shattered relationships. He shines his light and brings love and joy to the dark places of hate and sadness. He brings purity and holiness to even the most twisted and perverse lives. He brings peace in times of turmoil and purpose to those who hunger for a reason and meaning in life.

You may ask, "But can I *really change?" No matter what the naysayers of this world may want you to believe, Jesus brings the power and promise of radical and exciting transformation. When it comes to who we are and how we live our lives, Jesus makes all the difference in the world!*

Opening Illustration

Tell the story of Salomon (p. 122). How many people look at themselves and believe that there is no hope for them to change? How many people need to hear the message that Jesus Christ is in the business of transforming lives? Let the truth of God's Word (Phil. 4:13) sink into the hearts of those who are listening.

If Jesus is in the life-changing business, what is it he wants to do in our lives? We may grow anxious that God wants to steal our joy and put stifling limits on our fun. Nothing could be further from the truth. The difference that Jesus makes in our lives is a difference that leads to the very things our hearts long for. The changes he wants to make are the things we want the most but never seem to be able to attain on our own.

What is one of the greatest desires of the human heart? Intimacy! We all long to be in a relationship of total love, reckless surrender, and absolute transparency. Our heart yearns to be totally exposed and vulnerable with one we know will love us no matter what. This is the very kind of relationship that God offers us in Jesus Christ.

1. From Loneliness to Intimacy (Rom. 5:9–11; 2 Cor. 5:16–21; Eph. 2:12–13)

- Intimacy is the deepest longing of the human heart, and that is why so many popular songs strike this familiar chord. You may want to draw from the lyrics of a few popular songs that are currently on the minds of people. Why do people sing these songs over and over? These songs express their inner longings.
- Intimacy comes when we cultivate a relationship. Use the example of a healthy marriage. What does it take to nurture intimacy? Why would we think closeness with God would be any different?
- Tell the story of Indian evangelist Sadhu Sundar Singh (p. 124). After walking closely with Jesus, he was able to say, "Without Christ I am like a fish out of water. With Christ I am in an ocean of love."
- One of the joys of an intimate relationship with Christ is that it will never end (1 Cor. 15:54–55).

Relationship is not enough. We want our relationships to be filled with love and joy. True intimacy with one who knows us and loves us will bring a joy like nothing else this world can offer. When this relationship is with God, who is the author of love and joy, we find that his presence so fills us that there is a lavish overflow of these same characteristics into all of our relationships.

2. From Sadness to Joy (1 Cor. 13:1–7; 1 John 4:8, 16)

- Love and joy are bound to each other (Gal. 5:22). When God unleashes these in our lives, words can't begin to express what God means to us. Tell the story of the young believer who experienced this reality:

> A fairly new Christian was giving his testimony at a meeting, and it went smoothly until he came to describing God's love. He wanted to find a word that adequately described this amazing thing he had experienced. Finally he blurted out, "The staggerating love of God." There is no word called "staggerating" in the English language, but his joy over God's love was so intense that he needed to coin a word to express his feelings (pp. 126–27).

- Reflect on how God can take difficult or painful situations and turn them into something good (Rom. 8:28).

When God's love fills us and his joy overflows in our hearts, the changes in us begin to snowball—they begin small but then grow larger and larger. We can't stay the same. We don't want to! We long to be more like Jesus and to see his life growing inside of us.

3. From Sinfulness to Holiness (1 Peter 1:13–16)

- Expound on the deep meaning of Peter's call to holiness. You may want to look at the roots in Leviticus 11:44. In his chapter dealing with this call to a transformed life, Ajith Fernando mentions that in a study of the 2,005 verses of Paul's epistles, about 1,400 verses say something about holiness, godliness, or Christian character.
- God calls us to break from our habitual sins and surrender ourselves to him (1 John 3:9).
- Address the sobering reality that the Bible often warns us that people whose lives are characterized by sin will not be saved (1 Cor. 6:9–11; Gal. 5:19–21).
- With powerful and convicting words, Ajith Fernando writes:

> I believe that one reason why Christians do not take the call to be holy seriously enough is that our preaching and teaching have been defective. I believe that some Christians have not realized that racism and prejudice are completely incompatible with Christianity. This is why the evangelical movement has such a bad record in this regard. Perhaps our believers have not been clearly told that Christians simply must not do things like exploiting customers or employees, like lying and bribing, like disturbing neighbors, like being rude to spouses.

- If you have been pulling your punches as a preacher and if you have failed to call your congregation to holiness, confess it to them! Promise that you will be faithful to preach God's Word, and call each member of your congregation (including yourself) to walk in purity and holiness. Fernando does a great job of developing this call on pages 130–31.

In a world filled with turmoil and anxiety, we long for peace. We need to know with certainty that God is watching over us and that he will provide all we need. He is our heavenly Father, and we are his beloved children. He is the Good Shepherd, and we are his sheep. We can live with peace knowing that God will supply all we need.

4. From Turmoil to Peace (Phil. 4:6–7)

- Dig into Jesus' teaching on the peace that comes when we have our priorities straight (Matt. 6:28–34).
- You may want to have a church member share a brief testimony about how he or she has experienced God's amazing peace in a time that was somewhat difficult. This can be done live or on video, or you may wish to read a brief written testimony.

Though we could go on and on about the dramatic differences that take place in our lives when we know Jesus, we will look at just one more in this message. Again, the difference is one that answers a core desire of the human heart. We long for meaning and purpose in life.

We want to know that what we do with our days will really make a difference. God shows us that he has a plan for our lives that moves us from senseless wandering to lives of purpose and significance.

5. From Wandering to Purpose

- In this closing portion of the message, focus on two biblical images that help followers of Christ understand their identity and purpose in life. The first is our call to be Christ's ambassadors (2 Cor. 5:18–21). We are all gifted and called to share in God's ministry (Rom. 12:3–8). Are we living up to this high calling? Are we spectators or participants when it comes to Christian service and witness?
- Also reflect on the spiritual reality that we are children of God. We are his sons and daughters. We are part of the family of God (Rom. 8:14–17).

Closing Prayer

OTHER IDEAS FOR THIS WORSHIP SERVICE

Hymn Suggestions

"Holy, Holy" (Jimmy Owens)
"Let the Beauty of Jesus Be Seen in Me" (Albert Orsborn/Tom Jones)
"Take Time to Be Holy" (William D. Longstaff/George C. Stebbins)

Praise Chorus Suggestions

"Every Move I Make" (1996, Mercy/Vineyard)
"God Is the Strength of My Heart" (1989, Integrity's Hosanna! Music)
"The Happy Song" (1994, Curious? Music)
"In My Life, Lord, Be Glorified" (1978, Bob Kilpatrick Music)
"We Are an Offering" (1984, Bug and Bear Music)
"You Are My All in All" (1990, Shepherd's Heart Music)

Prayer Suggestion

You may want to include the following as a prayer in the service, print it in your church bulletin, or project it on a screen prior to the service as people are entering the sanctuary.

> *I'm part of the fellowship of the unashamed. I have Holy Spirit power. The die has been cast. I have stepped over the line. The decision has been made—I'm a disciple of His. I won't look back, let up, slow down, back away, or be still. My past is redeemed, my present makes sense, my future is secure. I'm finished and done with low living, sight walking, smooth knees, colorless dreams, tamed visions, worldly talking, cheap giving, and dwarfed goals.*
>
> *I no longer need preeminence, prosperity, position, promotions, plaudits, or popularity. I don't have to be right, first, tops, recognized, praised, regarded, or rewarded. I now live by faith, lean on His presence, walk by patience, am uplifted by prayer, and I labor with power.*
>
> —A YOUNG PASTOR IN ZIMBABWE, AFRICA, MARTYRED FOR HIS FAITH

Additional Scripture Texts

John 14:27
Philippians 4:6

Reflection

You may want to tell the story of Lee and Leslie Strobel as an example of changed lives (see sidebar on pp. 30–31). This contemporary story may strike a chord for many of your listeners.

SMALL-GROUP DISCUSSION RESOURCES

At the end of each chapter, the author has offered some questions for discussion and reflection. If you want to use this book or these sermons as a springboard for small-group discussion, here are a few more questions that may help in the process:

Biblical Understanding

1. Read Romans 5:9–11 and 2 Corinthians 5:16–21. Describe our relationship to God outside of Christ.
2. How does this relationship change when we come to God through Jesus Christ?

Theological Reflection

1. Both Romans and 2 Corinthians speak of reconciliation. What has God done to create an opportunity for reconciliation between us and himself?
2. God has called us to a ministry of reconciliation. Describe what this ministry might look like in your life at 3:00 on an average Monday afternoon.

Practical Application

1. Describe your life before you were reconciled to God. How have you changed?
2. The transformation God works in our lives does not happen all at once. He changes us over time. What is one area in which God is growing and changing you in this season of your life, and how can others pray for you to remain open to the transforming power of the Holy Spirit?

Chapter 7

POWER FOR CHRISTIAN LIVING: AM I ON MY OWN?

SERMON TITLE:

NO POWER SHORTAGE!

Opening Illustration

Tell the story of Stanley Mogaba. The Charles Wesley quote and Mogoba's response tie together this poignant story of the power of God to invade and transform a life (pp. 139–40).

I can remember the oil embargo and gas shortage in the United States in the early 1970s. Cars were lined up for blocks as they waited to get a few precious gallons of gas poured into their tank. For a time, you could get gas only on even or odd days based on your license plate number. Some people even drove to the gas station the night before and parked in line so they would be sure to get gas in the morning.

Why all the fuss? Because gasoline is a power source that impacts the whole economy of a nation. A gas shortage means higher prices, long lines, and possible rationing of the available supply, not only for car owners but also for truckers.

For decades scientists have researched other forms of power to replace gasoline. Can you imagine if they discovered a source of power that was clean, plenteous, and free? As consumers, we hope and pray that they do. What a breakthrough this would be.

As Christians, we have discovered a source of power that is limitless and free and has more potential for good than crude oil will ever offer. It is the amazing power of God's Holy Spirit! When we tap into this plenteous source of power, we will grow amazed at what God can do in and through us. (If you have personal memories of the gas shortage, tell your own story and relate it to how important it is to have a surplus of power.)

1. The Reality of the Holy Spirit's Presence

- Discuss the amazing promise of the Holy Spirit (John 14:15–27).
- Jesus says that the indwelling Spirit will bring power (Acts 1:8). We all long for the power and energy we need to live the Christian life to the fullest. Thus, we need to realize that the Holy Spirit is our primary source of this much needed power.
- Roger Frederickson makes a connection between God breathing his Spirit into the first man and Jesus breathing his Spirit into the church (p. 142). Look at this connection and help people recognize the personal investment God makes in his beloved children.

You have to plug in! No power source is worth anything until you plug into it. You can have huge reservoirs of gas, but until you put the nozzle in the tank and fill it up, the gas does no good. You can have a powerful electric supply, but until you plug in an appliance, it does not work.

This is also true for us as followers of Jesus Christ. God offers the power source of his Holy Spirit, but we need to plug in. When we repent of sin and receive the grace of God in Jesus Christ, the Holy Spirit comes to live within us. Yet we are also called to be continually filled with the Spirit (Eph. 5:18). We need to know that the Spirit dwells within us, but we also need to stay plugged in to the constant supply of power the Spirit offers.

2. The Powerful Work of the Spirit in Us

- The Spirit calls us to holiness (Ezek. 36:27; Eph. 1:4; 1 Thess. 4:7–8). God has given us all we need to walk in holiness. He has made it possible, but we have to allow the power of the Spirit to so fill us that we walk in obedience and holiness. We all have to keep growing in obedience to God. Maxie Dunnam brings this alive when he writes:

> Obedience is the key. While God has made provision for our holiness, he has also given us responsibility for it.

> Herein lies the struggle. We have deep desires to live a holy life, but we have given up on the possibility. We have struggled long and diligently with particular sins and moral weaknesses. We may have overcome blatant sins, yet we struggle with anger, pride, jealousy, lust, racism, and unconcern for the poor. If not lazy or slothful, we waste time; if not gluttonous, we eat too much; if not completely idolatrous, we often make a god out of money and material security; if not blatant liars, we slip into deceitful patterns and shade the truth; if not covetous of things, we find ourselves jealous of the position or popularity of others (p. 145).

— Reflect on the battle to live in holiness. Dunnam develops this beautifully on pages 144–48. You may want to develop the concept of being "as holy as I want to be."

- The Spirit gives us assurance.

  — Tell the story of John Wesley's Aldersgate experience (pp. 148–49). You may want to read this right from the book.

- We are the children of God not because we say so, but because God says so (Rom. 5:15–16).

When we fill up a car with gas, it does something! We can drive the car to run errands, get to work, and take kids to school or practice. A power supply exists to help us do something. When we plug in an appliance and tap into the electrical current, the goal is to open a can, microwave some popcorn, or turn on a light. A cause and effect dynamic is at work.

This is also true when we are filled with the power of the Holy Spirit. God's power fills us, but then it also flows through us—cause and effect. We move into action that gives glory to God and touches the lives of others. What are some of the supernatural things that begin to happen through the life of a Christian who is plugged in to the power of the Holy Spirit?

3. The Amazing Work of the Spirit Through Us

The Holy Spirit wants to do all kinds of things through our lives. Here we will focus on three key works of the Spirit.

- The power to overcome the power of the enemy (Eph. 6:10–18; Col. 1:13–14).
  - —The New Testament writers were clear about the call to spiritual warfare. Satan is real, and the existence of "unclean spirits" (Luke 8:26–39) is supported throughout the Bible. When the Holy Spirit is alive in our hearts, we grow in our ability to fight, resist, and overcome in the name of Jesus (James 4:7; 1 John 4:4).
- The power to extend forgiveness (Matt. 6:12–15).
  - —Tell the story of Corrie ten Boom (pp. 152–53). It is very fair to acknowledge that forgiveness can be difficult and even painful for the moment. Yet this is God's call on our lives, and it will never be realized until we allow the Holy Spirit to pour through us.
- The power we need for mission and evangelism (Acts 1:8).
  - —Read the Manila Manifesto produced by the Second International Congress on World Evangelization in 1989.

> The Scriptures declare that God himself is the chief evangelist. For the Spirit of God is the Spirit of truth, love, holiness and power, and evangelism is impossible without Him. It is He who anoints the messenger, confirms the word, prepares the hearer, convicts the sinful, enlightens the blind, gives life to the dead, enables us to repent and believe, unites us to the body of Christ, assures us that we are God's children, leads us into Christ-like character and service, and sends us out in our turn to be Christ's witnesses. In all this the Holy Spirit's main preoccupation is to glorify Jesus Christ by showing Him to us and forming Him in us.

What a great reminder that God is the primary worker in the call to evangelism. Yet we also live with the profound reality that we are in partnership with God in his missionary work.

— Take an honest look at your congregation. Look back over the last year, five years, and even ten years. Are you seeing people make genuine and life-changing commitments to follow Jesus Christ? If so, celebrate this reality and challenge your congregation to pray more passionately and share the Gospel more freely. If you have to admit that your church is not reaching lost people, address this with your congregation and call them (and yourself) to a new season of evangelistic outreach. I would strongly challenge you to read *Building a Contagious Church: Revolutionizing the Way You View and Do Evangelism* by Mark Mittelberg (Grand Rapids: Zondervan, 2000). It offers dynamic strategies and practical tools for building an evangelistically contagious ministry.

- Close by telling the story of the powerful work of God in Czechoslovakia in 1989 (pp. 154–55). God is on the throne, the Spirit is working in power, and the Lamb has won!

Closing Prayer

OTHER IDEAS FOR THIS WORSHIP SERVICE

Hymn Suggestions

"Breathe on Me, Breath of God" (Edwin Hatch/Robert Jackson)
"Come, Holy Spirit" (John Peterson)
"We've a Story to Tell to the Nations" (H. Ernest Nichol)

Praise Chorus Suggestions

"The Battle Belongs to the Lord" (1985, Fairhill Music)
"Change My Heart, O God" (1982, Mercy)
"Cry of My Heart" (1991, Mercy/Vineyard)

"He Who Began a Good Work in You" (1987, Birdwing Music)
"Let Your Spirit Rise within Me" (1982, Integrity's Hosanna! Music)

Prayer Suggestion

You may want to include a portion from the Nicene Creed (one of the Ecumenical Creeds) in a prayer.

> We believe in the Holy Spirit,
> the Lord, the giver of life.
> He proceeds from the Father and Son,
> and with the Father and Son is worshiped and glorified.
> He spoke through the prophets.

Additional Scripture Texts

John 14–16
Acts 2

Drama Suggestion

"Life Cycle," from *Sunday Morning Live*, vol. 3 (Grand Rapids: Zondervan, 1993).

Responsive Reading

Leader: What happens in our lives when we come to know the Father through faith in His only Son, Jesus Christ?

Congregation: We affirm that saving faith results in sanctification, the transformation of life in growing conformity to Christ through the power of the Holy Spirit. Sanctification means ongoing repentance, a life of turning from sin to serve Jesus Christ in grateful reliance on him as one's Lord and

> Master. We reject any view of justification which divorces it from our sanctifying union with Christ and our increasing conformity to his image through prayer, repentance, cross-bearing, and life in the Spirit.
>
> —From "The Gospel of Jesus Christ: An Evangelical Celebration"

SMALL-GROUP DISCUSSION RESOURCES

At the end of each chapter, the author has offered some questions for discussion and reflection. If you wish to use this book or these sermons as a springboard for small-group discussion, here are a few more questions that may help in the process:

Biblical Understanding

1. Read John 15:26–16:15. What promises did Jesus give concerning the Holy Spirit?
2. What is the work and ministry of the Holy Spirit? How have you experienced the Spirit of God ministering in one of these ways?

Theological Reflection

1. How does the Holy Spirit help us grow in holiness?
2. Describe how the Holy Spirit has given you assurance and confidence in your faith.

Practical Application

1. What is one spiritual battle you are facing right now? How can you be more intentional about plugging into the power of the Holy Spirit as you fight this battle?
2. Take time in the coming days to memorize the following verses: Ephesians 6:10–13; James 4:7; and 1 John 4:4. Let the truth of these passages form your understanding of God's power to help you stand strong in your faith against the attacks of the enemy.

Chapter 8

IS THIS LIFE ALL THERE IS? WHY HEAVEN IS WORTH THE WAIT

SERMON TITLE:

IS THIS LIFE ALL THERE IS?
WHY HEAVEN IS WORTH THE WAIT

Opening Illustration

Tell some of the story of Joni Eareckson Tada's life and how her experience has granted some unique and helpful insights into the hope of heaven (pp. 159–61).

We all have waited in line at a grocery store, fast-food restaurant, or amusement park and wondered how long it would take before we would have our turn. In fact, we seem to spend a lot of time waiting in lines. Have you ever found yourself asking whether what you are waiting for is worth the wait?

This is a question all of us should ask. If we are going to invest our hearts, lives, and time in something, we had better know that our investment is a wise one. If we are going to commit our lives to following Christ, it is fair to ask if heaven is worth the wait. The apostle Paul wrote:

> *If there is no resurrection of the dead, then not even Christ has been raised. And if Christ has not been raised, our preaching is useless and so is your faith. More than that, we are then found to be false witnesses*

> *about God, for we have testified about God that he raised Christ from the dead. But he did not raise him if in fact the dead are not raised. For if the dead are not raised, then Christ has not been raised either. And if Christ has not been raised, your faith is futile; you are still in your sins. Then those also who have fallen asleep in Christ are lost. If only for this life we have hope in Christ, we are to be pitied more than all men (1 Cor. 15:13–19).*

Yet Paul also wrote, "I consider that our present sufferings are not worth comparing with the glory that will be revealed in us" (Rom. 8:18).

1. Why Should Our Hearts Long for Heaven?

- Our broken lives will be healed (1 Cor. 15:50–57; Rev. 21:1–4). We all experience pain in this life: broken bodies, relationships, reputations, homes, promises, and hearts are scattered on the road of life. Our hope of heaven assures us that every tear will be wiped away and sorrow will end.
- Heaven is ultimate reality. Too often we buy into a vision of heaven that is based more on pop-Eastern religion than biblical Christianity. Heaven will not be some cloudy, ethereal, impersonal, disembodied existence. It will be more real and solid than anything we have ever experienced in this life. The biblical pictures of heaven are often filled with sensual images of sound, sight, and smell. These pictures help us realize that heaven is ultimate reality (Isa. 6:1–7; Rev. 21:1–22:5).
  - —C. S. Lewis portrays heaven in vivid and solid terms in two of his books. You may want to look at *The Great Divorce* (chap. 5) and *The Last Battle* (chaps. 15–16) for possible illustrations.
- We will be free at last (1 Cor. 15:42–44).
  - —We will be free from our perishable bodies and will receive new bodies. Take time to look at Paul's description of our new bodies in 1 Corinthians 15.
  - —We will be free from our battle with sin. Reflect on the deep freedom that we will experience when we no longer battle

temptation and the enticements of the enemy. We will have pure hearts and minds that never wander toward sin.

Is heaven worth the wait? Just a glimpse of heaven and all question is removed. When we begin to realize what awaits those who believe in God through faith in Jesus Christ, we discover that heaven is worth the wait. What is it that we can look forward to?

2. Heaven Is More Than a Place; It Is the Consummation of a Relationship

- The bride will meet her bridegroom (Isa. 62:4–5; Rev. 21:1–4).

  —Joni does a great job of portraying the holy city, the new Jerusalem, on pages 162–63.
  —When we think of the day that we will see our Lord face to face, the best image we can hold in our heart is the meeting of the bride with the bridegroom. The joy, excitement, and passion is beyond simple words. This is a moment of ultimate love (1 Cor. 2:9).

- In that day we will enjoy the fulfillment of a perfect love relationship for we will be together in the place we desire to be (John 14:2–3).

  —Are we "fitted" for heaven? We should be in the process of preparing ourselves to meet the bridegroom. This process involves seeking to live in holiness and abandoning things that entangle us and keep us from our beloved. For help in developing this concept, see pages 163–66.

- How do we get to heaven? (Rom. 7:24–25)

  —Discuss the vastness of space (pp. 166–67).
  —Yet heaven is as close as a prayer! Take time at this point in the message to give a basic gospel presentation. A helpful resource is chapter 11 of *Becoming a Contagious Christian* by Bill Hybels and Mark Mittelberg (Grand Rapids: Zondervan, 1994).

Don't wait too long to decide. Jesus has extended his offer of heaven to you. When we look at the thief on the cross who came to Jesus at the very last hour (Luke 23:39–43), we realize that it is never too late! God is the First and the Last, the Beginning and the End. Because he is the Lord of eternity, as long as there is life, there is still hope. Yet this is no reason to wait until the last minute to accept Jesus' offer. Eternity hangs in the balance. There is a real heaven, a real hell, and real people will spend forever in one place or the other.

3. Heaven or Hell? The Options Are Real and the Choice Will Last Forever

- Don't choose hell (read Rev. 19:11–16).

  — Share Joni's quote from pages 168–69.

  > This is not a pretty sight. The same mouth that spoke peace and reconciliation will one day use the sharp sword of judgment. The same eyes that glowed with compassion will one day blaze with fire. Finally, impenitent sinners will be judged, and anyone whose name is not found written in the Lamb's book of life will be thrown into the lake of fire. Is this my Bridegroom? Yes, this same Jesus is my Lover and Avenger. He is altogether loving in his justice, and just in his love. And because he is perfect, his justice is pure.

  — Quote C. S. Lewis: "There are only two kinds of people in the end: those who say to God, 'Thy will be done,' and those to whom God says, in the end, 'Thy will be done.' All that are in hell, chose it."
  — Give a challenge for people to consciously choose not to continue on a path toward hell.

- Choose heaven.
  — Close with a clear call to choose heaven. God has opened the door. We need to receive what he has freely offered through his only Son, Jesus Christ. Our salvation is by grace—always. But we must accept his gift of grace (Eph. 2:8–9).

Closing Prayer

OTHER IDEAS FOR THIS WORSHIP SERVICE

Hymn Suggestions

"Beyond the Sunset" (Virgil P. Brock/Blanche Kerr Brock)
"Face to Face" (Carrie E. Breck/Grant C. Tullar)
"What a Day That Will Be!" (Jim Hill)

Praise Chorus Suggestions

"All Hail, King Jesus" (1981, Glory Alleluia Music)
"Revelation 7" (1996, Dew Brothers)
"There's a Place (Because of You)" (1995, Kingsway's Thankyou Music)
"We Will Dance" (1993, Mercy/Vineyard)
"We Will Ride" (1994, Mercy/Vineyard)

Prayer Suggestions

The following prayers are from *Prayers of the Martyrs*, ed. Duane W. H. Arnold (Grand Rapids: Zondervan, 1990).

This is the end,
but for me
It is the beginning
of life.

—*Dietrich Bonhoeffer, a German Lutheran pastor who was executed on April 9, 1945, in the Flossenburg concentration camp by the personal order of Heinrich Himmler*

I have been too long
in this world of strife;
I would be with Jesus.

—*Julian of Brioude, beheaded in the third century for his faith*

Drama Suggestion

"Wait Until Halftime," from *Sunday Morning Live*, vol. 5 (Grand Rapids: Zondervan, 1994).

SMALL-GROUP DISCUSSION RESOURCES

At the end of each chapter, the author has offered some questions for discussion and reflection. If you wish to use this book or these sermons as a springboard for small-group discussion, here are a few more questions that may help in the process:

Biblical Understanding

1. Read 1 Corinthians 15:3–19. What are the implications for Christians if Christ has not been raised from the dead?
2. Read 1 Corinthians 15:35–57. Paul is absolutely confident that Christ has been raised from the dead. How will we be different after we are raised from the dead?

Theological Reflection

1. Paul was absolutely confident that Jesus Christ was risen from the dead, so why did he draw out all the implications for Christians if Christ had not risen?
2. How might the teaching of 1 Corinthians 15 speak to a person who lives under the dark cloud of believing this life is all there is or ever will be?

Practical Application

1. If heaven is more than just a place and is the consummation of a relationship with God, how can we begin to experience some of the glory of heaven today? What are you doing to deepen your intimacy with God on a day-to-day basis?
2. How might other Christians pray for you and encourage you in your commitment to deepen your love relationship with God?

Chapter 9

DOES THE WORLD REALLY NEED TO HEAR THE GOSPEL OF JESUS CHRIST?

SERMON TITLE:
DOES THE WORLD REALLY NEED TO HEAR THE GOSPEL?

I have seen it, and so have you. A young person or an adult has confidence and certainty in his abilities. He is sure he can do it—that is, until someone begins to question him. "There's no way you can run a marathon!" "You're going to sing a solo in church? Are you sure that's a good idea?" "Go back to college? You're in your 50s. Is that really necessary?" "Ask for a raise? Your boss is going to chew you up and spit you out!" "You want to be a what? A pastor? After the life you've lived? You had better stop and think about that a little more." The list could go on and on.

You were confident, ready to move forward in boldness. But then a cloud of doubt began to float over your head, and now you are under its shadow. "Maybe I can't. Maybe I shouldn't. What in the world was I thinking?"

Many things in life demand confidence, but none is more important than our confidence in the Gospel of Jesus Christ. Nothing in all the world deserves more confidence. And there is nothing the enemy of our souls wants to erode more than our confidence in the Gospel.

1. We Must Have Confidence in the Gospel (Rom. 1:1–10)

- It is essential that we have confidence in the truth of the Gospel. If we are not certain in the veracity of the Gospel, how can we bring the message of God's saving grace in Jesus Christ to the world around us?
- What happens when we don't have confidence in the Gospel?

  — We doubt the need to proclaim the Gospel.
  — We claim that all religions are basically the same.
  — Both of these lead to the same thing: an ineffective life and ministry. We muddle through with faint convictions and never really confront others with the life-changing message of the Gospel.

- We must have a radical confidence that the Gospel is not from men or simply a tradition developed by people (Gal. 1:11–12). It is the message of God for all people (pp. 176–77).
- The Gospel is the Good News! It is the best news in all of human history. When we know this, with bold certainty we grow excited and motivated to communicate this message to every person we meet.
- When we are confident in the Gospel, we have discernment to see and reject the false gospels that cry out for acceptance (see pp. 177–79).

  — prosperity gospel
  — political ideologies
  — social gospel

A young girl hears a boy in the back row of the choir whisper that she can't sing. All of a sudden her beautiful and developing voice grows quieter and quieter until she no longer dares to sing. She just lips the words she formerly sang with such joy.

The lie has won!

You see, her voice is truly wonderful. But she has heard the lie and allowed its tendrils to wrap around her soul and her vocal chords. Confidence has been eroded. The music has ended.

2. The Erosion of Confidence

Like every other area of life, if we hear enough people tell us we are wrong, we can begin to lose confidence. Even when we know the Gospel is true and the only hope for the world, the constant downpour of questions, ridicule, and opposition can wear us down over time. Examine some of the sources of opposition to the Gospel (pp. 177–82).

- Cultural resistance to Christian missionary and evangelistic work.
- The power of the media and the constant onslaught of anti-Christian images and messages.
- Battles from within our own ranks. Even those who claim to be Christians can resist the clear teaching of Scripture when it comes to the uniqueness of Christ and salvation in his name alone (Matt. 24:4–5; Gal. 1:6–9; 2 Peter 2:1–2).
- Belief that religion is enough. Many people are satisfied with any form of "sincere" religious devotion. They believe that if they are serious about personal religious convictions, that is enough to satisfy God. Yet they fail to remember the teaching of our Lord (Matt. 23:15).
- Name calling and public shaming. In our day, the ruling ideological god seems to be tolerance—that is, tolerance of every philosophy and lifestyle except Christianity! When evangelical Christians declare a bold belief that Jesus is the only way to the Father (John 14:6), they become the target of the tolerance-loving media, political leaders, and even some church leaders. The name calling begins! Evangelicals are said to be a bunch of religious bigots, intolerant hate-mongers, and unloving exclusivists. It is striking how profoundly intolerant these accusers are when it comes to Christians who believe Jesus is the only way. For a helpful discussion of the term *exclusivist*, see pages 179–81.

Who will sit down with that little girl and tell her the truth? Who will help her to open her ears to hear her own voice and realize that she has a precious gift from God? Who will reach into her strangling soul and tear loose the tentacles that are constricting around both her heart and voice? If she can hear the truth and believe the truth, then once again her voice can be raised in songs of joy and praise.

3. The Restoration of Confidence

It is time for Christians to stand up with boldness and declare that we believe the Word of God. Let the world hurl insults. Let the name callers give us their best shot! Jesus is Lord. He has risen, and he is the only sure and certain hope for the world. We need to cling to the truth with unyielding tenacity and never back off!

- The unique claims of Christ. He is both the center and the circumference (Luke 19:10). The goal of Christ's life and ministry was to win lost people. If we are going to bear his name, we can do no less.
- False shepherds and enemies of the cross (Jer. 23:1–4). We need to begin speaking the truth in love. If there are leaders in our churches, denominations, and training institutions who are false shepherds misleading the sheep, we need to speak the truth. To look the other way and remain silent is to allow them to continue destroying the flock of God. Confidence leads to action and bold declaration of the truth!
- An unyielding commitment to the Gospel and evangelism—the greatest love we could ever express. If we truly love people, we will tell them about the Good News we have received by grace. Withholding this truth is the most unloving thing we could ever do. Boldly and passionately telling others is the ultimate act of love.

Many years later a young man walks into a grand concert hall. He has come with friends to enjoy a night of instrumental and vocal music. As his eyes wander down the pages of the program, he sees a familiar name. A picture comes to his mind of a shy, red-headed girl from the front row of choir when he was a young boy, a girl he had ridiculed, mocked, and driven to silent tears.

This should be good, *he thinks with a cynical smirk on his face. To his astonishment, it is! She is confident, powerful, and poised. An invisible hand wipes the smirk off of his face as she sings. The confidence he tried so hard to destroy has returned, and her voice cuts through the air like a knife. The truth has won, and the song goes on!*

4. True Confidence in the Gospel Always Leads to Action

- Proclaiming the Gospel is a privilege *and* an obligation (Rom. 1:14–15). Tite Tiénou gives some helpful insight to this truth on pages 182–83.
- We must share the treasure of the Gospel. No Gospel hoarding! The Gospel is not some commodity we accumulate and hide away. It is a treasure that grows every time we give it away. As the confidence of the Holy Spirit fills our hearts, we long to give away this great treasure and watch it transform the lives of others just as it changed us.

Closing Prayer

OTHER IDEAS FOR THIS WORSHIP SERVICE

Hymn Suggestions

"For God So Loved the World" (Frances Townsend/Alfred B. Smith)
"Send the Light" (Charles H. Gabriel)
"Channels Only" (Mary E. Maxwell/Ada Rose Gibbs)

Praise Chorus Suggestions

"Champion" (1994, Kingsway's Thankyou Music)
"The Cross Has Said It All" (1996, Kingsway's Thankyou Music)
"History Maker" (1996, Curious? Music)
"I Could Sing of Your Love" (1994, Curious? Music)
"Shine, Jesus, Shine" (1987, Make Way Music/Integrity's Hosanna! Music)
"People of God" (1982, Singspiration)
"Shout to the Lord" (1992, Curious? Music)

Prayer Suggestion

Jim Elliot, a young man called by God as a missionary to the Auca Indians, was murdered by the very people he hoped to reach with the Gospel. As you prepare to pray for God's people the week you preach on this topic, reflect on these brief readings from Jim's personal journal. The spirit of confidence contained in these words is one we should all pray to have in our own hearts.

> *God, I pray Thee, light these idle sticks of my life and may I burn for Thee. Consume my life, my God, for it is Thine. I seek not a long life, but a full one, like you, Lord Jesus. (1948)*
>
> *Father, take my life, yea, my blood if Thou wilt, and consume it with Thine enveloping fire. I would not save it, for it is not mine to save. Have it, Lord; have it all. Pour out my life as an oblation for the world. Blood is only of value as it flows before Thine Altar. (1948; from Elisabeth Elliot,* Shadow of the Almighty *[New York: Harper and Row, 1958])*

Additional Scripture Texts

Matthew 28:16–20
Acts 1:7–8

Responsive Reading

Leader: Jesus said, "I am the way and the truth and the life. No one comes to the Father except through me." In light of Jesus' teaching, what can we confidently affirm?

Congregation: We affirm that Jesus Christ is the only way to salvation, the only mediator between God and man.

Leader: What implications does this have for those who observe the rituals and traditions of other religions?

Congregation: We deny that anyone is saved in any other way than by Jesus Christ and His Gospel. The Bible offers no hope

> that sincere worshipers of other religions will be saved without personal faith in Jesus Christ.
>
> —FROM "THE GOSPEL OF JESUS CHRIST: AN EVANGELICAL CELEBRATION"

Reflection

You may want to use the following quote from the Statement on the cover of your bulletin or project it on a screen before your service starts to help people begin reflecting on the theme of the message.

> Salvation is a Trinitarian reality, initiated by the Father, implemented by the Son, and applied by the Holy Spirit. It has a global dimension, for God's plan is to save believers out of every tribe and tongue (Rev. 5:9) to be his church, a new humanity, the people of God, the body and bride of Christ, and the community of the Holy Spirit. All the heirs of final salvation are called here and now to serve their Lord and each other in love, to share in the fellowship of Jesus' sufferings, and to work together to make Christ known to the whole world.

This quote is from an excellent book called *Four Views of Salvation in a Pluralistic World*, ed. Dennis L. Okholm and Timothy R. Phillips (Grand Rapids: Zondervan, 1996). It may help you as you study for this sermon.

SMALL-GROUP DISCUSSION RESOURCES

At the end of each chapter, the author has offered some questions for discussion and reflection. If you wish to use this book or these sermons as a springboard for small-group discussion, here are a few more questions that may help in the process:

Biblical Understanding

We have all seen warning signs, such as "Beware of Dog," "Roads May Be Icy," "Dangerous if Swallowed." Read the following passages and put them in your own words. How would you post these on a warning sign for other Christians to read?

Jeremiah 23:1 (a warning from Jeremiah)
My sign would read:
Matthew 24:4–5 (a warning from Jesus)
My sign would read:
Galatians 1:6–9 (a warning from Paul)
My sign would read:
2 Peter 2:1–3 (a warning from Peter)
My sign would read:

If you are doing this study in a small group, tell participants what some of your warning signs would say. Why do you think God posts so many signs throughout the Bible about false teachers?

Theological Reflection

1. What are some of the false teachings and philosophies that seem to be growing and flourishing today?
2. How do these false belief systems differ from the true Gospel of Jesus Christ?

Practical Application

1. Tell about one person who has helped you grow more confident in the Gospel. What can you do to bolster the confidence of other Christians as they seek to hold to the Gospel?
2. If you are aware of someone who is teaching what is contrary to the Gospel, what could you do to gently restore and correct them? Why is speaking the truth in love so important in these situations?

Chapter 10

HOW CAN I SHARE MY FAITH WITH OTHERS?

SERMON TITLE:

HOW CAN I SHARE MY FAITH WITH OTHERS?

Opening Illustration

Open by telling a story about sometime when you (or someone else) had an unexpected, split-second opportunity to talk about spiritual things and share the Gospel. You may want to read the story told by Lee Strobel (pp. 187–88), tell a story from your own life, or ask a church member to give a personal testimony. A church member's testimony could be prepared in advance and given live or videotaped. Tell the congregation that these moments come along often, but we need to decide if we are going to walk through the door God is opening before us.

- When we say yes to these opportunities, we find joy, invigoration, and meaning in life. You may want to use the image of a movie (black and white or color) from page 188.
- Jesus was emphatic about how we should respond at these moments (John 20:21).
- We need to remember that we are never alone in this great calling. God is the primary evangelist. His Spirit will fill and lead us (Mark 13:9–11).

Eight Practical Steps for Sharing Our Faith

If you have video projection capabilities, I would strongly encourage projecting the eight key points of this sermon on a screen for the congregation to see. You also may want to project some of the key verses. Another option is to hand out a sermon outline (or print it in your worship bulletin). This sermon closely follows the content of chapter 10 of *This We Believe* and relies heavily on Lee Strobel's approach to evangelism.

1. Ask God to Increase Your Love for Lost People (Luke 15)

- Spend time reading and meditating on Scriptures that help you see Jesus' heart for the lost. Encourage church members to spend time regularly reading and reflecting on the four Gospels.
- Ask God to give you a new passion for the lost. Pray often for a heart that is broken for the lost condition of those who do not know God through Jesus Christ.

2. Pray Consistently for the Spiritually Lost

- Expound on Luke 23:34 and the meaning of Jesus' prayer. John Stott's exposition of this passage from pages 190–91 is very helpful.
- Get practical by writing down the names of at least three people you will pray for consistently, specifically, and fervently.
- Challenge people to never give up hope! Tell a story from your life or ministry about a time when people prayed for a long time and finally saw a loved one or friend come to faith in Christ. You may want to use the story Lee Strobel tells on page 191. You could also read a brief testimony from a church member or invite someone forward to tell his or her story.

3. Reach Out in a Way That Fits You

- Recognize that there are numerous styles of evangelism. God has not made us with a one-size-fits-all approach.
- Give a brief look at the six styles (see p. 192). You may also want to read chapter 9 of Bill Hybels and Mark Mittelberg's book *Becoming a Contagious Christian* (Grand Rapids: Zondervan, 1994).

4. Build Bridges of Friendship with Lost People

- Study Jesus' example (Luke 19:1–10; John 4:4–30, 39–42).
- Have a no-strings-attached attitude. Love people where they are even if they don't respond to the Gospel.
- Drop hints early that you are a Christian. Let people you meet know that your Christian faith is core to who you are.
- Spend time with others.
- Learn to listen.
- Be sure that you influence others and that they don't drag you down. Jesus spent time with tax collectors and sinners (Matt. 9:10–11), but he influenced them; they did not entice him to engage in their sinful ways. If you are not spiritually strong enough to stand your ground, then there are certain situations you should not enter.

5. Don't Just Share Your Faith—Show It

- Live a humble and authentic life. Know that seekers have a hypocrisy radar that is always on! Your lifestyle and words need to be consistent (Matt. 5:14–16).
- Actively work at serving your friends who don't yet know Christ (Matt. 5:16; Mark 10:45).

6. Be Ready to Tell Others How You Met God

- Be ready to give a brief and clear telling of your story of faith.
  - —Describe your life before you knew Christ. If you became a believer at a young age, you can reflect on where you think your life would have gone without Christ. Simply by looking at your greatest areas of struggle and temptation, you can get a pretty good sense of where your life may have headed.
  - —Tell about how you became a Christian. How did you come to a place of praying to receive Jesus as the one who forgives you and leads your life?
  - —Rejoice in how different your life is because of Christ. People need to know that God has the power and the desire to transform lives.

- Be careful not to become preachy or overbearing. Simply tell about what God has done and is doing in your life.

7. Be Prepared to Explain God's Message (1 Peter 3:15)

- There are many simple ways to present the core message of the Gospel:

  —the Roman Road (see pp. 197–98)
  —Do Versus Done (see p. 198)
  —the bridge illustration (see the book *Becoming a Contagious Christian*, pp. 156–59)

- Reflect on the reality that a bold witness could bring some minor tension but virtually never the kind of persecution others have faced through history.

8. Take Risks to Reach People with the Gospel

- Be ready to count the cost and take some risks. In Luke 19, Jesus got up close and personal with Zacchaeus even though Zacchaeus was considered an outsider and a sinner. Jesus went to dinner parties with tax collectors and sinners, associated with women of questionable reputation, and touched people with leprosy. He took risks because he longed to reach those who were lost. Reaching people with the Gospel always has been and always will be risky business.

Closing Prayer

OTHER IDEAS FOR THIS WORSHIP SERVICE

Hymn Suggestions

"I'll Go Where You Want Me to Go" (Mary Brown and Charles E. Prior/Carrie E. Rounsefell)
"Living for Jesus" (Thomas Chisholm/C. Harold Lowden)
"Rescue the Perishing" (Fanny J. Crosby/William H. Doane)

Praise Chorus Suggestions

"Can a Nation Be Changed?" (1996, Kingsway's Thankyou Music)
"I Will Sing of the Mercies" (1992, Word Music)
"Knocking on the Door of Heaven" (1996, Kingsway's Thankyou Music)
"Shine, Jesus, Shine" (1987, Make Way Music/Integrity's Hosanna! Music)
"Song for the Nations" (1986, 1992, Integrity's Hosanna! Music)
"We Want to See Jesus Lifted High" (1993, Kingsway's Thankyou Music)

Prayer Suggestion

Consider having a time of silent prayer for those who are lost. Often we fill our services with so much activity that there is no time for silence. Give direction for various areas of focus and then leave time for silent supplication. You may want to begin close to home and then move in concentric circles outward. Pray for those in your home and immediate family, in your neighborhood, in your workplaces and schools, in your community, in your nation, and finally for people all over the world.

Additional Scripture Text

Luke 15:11–31 (You may want to read this passage using four different readers: narrator, father, prodigal son, and the older brother.)

Responsive Reading

Leader: What does Jesus command all who follow Him?

Congregation: We affirm that Jesus Christ commands his followers to proclaim the Gospel to all living persons, evangelizing

	everyone everywhere, and discipling believers within the fellowship of the church.
Leader:	What does this include?
Congregation:	A full and faithful witness to Christ includes the witness of personal testimony, godly living, and acts of mercy and charity to our neighbor, without which the preaching of the Gospel appears barren.
Leader:	Is it enough to simply live a good life and hope this will be an adequate witness?
Congregation:	We deny that the witness of personal testimony, godly living, and acts of mercy and charity to our neighbors constitutes evangelism apart from the proclamation of the Gospel.

—From "The Gospel of Jesus Christ: An Evangelical Celebration"

SMALL-GROUP DISCUSSION RESOURCES

At the end of each chapter, the author has offered some questions for discussion and reflection. If you wish to use this book or these sermons as a springboard for small-group discussion, here are a few more questions that may help in the process:

Biblical Understanding

1. Read Luke 15:3–32. What do these three stories have in common?
2. What do you learn about the heart of God from these stories?
3. What do you learn about human need from these parables?

Theological Reflection

1. Here are three titles for the parable found in Luke 15:11–31. Pick one of them and reflect on what you learn from this main character.

The Prodigal Son
The Forgiving Father
The Angry Big Brother

Practical Application

1. What is one roadblock or hindrance that keeps you from sharing the Gospel with others? What are you doing to remove this roadblock and to become bolder and more consistent in your witness?
2. Name one person you know who clearly and consistently models being a good witness to nonbelievers. What is it about that person's life that you would like to learn to emulate?

Chapter 11

THE EVANGELICAL FAMILY: ITS BLESSINGS AND BOUNDARIES

SERMON TITLE:

THE EVANGELICAL FAMILY: ITS BLESSINGS AND BOUNDARIES

Opening Illustration

- Tell a story about a time when you experienced a deep sense of family connectedness in your blood family or in the family of God. Reflect on how rich and satisfying such moments are, for God has made us for community, for life together. In such moments we can echo the words of the psalmist.
- Read Psalm 133.
- Pray for a deep commitment to unity in the body of Christ that is based on the truth of God's Word. Confess where we often settle for pseudo-community that is based on pleasing people and seeking a false peace rather than holding to the truth of God and his Gospel. Ask for a renewed courage to hold fast to the truth so tenaciously that genuine unity will grow out of the truth.
- Take a moment to explore the vivid imagery of Psalm 133. Joseph Stowell does an excellent job of developing a number of images (anointing oil, the place of Aaron, and the dew of Mount Hermon) on page 206.

- What was true for the people of Israel is true for the church today. A supreme pleasantness and joy invades our lives when we are walking in true unity with our brothers and sisters in Christ. Since God calls us to unity and our hearts yearn for unity, it is time that we seek true unity with all our hearts.

Have you ever watched two siblings fight over the remote control for the TV? You would think you had just entered a war zone. Words are hurled like missiles, emotions flare, and eyes blaze with fiery anger—all over which program they will watch. Let's admit it: much conflict in families is over trivialities. This can also be true in the family of faith. Unity—true unity—is tougher than it looks. If we are going to get along and walk hand in hand, we need to realize it is going to take a concerted effort.

1. Unity in the Family—It's Tougher Than It Looks!

- The world is watching us. We claim to love each other in the name of Jesus. We claim to be a family. So when non-Christians see conflict and dissension among us, our witness is severely compromised. This is why God is so serious about calling his people to unity.

  — Proverbs 6:19: God hates a spirit that stirs up dissension.
  — John 13:34–35: God calls us to walk in love with one another.
  — Galatians 3:26–28: When we walk with Jesus, we find a level of unity beyond what we ever could achieve or even imagine without him.
  — You may want to look at the call to love in 1 Corinthians 13. Remember, this was written to a church that was dealing with intense bouts of disunity and inner turmoil.

- If we are going to seek unity, we need to identify some of the natural hindrances we will face.

  — Demanding our own way is a sin that all of us can fall into. When we complain that things are not as we wish, when we jealously protect our traditions, when we are motivated by pride, and when we see the church as a place for flexing our muscles and exercising power, we are bound to bring disunity in the church. Matthew 20:20–28 gives an account of how this happened among Jesus' disciples (pp. 208–9).

—Another hindrance is prejudice. When we allow prejudice to grow in our own hearts or among followers of Christ, we can expect division in the body. Jesus modeled an inclusive and accepting life as he reached out to women, lepers, tax collectors, and many other people who were outside of his culturally designated social circle (see, e.g., John 4:4–28).

"You two kiss and make up!" "You boys shake hands, say you're sorry, and go play nicely!" "Stop fighting and give your sister a hug!" These parental mantras have echoed through the ages. Yet too often parents are creating a pseudo-peace that will crumble the moment Mom and Dad are out of sight. Establishing genuine peace involves digging in and discovering where the conflict comes from. It means knowing the truth and telling the truth even when it hurts. In a family, pseudo-peace leads to pseudo-unity, which is actually no unity at all.

This is also true in the evangelical family. In recent years we have become enamored with signing formal agreements that claim we are united. We pat ourselves on the back and claim we have taken great strides toward unity. We look the other way when it comes to serious doctrinal differences as we "shake hands and make up." If these overtures are a reflection of real unity based on a serious grappling with the truth of the Gospel, then all praise be to God. However, when they are shallow efforts that only create pseudo-unity, we actually damage the body of Christ and shame the name of our Savior. Only unity rooted in the truth of God's Word and the unchanging Gospel of Jesus Christ will last.

2. The Road to Unity in the Family: The Truth, the Whole Truth, and Nothing but the Truth

- Consider giving a copy of "The Gospel of Jesus Christ: An Evangelical Celebration" (with the preamble) to each person in your congregation. If recipients wish to learn more about this Bible-based statement, direct them to thiswebelieve.com. This document is a great example of an effort to develop a statement of faith that is rooted in Scripture, committed to the truth, and unbending when it comes to the current pressure to compromise for the sake of "unity."

- On pages 209–15 of *This We Believe*, Joseph Stowell gives a brief but clear exposition of the importance of unity but also of the greater importance of our commitment to the truth. He says:

> As important as unity is, it is not our most important value. Jesus Christ taught that truth transcends unity as a priority. It is critical to recall that in Christ's high priestly prayer, before he prayed that we would be one, he prayed that we would be set apart in the truth (John 17:17). From God's point of view, truth is not only more important than unity, but is in fact the basis for unity. The Bible does not know a unity that is just for unity's sake. Authentic Christian unity is a unity forged in a common cause, a common conviction, a common interest. Biblical unity is forged in our mutual bondedness to the truth in Christ, "the way and the truth and the life" (John 14:6). When we embrace the truth, we are free to embrace one another in the truth.

—Yet we live in a day of relativism and pluralism, when many would claim that there is no absolute or ultimate truth. In our politically correct world, we need to cling to the truth even if others are abandoning it! Stowell develops the implications of proclaiming absolute truth in a postmodern, broken world on pages 211–12.

- Charles Spurgeon added his voice to this discussion years ago when he wrote:

> To remain divided is sinful! Did not our Lord pray "that they may be one, even as we are one"? (John 17:22). A chorus of ecumenical voices keep harping the unity tune. What they are saying is, "Christians of all doctrinal shades and beliefs must come together in one visible organization, regardless. . . . Unite, unite!" Such teaching is false, reckless and dangerous. Truth alone

> must determine our alignments. Truth comes before unity. Unity without truth is hazardous. Our Lord's prayer in John 17 must be read in its full context. . . . "Sanctify them through thy truth: thy word is truth." Only those sanctified through the Word can be one in Christ. To teach otherwise is to betray the gospel (pp. 212–13).

- The Scriptures plainly indicate that there are core doctrines we cannot compromise without endangering the very life and health of the church. Two of these are the doctrine of salvation and the doctrine of Christ. Joseph Stowell gives great illustration and biblical exposition of this on pages 213–15.

Fractured families, broken marriages, and shattered hearts litter the landscape of this nation. Building a strong and healthy family is tough. Church families, sadly, are not much different. They are torn by dissension, factions, and pseudo-community. For the church of Jesus Christ to function as a healthy and united family, we must take some specific steps.

3. Building a Strong Family: Steps Toward Unity

- We must become habitual, bold truth tellers. Like the child in "The Emperor's New Clothes," someone must stand up and cry out, "The king has no clothes!" If we are committed to move toward genuine and lasting unity in the church, we can settle for no cheap imitations. Accepting false teachings and theologies will never lead to unity. There must be no more joining of hands in mock ecumenical fellowship with those who deny Christ as the only way to salvation. Our unity must be based on the truth of the Word of God alone. As Joseph Stowell puts it:

> While some would wish that evangelicals and other Christians were not so unbending about these matters, it is simply the case that there can be no true unity without a clear articulation of the truth regarding salvation. If we strive for unity apart from a pure Gospel, we will

> have done the Gospel a tragic disservice and will have confused many about their own eternal destiny (p. 217).

- We can't be fighting over peripheral issues. We must agree on core issues. On issues such as mode of baptism, church polity, end-times schemes, and other topics we can't allow division. We stand together in Christ. We major on the majors and minor on the minors. In Ephesians 4:1–16 the apostle Paul gives clear exhortations for how we can "keep the unity of the Spirit through the bond of peace" (v. 3).
- Close with a vision of what this family can look like. Our hearts yearn to find a place we can call home, a community of believers who are united in the truth. Stowell says:

> Evangelicals, then, are a family united in the Gospel of Jesus Christ. We come from many nations, races, economic circumstances, denominations, and churches. The geographical boundaries for the family are as large as the world itself. But the doctrinal boundaries are circumscribed by a commitment to the Gospel of Jesus Christ in particular, and to the historic tenets of orthodox Christian truth in general, as described in Holy Scripture (p. 218).

Closing Prayer

OTHER IDEAS FOR THIS WORSHIP SERVICE

Hymn Suggestions

"Blest Be the Tie" (John Fawcett/Hans G. Naegeli)
"The Family of God" (Gloria and William Gaither)
"They'll Know We Are Christians by Our Love" (Peter Scholtes)

Praise Chorus Suggestions

"Believer" (1996, Kingsway's Thankyou Music)

"Bind Us Together" (1977, Thankyou Music)
"Chosen Generation" (1978, Sound III, Inc.)
"One Voice" (1989, Integrity's Hosanna! Music)
"There Is a Louder Shout to Come" (1996, Kingsway's Thankyou Music)
"We Believe" (1986, Thankyou Music)

Prayer Suggestion

Although the Nicene Creed is not as familiar as the Apostle's Creed in many churches, consider reading it to the congregation or reciting it in unison as you prepare for prayer. Let the structure and content of this great statement of faith give shape to your time of prayer.

Additional Scripture Texts

John 17 (reflect on the relationship of the truth and the call to unity)
2 Corinthians 5:19–21

Other Ideas or Suggestions

If you have projection capabilities in your sanctuary, you may want to show a collection of pictures of your congregation members. This could be done during the offering with a song that reflects on the joy, value, and blessing of the family of God. Celebrate the unity and love you experience as a body.

SMALL-GROUP DISCUSSION RESOURCES

At the end of each chapter, the author has offered some questions for discussion and reflection. If you want to use this book or these sermons as a springboard for small-group discussion, here are a few more questions that may help in the process:

Biblical Understanding

Read Jesus' prayer in John 17. What does Jesus pray for:

Himself?

His disciples?

Those who will come to faith through the ongoing work of the disciples (believers today)?

Theological Reflection

As you read this prayer, what do you learn about:

The relationship of truth and unity?

The heart of Jesus?

God's vision for the church?

Practical Application

1. What is one thing your church can do to partner with other local congregations who believe the Gospel as you seek to reach lost people in your community?
2. Jesus said: "Therefore, if you are offering your gift at the altar and there remember that your brother has something against you, leave your gift there in front of the altar. First go and be reconciled to your brother; then come and offer your gift" (Matt. 5:23–24). If you are experiencing disunity with a brother or sister in Christ, how can your small group pray for you and encourage you as you seek restoration in this relationship? (Remember, you don't need to tell the name of the other person or all of the details. Simply allow your group members to pray for you and check in with you to see if you are being faithful to seek reconciliation in this relationship.)

Chapter 12

THE BIG PICTURE: DOES GOD HAVE A PLAN FOR THE WORLD?

SERMON TITLE:

THE BIG PICTURE:
DOES GOD HAVE A PLAN FOR THE WORLD?

Opening Illustration

To understand God's plan for the world, we need to see the big picture. A close-up look will never do, for God's plan is as big as the one who made the heavens and the earth. Use a word picture that shows the need to step back and see the vastness of what God has planned for those he loves. You may want to use the illustration on page 221 of the drawings on the Nazca plains of Peru. Or you may want to use the image of a giant mosaic with thousands of small pieces of stone and glass: if you stand close, you can appreciate a few stones, but you can't see the big picture. The same is true of a beautiful tapestry. Looking at a few of the strands of thread tells you very little about the image you will see when you step back and let your eyes survey the entire work. These illustrations help us see that we need to get a bird's-eye view of God's plan for the world.

- Read John 3:16–21.

1. A Survey of the Big Picture

- As you prepare to study John 3:16, share some preliminary insights to help prepare the congregation. Timothy George gives an excellent preview on pages 222–23.
- There is purpose and direction in the Christian faith. Life is not some endless, cyclical repetition of the same meaningless activities. In Christ we are part of a linear progression of actions and activities that are ordained by God and heading toward a glorious and joy-filled consummation.
- The Bible is not some eclectic collection of unconnected stories. It is the revelation of God that has a coherent unity and message we all need to hear. It is living, active (Heb. 4:12), and infused by the Spirit of God. George communicates this powerfully when he writes:

> Some people try to study the Bible the way a geologist might study a piece of petrified wood in a lab—interesting perhaps, but cold, inert, dead. To them the Bible's story line is a "myth," a fanciful, made-up history. But if you read the Bible without such blinders, you may discover something quite different. The Bible is a living book. You cannot read it and put it down the way you might the sports page or a Stephen King novel. It addresses you, provokes you, questions you, commands you, calls out to you. It has your number. Slowly you come to see, as Christians have through the centuries, that what the world calls "myth" is really a true and trustworthy account of your life and of life itself (p. 222).

- Our worship as Christians makes sense only in light of God's plan for history and the certainty of the resurrection of Jesus and his promised return.

The rest of this message is an exposition of John 3:16. This familiar and powerful verse of Scripture contains the heart of the Gospel. I would encourage that you pause at this point in the message and pray for a powerful presence of the Holy Spirit. Pray for closed ears to be opened and for hearts of stone to become hearts of flesh. This sermon has a dual purpose: (1) to help believers clarify the core message of the Gospel in a way that they can communicate to others and (2) to present the Gospel to any persons gathered with you for worship in a way that they can both understand and respond to.

The following format is drawn directly from chapter 12 of *This We Believe*. Read this chapter closely as you prepare to preach this sermon.

2. According to Plan ("For God so loved the world . . ."; pp. 223–27)

- The scope of God's plan: It began before time (John 1:1ff.).
- The nature of God's person: perfect community and perfect love (1 John 4:8). God's plan is not based on some primal need he has for us to love him. It grows out of the perfect community God has within the Trinity and his character that is overflowing with love.
- God is not some disconnected, disinterested prime mover. He is deeply involved in every part of his creation and every aspect of our lives (Matt. 10:29–30). Timothy George develops a vivid contrast you may find helpful (pp. 225–27).

3. The Crux of History ("... that he gave his one and only Son . . ."; pp. 227–31)

- From the very beginning there has been confusion over who Jesus is (Matt. 16:13–16). This persists in our day. Jesus himself pointed to the inability of many to understand all that Moses and the prophets spoke of him (Luke 24:25–27).
- The Word of God is clear about who Jesus is. Timothy George gives a powerful collection of biblical images and titles for Jesus on pages 228–29:

> Jesus is the last Adam, the seed of Abraham, the son of David, and the true Prophet. He is the Servant King whose greatness exceeds that of Solomon (Luke 11:31). He cleanses the house of God, identifying himself as

the true temple (John 2:13–22). When he is taken to Egypt as a baby, he reenacts the Egyptian bondage experienced centuries before by the people of Israel. His going up to Jerusalem to suffer and die is the new Exodus. He is the paschal lamb whose poured-out blood brings rescue and redemption. With the coming of Jesus, God's reign has arrived. God's kingdom, Jesus announced, is now "among you" (Luke 17:21). Satan has been routed, as Jesus' work as an exorcist shows (Matt. 12:28). All that God has promised in the Old Testament Jesus fulfills. As the apostle Paul puts it, "Whatever God has promised gets stamped with the Yes of Jesus. In Him, this is what we preach and pray, the great Amen, God's Yes and our Yes together, gloriously evident" (2 Cor. 1:20 THE MESSAGE).

- The Nicene Creed declares it powerfully. Jesus is "the only-begotten Son of God, begotten of his Father before all worlds, God of God, Light of Light, Very God of Very God, begotten not made, being of one substance with the Father, by whom all things were made: Who for us and our salvation came down from heaven."
- The death of Jesus was God's foreordained plan. No person, political system, or random series of events put Jesus on the cross. It was the ultimate sacrifice of God's love for his children. George puts it succinctly: "It is important to say emphatically that God does not love us because Jesus died for us; rather, Jesus died for us because God loves us."

4. The Progress of the Gospel (". . . that whoever believes in him shall not perish . . ."; pp. 231–34)

- In the beginning of the book of Acts we find the new beginning. When Jesus ascended and the Spirit descended, the last days began. We are not alone; the Holy Spirit is with us and in us, calling us to Gospel action (John 14:15–21).
- Look at the rapid and intentional spread of the Gospel in the early centuries of the first millennium. With no communication

systems, cell phones, or e-mail, the message of Jesus spread like wildfire across the face of the earth (pp. 232–34).

- What price will we pay for the continued spread of the Gospel? Many have been martyred in the past and many continue to offer their lives for the Gospel (p. 234). Are we willing to take up the banner and bring the message of God's love in Jesus Christ to our generation no matter what the cost? Are we willing to cross cultural barriers and reach even those who resist or do not believe they need Christ?

5. Homeward Bound ("... but have eternal life"; pp. 234–36)

- Look at the sacraments of Baptism and the Lord's Supper, noticing how they point to heaven and the hope that lies ahead (p. 235).
- God, and only God, knows when the end will come. Yet we can know what will happen. Timothy George puts it this way:

> At some definite point in the future—and only God knows when that will be—Jesus will return to consummate the drama of redemption. Satan will be conquered, and Jesus will reign on earth in a world filled with justice and peace. At the resurrection, we shall receive new transformed bodies, comparable to the body Jesus himself had after he came back from the dead (1 John 3:2). There will be a final solemn separation when the wicked are forever banished from the presence of God in hell.

- As we travel on this journey homeward, we are called to invite others to join us. God has done the work and extended his love. Jesus has paid the price. The Holy Spirit is calling and prompting. We simply need to walk in the flow of what God is doing and offer what he has already earned for all who will believe!

Invite people to respond at the end of this service. Your church tradition may make this feel very natural, or it may seem quite new to others. If your tradition includes an altar call on occasion, this would be a great time to extend this public challenge. You will want to be sure you have trained and godly leaders ready to talk with people, pray with them, and follow up on their spiritual growth.

If your church would not feel comfortable with this kind of public approach, consider inviting people to come forward after the service (or to meet in another designated place in the church) to meet with a pastor or church leader.

Another possibility is making commitment cards available in your church programs or bulletins. These cards could involve a number of kinds of commitments such as:

- I desire to make a first-time commitment to Christ.
- I desire to rededicate my life to Christ.
- I commit to pray daily for three people who don't know Jesus Christ.
- I am willing to be part of an evangelism ministry that will reach out with the love of God in Jesus' name.

Have people write their names and phone numbers on these cards so that you can follow up on their responses. These can be placed in the offering plates or given to ushers as people leave the sanctuary.

After this series on the core of the Gospel of Jesus Christ, it just makes sense to finish with a tangible call to action and commitment.

Closing Prayer

OTHER IDEAS FOR THIS WORSHIP SERVICE

Hymn Suggestions

"All People That on Earth Do Dwell" (William Kethe/*Genevan Psalter*)
"Christ for the World We Sing!" (Samuel Wolcott/Felice de Giardini)
"For God So Loved the World" (Frances Townsend/Alfred B. Smith)

Praise Chorus Suggestions

"Be Exalted, O God" ("I Will Give Thanks)" (1977, Scripture in Song)

"Believer" (1996, Kingsway's Thankyou Music)
"Did You Feel the Mountains Tremble?" (1994, Curious? Music)
"I'm Forever Grateful" (1986, People of Destiny International/Pleasant Hills)
"Let Your Glory Fall" (1993, Mercy/Vineyard)
"Pre-Revival Days" (1997, Little Misty Music/Kingsway's Thankyou Music)

Prayer Suggestion

The third and least known of the ecumenical creeds is the Athanasian Creed. The first half of the creed gives a powerful and detailed description of the Trinity. The second half of the creed focuses on the person of Jesus Christ. It begins with the strong words:

It is necessary for eternal salvation
that one also believe in the incarnation
of our Lord Jesus Christ faithfully.

Now this is the true faith:

That we believe and confess
that our Lord Jesus Christ, God's Son,
is both God and human equally. . . .

The creed then goes on to explain the true nature and work of Jesus Christ. As you prepare to lead in prayer during this service, you may want to read a portion of the Athanasian Creed (particularly the second half). Let this shape your prayer. End with celebration and praise for Jesus Christ, our hope of salvation.

Additional Scripture Texts

Matthew 28:18–19
Luke 24:47
1 Corinthians 9:19–22

Responsive Reading

Leader: To whom should Christians preach the Gospel?

Congregation: We affirm that the church is commanded by God and is therefore under divine obligation to preach the Gospel to every living person.

Leader: Is there any person or group of people beyond the reach of the Gospel?

Congregation: We deny that any particular class or group of persons, whatever their ethnic or cultural identity, may be ignored or passed over in the preaching of the Gospel. God purposes a global church made up from people of every tribe, language, and nation.

—FROM "THE GOSPEL OF JESUS CHRIST: AN EVANGELICAL CELEBRATION"

SMALL-GROUP DISCUSSION RESOURCES

At the end of each chapter, the author has offered some questions for discussion and reflection. If you wish to use this book or these sermons as a springboard for small-group discussion, here are a few more questions that may help in the process:

Biblical Understanding

1. Read John 3:16–21. This passage has some vivid contrasts (light and darkness, eternal life and condemnation, belief and rejection). What do you learn about God as you look at these contrasts?
2. What do you learn about human beings?

Theological Reflection

1. As you look at John 3:16–21, what do you learn about the eternal implications surrounding what we choose to believe concerning Jesus Christ?

2. Discuss what biblical and theological response you would give to a person who says, "The Bible never makes serious claims that anyone will be separated from God for lack of belief," or "A truly loving God would never condemn anyone to hell for eternity!"

Practical Application

If God has revealed his love for the world through radical and sacrificial action (the sending of his one and only beloved Son), what can you do in the coming week to show the love of God to a person in your life who is not a Christian?

BUILDING
A
CONTAGIOUS
CHURCH
REVOLUTIONIZING
THE WAY
WE VIEW AND DO
EVANGELISM
MARK MITTELBERG

BECOMING A
CONTAGIOUS
CHRISTIAN
BECOMING A
CONTAGIOUS
CHRISTIAN
BILL HYBELS
& MARK MITTELBERG
BECOMING A
CONTAGIOUS
CHRISTIAN
LEADER'S GUIDE
Communicating Your Faith in a Style that Fits You
MARK MITTELBERG, LEE STROBEL & BILL HYBELS
BECOMING A
CONTAGIOUS
CHRISTIAN
PARTICIPANT'S GUIDE

The "Pastor's Field Manual"

Pastor's Bible

You never know what a day will bring. As a pastor, though, you've got to be ready for anything. Bedside visits, weddings, funerals, church conflict, discipleship and doctrinal issues . . . when others depend on you for help, answers, and wisdom, it's nice to know where to obtain them yourself, quickly and easily. The *NIV Pastor's Bible*. Like a mobile resource library for on-the-go pastors, elders, and church workers, it travels light but delivers a ton of information—exactly what you need, when you need it.

The *NIV Pastor's Bible* takes you straight to God's Word for insights on a broad array of topics. Zondervan has made a point of thoroughly understanding your needs and concerns in order to bring you the most practical, helpful, on-the-spot pastoral resource possible.

The NIV Pastor's Bible *Features*:
A 64-page resource section covering every conceivable aspect of public ministry—far too much to list here, but a small sampler would include:

- Special needs: bedside conversions, suicides, miscarriages, and more
- Answers to tough questions
- How to cope with change
- Outlines and ideas for church events: baptisms, infant dedications, new members, and more
- Concordance, maps, and indexes
- How to handle church conflict
- The Plan of Salvation
- Wedding and funeral services
- Complete text of today's best-selling translation, the New International Version
- Light, easy-to-carry Thinline edition
- Large, highly readable type
- NIV Translation

Black Top-Grain Leather
ISBN 0-310-91093-5

ZondervanPublishingHouse
Grand Rapids, Michigan

A Division of HarperCollins*Publishers*

Want to reach Postmoderns? Then learn to speak their language.

SoulTsunami

Sink or Swim in New Millennium Culture

Leonard Sweet

A mountainous wave of change known as post-modernism is threatening to wash the church away. We can either deny its existence—and drown. We can fight it—and lose. Or we can do as Leonard Sweet suggests—recognize the unprecedented opportunities it presents and chart a course across the waters.

> *"While the world is rethinking its entire cultural formation, it is time to find new ways of being the church that are true to our postmodern context. It is time for a Postmodern Reformation."*
>
> — LEONARD SWEET

Hardcover
ISBN 0-310-22762-3

Audio
ISBN: 0-310-22712-7
www.SoulTsunami.com

The Church on the Other Side

Doing Ministry in the Postmodern Matrix

Brian D. McLaren

What does the church need in order to make it on the other side of the postmodern transition? More than just a change to the latest ministry model. It needs an entirely new philosophy of ministry that's prepared to meet change as it comes. This revised and expanded edition of *Reinventing Your Church* explains postmodernism in a way that even laypeople can understand. It is a book of clear, creative thinking, passionate activism, and inspiring hope.

> *"The church on the other side never expects to 'get it right.' It assumes that as long as the church grows, it will have to adapt and change and learn."*
>
> —BRIAN MCLAREN

Hardcover
ISBN 0-310-23707-6

Worship Evangelism

Inviting Unbelievers into the Presence of God

Sally Morgenthaler

Rediscover worship. Tear down walls the church has built against it. Learn how to mix worship *and* evangelism. *Worship Evangelism* investigates the true nature of worship and its place in winning nonbelievers to Jesus Christ.

> *"In these days of unprecedented distraction and compromise, in a society that deifies human knowledge, competence, and bravado, the still, small voice of God is beckoning to us, calling to us as leaders and as children of the Most High to do what we were created to do: worship."*
>
> —SALLY MORGENTHALER

Softcover
ISBN 0-310-22649-X

We want to hear from you. Please send your comments about this book to us in care of the address below. Thank you.

ZondervanPublishingHouse
Grand Rapids, Michigan 49530
http://www.zondervan.com